LENNON REVEALED

ALSO BY LARRY KANE:

Larry Kane's Philadelphia

Ticket to Ride:
Inside the Beatles' 1964 Tour
that Changed the World

LENNON REVEALED

BY LARRY KANE

RUNNING PRESS
PHILADELPHIA · LONDON

FOR DONNA, MICHAEL, ALEXANDRA AND DOUG.
AND TO THE MEMORY OF JOHN LENNON.

Library of Congress Control Number 2005903223

ISBN-13: 978-0-7624-2364-4
ISBN-10: 0-7624-2364-1

Cover and interior designed by Matt Goodman
Edited by Greg Jones
Photo research by Susan Oyama
Typography: Garamond

DVD produced by Center City Film and Video, Philadelphia, PA

This book may be ordered by mail from the publisher.
Please include $2.50 for postage and handling.
But try your bookstore first!

Running Press Book Publishers
125 South Twenty-second Street
Philadelphia, Pennsylvania 19103-4399

Visit us on the web!
www.runningpress.com

TABLE OF CONTENTS

FOREWORD

I knew John Lennon. Not as much as some, but not as little as most. He was an inspiration to me and millions of others searching for truth, peace, and love. He spread the word through his music first, then by his actions. John set the tone for an entire generation to make a difference, and even when we fell short, he started chipping away at it.

I have read dozens of books on John's life, and this book has come the closest to the "truth" as far as I'm concerned. Larry Kane has put together not just his own personal thoughts on John Lennon, his friend, but has compiled an incredible lineup of interviews from John's closest friends and family. Not at all cautious, Larry has gone for what I think John would have wanted . . . the bloody truth!

You read that John Lennon was a bastard, a genius, a womanizer, a thinker, a poet, funny, cynical, sad, and a lot more. I know how *I* knew him in L.A. in the seventies: he was lost, angry, and missed Yoko more than music. He would have given anything just to go home. My friend, Harry Nilsson, was good at causing trouble, and John was looking for it. I was just a young musician hanging out with my idol. I wanted to *be* him, and I remember he would always let me ask one Beatles question every time I was with him . . . then he would tell me to f%#k off!

One drunken night, John put his arm around me and said, "Hudson," (I don't think he knew which Hudson brother was which) "keep looking for the truth, and when you find it, tell me where it is." I will never forget that moment.

There are a million moments like that in this book. I thought I had read it all, seen it all . . . hell, I'm Ringo's producer! I thought I had all the stories—WRONG! Larry Kane revealed things I never dreamed of. On the North American tours of '64 and '65, John trusted Larry, so he opened up parts of his heart that maybe only Paul, George, and Ringo were privy too. When I read the account of John and Larry meeting for the first time, I had to laugh out loud because the impression that Larry gives is that of a hard-core news reporter—suit, tie, low monotone voice—and he has the demeanor of a Republican. Well, looks can be deceiving, and I was wrong When you read this book, you see a man with great conviction, passion, humor, integrity, and honesty—John Lennon's kind of guy. That's why they stayed friends over the years: trust.

Larry's perspective and insights throughout this book kept me completely captivated. I relished the many nuances he revealed about the man who changed my life, and learned the kind of details that any fan would love to read about—Mario the young confidant who passed John's letters to Yoko and May; Petula Clark singing on "Give Peace a Chance"; Yoko's presence in John's life even through his "Lost Weekend"; and so much more. I could go on and on, but I won't. Just read the bloody book and make your own mind up!

I only know one thing for sure: I loved John Lennon, and this book makes me love him more.

—Mark Hudson, Los Angeles, 2005

PREFACE

WHO WAS JOHN LENNON AND WHY DO WE CARE?

Brash. Sensitive. Sexually empowered. A bad father and a good father. A dead poet whose language resonates with life. A rebel with more than a few causes. A rock star who entered new galaxies. Husband. Lover. Freedom fighter. Thinker, drinker, drug user and abuser. Guitarist, pianist, mouth organist. A singer of songs that haunt the mind and infuse the blood with tingles of joy and fear. A writer. A friend. A lost soul. A teacher and a student. A tiger with an intimidating roar and a cat with a soft, gentle purr. Legend in life. Icon in death. And to many, a puzzle. But was he really?

LENNON REVEALED?

For years before and for a quarter of a century *after* his life, pundits and politicians, reporters and would-be-reporters have tried to determine: who was John Lennon? This project intends to do more—to reveal John Lennon as a man, not just a myth; to slice through the myriad legends that accompanied his magnificent and creative presence; and to discover the real person through the visions and memories of people who knew him. It is a complicated journalistic assignment, fraught with attempts by people to carefully protect their own memories and overwhelmed by people who still have agendas.

What you will find in this book is an unfettered report from all angles and every point of view about a man whose physical presence is gone, but whose talent and message still live into this century and beyond.

First, a few thoughts on how I got to this particular place.

Reporters are impressionists. Our works do not appear on canvasses, but reflect the imprints on our minds. And in 1964, my twenty-one-year-old

mind held a very ambivalent impression of the assignment I had captured—
to travel with and report on the Beatles throughout their first tour of North
America. Trained as a hard-driving, aggressive gatherer of information, I
viewed the coverage of the Beatles tour as a job for someone with a more nar-
row view of the world, maybe even someone with rhythm and knowledge of
music—both of which were foreign to me. I did play the accordion as a
child, but, well, it was the accordion, and I was not very good. Frankly, as a
hard news radio reporter, I would rather have covered a bank robbery than
travel with a band, any band.

Admittedly, the assignment was my fault. The radio station management
had initially asked me to secure a short interview with the Beatles in what
would be their closest tour stop to Miami, the Gator Bowl in Jacksonville,
Florida. My letter to Beatles manager Brian Epstein included a business card
that listed all seven of my company's radio stations, six of them oriented to
black audiences who were hardly Beatles fans. Epstein did not know I was so
young, but he did believe, mistakenly, that I was some sort of radio mogul
in control of multiple stations. When the invitation came to travel in their
official press party on the entire tour of North America—thirty-two shows
in twenty-five cities—I was flabbergasted. I was also immediately determined not to go. My negativity was informed not only by my lack of interest in the subject, but, more importantly, by the death of my mother that
summer at the age of forty after a battle with multiple sclerosis. Her death
was—and still is—the worst thing that has ever happened to me. Eleven
years later, John Lennon would mark her life and death in a special way. In
the meantime, I had to decide what to do. Fate does not wait for indecision;
indecision is a fault line for great reporting careers.

Reluctantly, I went forward. With five years of radio news reporting and
anchoring behind me, I tackled what I believed at the time to be a wasted
and vacuous assignment, covering what would become known as the biggest
tour in the history of music—the Beatles' "invasion" of America and
Canada. It would be the first of their two tours that I would cover in full. In

the end, I would watch sixty-three Beatles concerts, witness their work on a movie, engage in countless hours of conversation with the four lads who would make so much history, and see my life and my viewpoint of what is and isn't news change forever. In the ensuing years, I have covered twenty-one political conventions, several superpower summits, seven different presidents, disastrous hurricanes and earthquakes, military combat, and the everyday ups and downs of ordinary people. Ultimately my career would take me to Philadelphia, where I anchored the TV news for thirty-seven years.

My book, *Ticket to Ride: Inside the Beatles 1964 & 1965 Tours that Changed the World,* was an insider's account of those tours and of my personal experiences with the Beatles. Many readers got the idea that I liked John Lennon. What was not to like? Here was a man with supreme talent, rage, individuality, frailties, charisma, and conviction who was looking desperately for places to deposit the waves of love roiling inside of him. My impressions of and reporting about the life of John Lennon in this book are based not only on my own extensive experiences, but rely heavily on the thoughts of other people who encountered John in many capacities throughout his life. I also performed exhaustive investigative research to help locate the pieces of his life that escaped me after two tours practically living with the boys, many phone conversations with John, and personal contact through special events that occurred over a period of seventeen years.

There is a subculture of Beatles journalism that seems to require authors to claim that they are the best and brightest on the subject. Despite this air of propriety over who has the real story, my circle of Beatles-connected friends is devoid of any such pettiness. But I bring up the subject of cooperation because I do not presume to be the only source of accurate information on the life of John Lennon. Each view of John's amazing life brings us something new. My reporting of Lennon and his adult life will no doubt vary from others, but it is mine.

AUGUST 18, 1964. JOHN LENNON INSULTING MY ATTIRE AND HAIR-STYLE ON OUR FIRST MEETING AT THE SAN FRANCISCO HILTON.

LENNON : *What's wrong with you. You look like a fag ass.*
KANE: *Better than looking like a slob like you.*

The man I met and traded insults with on that summer afternoon has been depicted as rude, abrasive, hostile and unpredictable by many writers and would-be experts over the years. My view is different, firmly rooted in the belief that John Lennon was all that and more, the "more" being an extremely centered and bright intellectual who gave so much more than he took back. Some people may wonder how a man who had gone to such extremes in his own life could affect others in such a profound and positive way. I believe it is all a case of mistaken identity. John is not the only thing we see in this book. We see ourselves—our potential for good and our propensity to screw things up. That is what living is all about. John's life, like all of our lives, was colored by serious and often debilitating flaws, some of which thwarted his creative process and threatened his very existence. And yet his talent and message prevailed.

If you're looking for a psychological profile—including facts like the baby formula he was fed or his achievements in grade school—perhaps you'll want to look elsewhere. And there are plenty of places to look.

What you'll find in this book is an honest and multi-layered portrayal of a man who affected us all in different ways, and who remains a cultural icon to millions. This work does not attempt to detail the week-to-week conflicts of John Lennon's psyche, but rather to find out how certain human frailties shaped a being that enriched so many others. It ultimately seeks to shed light on the truth, and sometimes to dispel long-standing myths about John—his loves, his sexuality, his rage, his alleged campaign against the United States, and more.

This is a true story; nothing is held back. Different points of view are not suppressed in the usual enthusiastic orgy of denial and memory lapse. It is my hope, through objective reporting, that in the pages of this book and in the enclosed DVD, John will come back to life for the reader, along with his expressions, sense of humor, and sheer honesty.

I do have to make one confession of a fact that made my job even harder. With all the brilliance, irreverence, craziness and confusion, the totality of his talent and the reality of his being, I fundamentally and honestly really liked the man. After all, more than just about anyone I've met, he taught me by example that bullshit and superficiality are a terrible waste of time. Yet, despite my respect and unfettered enthusiasm for John and what he left behind, there is no glossing over the truth of his life here. All the periods of John Lennon's life were marked by amazing candor. Truth, sometimes to his detriment, was his calling card—in his statements, music, and writing. This book lives up to his standards and legacy. It would be hypocritical to write the story of Lennon's adult life by glossing over the inadequacies and flaws that he refused to whitewash in his own lifetime. After all, as Yoko Ono told me as I interviewed her for this book, "He didn't want people to just adore him. He wanted people to know what he is made of."

This book is a celebration of his life, but in the spirit of Lennon, none of the challenges he tried to overcome will be ignored. He was, in spite of all his genius and accomplishment, a troubled man seeking his own truth. I have sought the truth here about John Lennon, with no apologies and no regrets, just wonderful and painful memories.

My story begins with the end, and reveals how that fateful night shaped some of the participants in this story. It ends with John's personal triumph, and then is poignantly accentuated in the beautiful writings of Lennon followers from across his universe.

John Lennon somewhere over Pennsylvania on the flight from Philadelphia to Indianapolis.

KANE: *John, people loved you in Philadelphia tonight.*

LENNON: *What's the fuss, Larry. I'm only an ordinary person doing fucking extraordinary things. Get the picture, Larry?*

I got the picture all right—a teenage prodigy, a man leading the greatest rock band of all time, a flawed human being desperately trying to find his way and—in the midst of a dark hole of despair—a human being who ultimately experienced the triumph of the human spirit.

The irony of it all is that John Lennon is bigger in death than he was in life. And believe me, he was big in life.

Larry Kane
Philadelphia
September 2005

ACKNOWLEDGMENTS

Putting together a work like this requires an extraordinary amount of help.

I begin with the core group that assisted me so consistently. My thanks to the team at Running Press: Editorial Director Greg Jones who is a giant among editors, Publicity Director Sam Caggiula, and the management team of Publisher Jon Anderson, former Publisher John Whalen, former Publisher Buz Teacher and former Associate Publisher Carlo DeVito. Staffers Marjorie Morrison and Tina Camma made doing business so pleasant. Art Director Bill Jones and designer Matthew Goodman were so creative. Susan Oyama's work on the photographs was, as usual, first class. The help of researcher Jennifer Rumain was invaluable. And Warren Mellnick did a great job in helping me produce the enclosed DVD, along with the talented staff at Center City Film and Video in Philadelphia, PA.

My good friend Paul Gluck, Vice President and Station Manager at WHYY TV, Radio and Internet, as usual was instrumental in providing valuable input.

The people who assisted me in getting good solid information, along with the interview subjects, are quite a group: Yoko Ono, undaunted and candid, provided invaluable insight. May Pang was delightful to deal with and insightful in her view of John's life. Pauline Sutcliffe and Diane Vitale, a dynamic duo who brought me and the reader much closer to the legacy of Stuart Sutcliffe. Joe Johnson, host of *Beatle Brunch* (www.brunchradio.com) was the key in soliciting input for the special interactive session at the conclusion of the book. Joe is a wonderful friend. Denny Somach, pop impresario, was incredible. And that is an understatement. The Los Angeles host of Breakfast with the Beatles, the incomparable Chris Carter, offered such keen insight. Martin Lewis, the king of all things British, offered his usual expertise and fluidity. Walter Podrazik, a wealth of knowledge, shared it with me. I want to thank John Stevens, noted professor at Berklee School of

Music in Boston. Andre Gardner, host of *Breakfast with the Beatles* in Philadelphia for his special editing work on this book (as well as his brilliant interviewing skills on the enclosed DVD), and Mark Lapidos, founder of the Fest for Beatles Fans, who was such a great help in connecting the dots. Much thanks to Shelley Germeaux of *DayTrippin* magazine. In the United Kingdom, Mark Lewisohn, Tony Barrow, and Tony Bramwell, Beatles experts all, kept me right on target. Pete Best's insights at the Fest for Beatles Fans were invaluable, as were Al Brodax, producer of the Yellow Submarine, and Paul Saltzman, whose pictorial account of the Beatles in India remains a best seller. Tony Perkins of ABC's *Good Morning America* provided an inspirational boost.

The music industry was well represented. Mark Hudson, producer for Ringo and others, is a gem of knowledge and intuition, as is Alan White, drummer for "Yes", and a man who accentuated the Lennon sound in the seventies. It was a pleasure to talk to Alan, one of the greatest drummers of all time. Photographer Bob Gruen, a close friend of John's, had invaluable information, along with photographer Allan Tannenbaum, whose picture graces the cover of this book. Legendary talk show host Geraldo Rivera and his long-time producer and confidante Marty Berman gave us a close-up view of John at work in the public sector, as did John's friend Mario Casciano. Radio broadcaster Paul Drew provided interesting accounts of John's comeback. My old friend Scott Regan has such a great knowledge of John's music. Author Bruce Spizer, whose own chronicles of Beatles history are legendary, gave me assistance at a critical time. John's final days were given special meaning by Michael Allison, the tree man and film producer who became a special friend of John.

Thanks also go to Lauren Lipton at KYW Newsradio. Joan Erle, research director at NBC 10 in Philadelphia, and Lawana Scales, program director at the same station. John Trusty, a friend from the Chicago area, is owed much thanks for his memories of John. Former Apple employees Linda Reig and Arlene Reckson are owed a debt of thanks. My gratitude to broadcasters

Dennis Elsas, Dave Sholin and New York anchorman Ernie Anastos, along with producer Allan Weiss who shared his memories of a fateful night. Thanks go to Lynne Sherrick, Damon Sinclair, Alan Steckler, Jeffrey Michelson, Dennis O'Dell, Scott Bluebond, Gene Vassal, Anne Gottehrer, veteran producer Vince Calandra, and distinguished Professor Leon Wildes, the man who fought John's legal battle to stay in America.

I would like to thank Paul McCartney and Ringo Starr for all the wonderful quotes over the years. And I cherish the memories in this book of the late George Harrison, Derek Taylor, Malcolm Evans, and Brian Epstein.

To Sean and Julian Lennon, I hope that this work finally clarifies what has been a conflicted view of your father's extraordinary life.

Norman Einhorn has been a constant source through his keen insight and sense of humor.

Finally, and foremost, I would like to thank my wife Donna, son Michael, daughter Alexandra, and son-in-law, Douglas Weiss, for their love, support, and patience.

ONE:
Murder at the Dakota

"I am going into an unknown future, but I'm still all here.
And still, where there's life, there's hope."
—*John Lennon, interviewed by Dave Sholin of the RKO
General Radio stations, Monday afternoon, December 8, 1980*

This is the story that defines what John Lennon was all about, and it begins with the end—his assassination on December 8, 1980. To comprehend the impact of John Lennon, it is imperative to understand just how his death affected people everywhere. And how the sudden end was really the beginning of another life.

Memory is a mind game. You think you remember what happened years ago in your life, but it takes hard mental digging to recall how it really was. Sometimes you may be right on target; other times distortion clouds the memory. Yet, there are certain events where the mood of the moment remains and can come back to bring you chills inside, and suddenly, with not much effort, you remember exactly how you felt. For Americans in the 1960s, there was the JFK assassination: everyone remembered exactly where they were and how they reacted when they heard the news. It wasn't until early December 1980, that such a universal pall would fall over the masses again. John Lennon's murder, in fact, touched the entire world.

It was an event that stunned even the most hard-nosed and stubborn peo-ple who ply the newsgathering trade. For this reporter, it was even worse, because I had spent countless hours in Lennon's presence—in the capacity of reporter and professional friend—from the first time he set foot in America in 1964 until shortly before his death. It was a journey that I neither desired nor expected, but one that has had tremendous impact and resonance. In retrospect, it was a dream job to be able to get so close to one of history's greatest dream makers. But, as has been the custom throughout history, the dream makers often run into the dream killers. And so it was outside the Dakota Apartments, John Lennon's home, on that fateful December evening in 1980.

❖

A hundred years before the end of John Lennon's life, construction began on the Dakota building at Seventy-second Street in Manhattan. The location was desirable because the Upper West Side was not heavily populated at the time, and the structure would stand just west of Central Park, the first urban landscaped park in America. From 1880 to 1884, construction engineers worked to complete the fashionable edifice. The proximity of the park was a new attraction in New York. Despite all of its newfangled creature comforts and location, it would be years before the Dakota would be solvent.

The Dakota is seemingly an odd name for an apartment building in the heart of America's largest metropolis. Legend says the name came from the fact that the neighborhood was so sparse at the time of its groundbreaking that it resembled the Dakotas of America's West. The name was given more direct physical representation when, during construction, high above the Seventy-second Street entrance, a statue of a Dakota Indian was erected. It has kept silent watch over the building since it opened in 1884. The build-ing's haunting motif, designed by the architect of the Plaza hotel, includes high, dramatic ceilings and floors with inlaid oak and cherry. Over the years it's been described as a Victorian Kremlin. The people who live there say the three-foot-thick walls, the forty-nine-foot-long drawing rooms, and the enriched sense of privacy and luxury is unique in Manhattan. As the twentieth century began, more and more apartment buildings were constructed on the Upper West Side. Eventually, Seventy-second Street became a major thoroughfare with the dawn of the automobile and the allure of numerous fashionable neighborhood restaurants.

The Dakota was well known for housing the famous and the artistic. The rigidity of its outside architecture contrasted with the inner luxury. Actors Boris Karloff, Lauren Bacall, Jose Ferrer, Judy Garland, and legendary composer Leonard Bernstein lived much of their lives there. Yet beyond its glamorous past and its haunting architecture, the Dakota would achieve a new and dark dimension of celebrity on the night of December 8, 1980.

❖

Alan Weiss passed the Dakota often. On the way to his job as the 6 p.m. news producer at WABC-TV on West Sixty-sixth Street, he would look up at the building and know that one of the idols of his generation was living inside. Weiss was a Beatles fan. He was particularly a John Lennon fan. Fate would have it that he would meet his idol in the twilight moments between life and death, and more than any person in the vast universe of mourners, get a genuine and unedited glance at the tragedy of murder. He remembers how his own close call with tragedy on December 8, 1980, would seal that fate:

"I had a date that night, and I had to get to a cash machine. Normally when I ride my motorcycle, I buckle my helmet. But because I was just coming across Central Park, I got on my bike and I didn't buckle my helmet. I'm getting to the outer drive that takes you out of the park on Fifty-ninth Street at Seventh Avenue. I'm making a right turn and a taxi on the inside of me is supposed to make a right turn but instead he decides he's not going to and he tries to get in front of me and I hit him at thirty miles per hour, slam over my handlebars, crack the windshield on the taxi, and end up on the ground. I slam my head against the ground, but my helmet wasn't buckled. My helmet gets knocked off and I slam my head a couple of more times like a stone skipping on water, and I finally stop spinning on the middle of the ground and I look up and all these cars are coming around the corner."

Today, Alan Weiss is a successful independent producer in New York City, creating, among other things, edgy documentary news broadcasts. Yet nothing he has filmed could match the intensity of what he would experience that night. The shock of a serious accident was followed in short order by a different kind of anguish.

❖

Almost at the same time that Alan Weiss lay crumpled on the pavement, John Lennon and his wife Yoko Ono were on their way home from the Hit Factory, a famous recording studio in Midtown Manhattan. The couple had spent an unusually long day at home tending to business matters, interrupted only by a prophetic interview with Dave Sholin, a programmer for the RKO Radio Network. Sholin was in New York specifically to conduct this interview with John and Yoko for his original radio series on famous couples. It was the first interview with Lennon for Sholin; it would be the last for John Lennon. Sholin remembers:

"It was a mesmerizing experience. On the afternoon of December 8, 1980, I took my shoes off, as was the custom in the Lennon household, sat down in a plush couch, and as my engineer assembled the equipment, stared at the ceiling. It was like looking at the sky; the ceiling was painted in beautiful clouds. I was in their world now, and a bit nervous, but record producer (and budding multimedia mogul) David Geffen had told me it would be all right. I thought we'd be there an hour. At around one o'clock, Yoko Ono came out to greet us with a great deal of warmth. I began the interviews with Yoko, and a few minutes later, John came in and said, 'Hey, here I am. Are you ready for me?' We started at one and didn't finish until after four. John loved it so much, he said he wished he could blow off the recording session. It was a great interview."

Sholin's interview with John was revealing. Combined with his recent return to making music, much of what Lennon said in that interview was a public tip that John Lennon's life may have been in transition:

"We're either going to live or we're going to die. If we're dead, we're going to have to deal with that; if we're alive, we're going to have to deal with being alive. So worrying about whether Wall Street, or the Apocalypse is going to come in the form of the great beast, is not going to do us any good day-to-day. . . .

"The thing the sixties did was show us the possibility and the responsibility that we all had. It wasn't the answer, it just gave us a glimpse of the possibility . . . and possibly in the eighties everyone will say, 'Okay, let's project the positive side of life again. . . .'

"I don't want to have to sell my soul again, as it were, to have a hit record. I've discovered I can live without it, and it makes it happier for me. . . . We feel like this is just a start now. . . . *Double Fantasy,* this is our first album. I know we've worked together before . . . but this is our first album. . . . I feel like nothing has ever happened before today. . . .

"You have to give thanks to God or whatever is up there that we all survived . . . the tremendous upheaval of the whole world. . . . But the world is not like the sixties, the whole world's changed. I'm going into an unknown future, but I'm still all here. And still, while there's life, there's hope."

This intense final interview gives us a glimpse of a man emerging anew just hours before his death, exiting a five-year hiatus at home, composing again, seemingly at peace with himself, and prepared for anything. A man who had always been possessed by the evils borne of insecurity appeared ready for a new fate. Or so it seemed.

Dave Sholin was pleased. A few minutes after 4:30 p.m., he looked out across the Seventy-second Street sidewalk as his crew packed up. Across the street, on the south side, he spotted a couple of young men. One of them came up and asked, "Did you just interview John Lennon?" Before he could answer, the man walked away. Sholin says there was no doubt—because the face has haunted him forever—that the man, soon to join the rogues' gallery of cowardly assassins, was Mark David Chapman.

As Chapman walked away, John and Yoko emerged from the Dakota looking for a cab. Sholin offered them a ride to the recording studio. He was determined to make a 6:30 p.m. flight to his home in San Francisco, but how could he not give a lift to John Lennon and Yoko Ono? Sholin recalls the ride:

"I wish I had the tape recorder rolling in the van. John was so animated, so happy. He was on top of the world. Yes, he looked thin, but healthy, and I was thrilled to give him a ride, to be a part of his day. I thought of his sitting in that single chair in the apartment and how he loved talking about *Double Fantasy*, and how all of this was sort of a coming out. He talked about the rumors of a rift with Paul McCartney. He said it wasn't true, that he loved Paul. And I believed him. And then he started breaking into some singing of hard rock songs; this was a happy man. As he climbed out of the van, he waved and Yoko blew a kiss in the air. We raced toward Kennedy airport, and we made the plane by a few minutes, which turns out to be a case of odd timing considering what would be. As the plane headed westward, I felt good about the interview. After years of seclusion, John Lennon let it all out for me. He seemed, by appearances, confident and hopeful. I felt happy for John Lennon."

Hours later, Dave Sholin was airborne over the Rocky Mountains, thrilled with his day, and eager to listen to his interview with John and Yoko. He was tired but at peace, comforted by a job well-done that turned out to be more than he asked for. He settled into a light sleep at about the same moment Alan Weiss lay quite unsettled and in great physical pain back in the emergency room at Roosevelt Hospital in New York City. Weiss recalls:

"I'm lying in the gurney, the doctor comes over, and she indeed is beautiful, and she looks at me and says, 'You know, I'll take you in for x-rays. I have to see what's wrong with you.' I said, 'Fine.' She says, 'You're lucky. We're slow tonight.' She had no sooner said that and all of a sudden a man comes running in screaming, 'We have a gunshot, we have a gunshot! Gunshot in the chest!' And she says, 'When's he coming in?' 'Hitting the door right now!' And the door slams open. Six cops come running in with a stretcher between them. And she looks at me and says, 'Alan, I'm sorry. I gotta go take care of this.' So I'm lying there on the gurney and these guys run right into the room and I'm lying outside of it. So I'm lying there, my eyes are closed, two cops come out and one says to the other, 'Jesus, can you believe it? John Lennon.' And I open my eyes and I look up at these two cops standing over my bed and I said, 'I'm sorry sir. What did you say?' They walk away and . . . now people are flying in and out of this room and they're carrying blood, gauze, and all sorts of other things and I'm trying to speak to them, saying, 'Excuse me. Who's in there?' And no one will talk to me."

❖

The official case number of the New York City Police Department, dated December 8, 1980, was 14854. At approximately 10:52 p.m., police officer Stephen Spiro arrived at the Seventy-second Street archway entrance to the Dakota where he found John Lennon gravely wounded, and a young man sitting a few feet away reading the J.D. Salinger novel *Catcher in the Rye*. As rescue crews arrived on the scene and quickly moved John to nearby Roosevelt Hospital, officer Spiro arrested the suspect, identified as Mark D. Chapman, last known residence in Honolulu, Hawaii, and confiscated a .38 caliber snub-nosed revolver. The official police report, written early the next morning, read, "The victim was shot with the described weapon; the named suspect causing the victim's demise."

The police report did not explain that the cowardly Chapman shot John in the back. Assassins, many of them, always seem to act from the rear, perhaps afraid to stare their victims in the eye. At 8:02 a.m. on December 9, Mark D. Chapman was arraigned and charged with murder. He had on him the Salinger book and $2,201.76 in cash. It was apparent from the attack, the disposition of the attacker, and the casualness of his arrest that Mark Chapman had come to kill. By December 14, according to the Twentieth Precinct detective's report, the case was closed, pending court disposition.

The official report on any violent episode deals with the facts at hand. But there is more to this story. First of all, it has been noted that Mark David Chapman assumed a military firing position. He sprayed six bullets at John Lennon's back. It is amazing, almost miraculous, that Yoko Ono escaped injury. The officially described crime scene conjures images of a passive Chapman reading his book upon the police arrival. But in between his savage act and the arrival of Officer Spiro, Chapman had paced the area restlessly, waving his revolver back and forth. As John was helped up the stairway to the Dakota security office, Chapman remained agitated and shouted warnings at the doorman and other observers before he sat down to read. Within minutes, police carried John from the security station down to a patrol car and gently placed him in the back seat. The car raced to Roosevelt Hospital even as the killer was led away.

Yes, it is true that Chapman had sought an autograph from John earlier in the day. And Lennon, ever approachable, fulfilled that request by signing Chapman's copy of *Double Fantasy*. John, in fact, asked Chapman if that was all he wanted. Chapman replied, "Yes, thanks John."

Obviously that was not all he wanted. When they led him away from the scene of his horror, that innocent-looking twenty-five-year-old had a smirk on his face that revealed his inner demons. The dream killer may have been reading a book about rebellion, but he was nothing but a gutless, cold-blooded murderer who shot the dream maker in the back. Case over? Not so fast. In every public tragedy there is a personal cost: a cost to the next of kin.

And in the case of John Lennon and his extended family of fans, that personal cost was unimaginably immense.

Imagine all the people. . . .

❖

John Lennon, whose enormous talent was at times fueled by bouts of hopelessness and insecurity, could never imagine the scene at the Dakota. Nor could he imagine the dramatic effort to save his life, or the terrible suffering of his wife.

On the way to the hospital, Yoko Ono pleaded with police officer Anthony Palma, "Tell me it isn't true!" The officer later said she was "very hysterical." At Roosevelt Hospital, doctors attending Alan Weiss moved to attend to the incoming shooting victim. As the pieces quickly fell into place, Weiss realized that he was witnessing the unbelievable.

"And I hear crying and I look up and there is an Asian-looking woman in a full-length mink coat on the arm of this huge motorcycle-jacketed police officer coming in. I don't know if that's gotta be Yoko Ono. It's gotta be John Lennon. So I realized that I had to get up and make a phone call and so, maybe when the adrenaline starts flowing, suddenly the injury disappears.

"So I got up and I was able to hop down the hallway. There was a glass door and outside of the glass door was a pay phone. I'd been to the hospital many times before. I knew the layout. And I was about to go through the doorway when a security guy grabbed me, says, 'You can't leave.' 'What are you talking about—I can't leave. This is a public place. I'm leaving. I'm checking myself out.' 'No, you can't leave.' And he pulled me right from the door. At that moment, the cop who brought me in at the other end of the hospital comes in the other end of the corridor; he sees me and comes running and he says, 'Mr. Weiss, what are you doing standing up? We had to take the stretcher apart to bring you in.' I said, 'Didn't you hear?' He said, 'Didn't we hear what?' 'Didn't you hear John Lennon's been shot?' He said,

'Who told you that?' I said, 'No one exactly told me that; I just heard these cops talking about it.' He said, 'Alan, you're crazy. You banged your head. Would you come lay down?' I said, 'Sure, but do me a favor? Would you let me just call my office?'

"So the cop leans over, takes the Centrex phone from the nursing stand, dials my office, I get Neil, the producer, on the phone. I say, 'Neil, it's Alan.' He says, 'Hey, Alan. I heard you had an accident; how are you?' I said, 'Neil, I think John Lennon's been shot and he's here at Roosevelt.' So they take me back to my gurney; I'm sitting on the edge of my gurney watching them working on John Lennon inside the room. And he's stark naked and his legs are facing me, and there were doctors and stuff was hanging out. . . . John Lennon was an idol, an absolute idol. I adored the Beatles—grew up with them and particularly liked John Lennon so no, I was not feeling much pain."

Weiss was a trained journalist, but also a human being with feelings. While he reported the possible death of John Lennon, he could not and did not detail the horrifying scene unfolding before him, just a few feet away.

"I could see his chest. To me, his chest looked open; I could be wrong. It might have just been that there was blood on his chest. They were clearly working on him. So they wheel me out of the emergency room and they put me in a room right outside and I'm lying there. And I must have been there for about fifteen minutes. And the music that's played on the house system plays 'All My Loving' or 'Till There Was You' . . . I have it written down. Four minutes after that was over, I heard the screaming, 'No! No! Oh, no!' And a door opens up and Yoko Ono comes out hysterically crying on the arms of David Geffen. They walked down the hall together . . . and it was . . . sadly . . . over."

❖

With the time difference, radio interviewer Dave Sholin was tired when he reached San Francisco International Airport. He motored his car along an expressway and tuned into his home radio station, KFRC, which was playing a variety of Beatles songs. That was the first tip that something was not right. Sholin recalls:

"The station never played Beatles songs. I knew something was up. I drove faster. The news came on and I had an explosion of chills. I thought I was dreaming. Somewhere between the Hit Factory and my arrival in San Francisco, John stopped breathing. Opening the door of my apartment, I could barely walk. Weak. That's what I felt. It was so surreal, so frightening. I sat by myself, still in shock. Within half an hour, the phone rang and for forty-eight hours I talked about the last interview to the *Today Show, Good Morning America* and scores of reporters. I've been talking about that interview ever since. But I will never forget the moment I found out. And the loneliness I felt."

❖

Lonely. Haunted. Surreal. The words and emotions still flow about that fateful night, as if individuals lost a piece of themselves that's been replaced by a longing which never ceases. And while the words have told the story, the images provide the physical connection. Pictures, seen through the lens of a photographer, reveal humor, grief, joy, despair, and hope. No human being has taken more photographs of John Lennon than Bob Gruen.

On the night of December 8, 1980, Bob Gruen was at home in New York City's West Village printing his latest batch of family photos for John and Yoko. Bob was a young celebrity photographer who was making a name for himself. Working in the darkroom, he was excited about his pictures. He hoped to deliver them to the Dakota at 1 a.m. The hour was not unusual for the Lennons, who lived by their own standard of time.

Gruen was six years younger than John but compatible with him in the temper of the times. John Lennon had few male buddies. It was a fact of his life that he bonded more easily with females. Gruen was an exception. He was one of John Lennon's closest friends and had become, in effect, the family photographer for Yoko and John. Yoko, always possessive and careful about who John spent time with, was comfortable and secure about the friendship with Gruen.

While Gruen put the finishing touches on his latest batch of shots, he got an urgent call from the doorman.

"I was here printing pictures I had taken of [John] two days earlier. Late as usual, I was supposed to get to the studio. It was around eleven o'clock I think and I was just finishing the last couple of prints I had to wash, then dry, and run up to the studio by midnight, show it to John and Yoko, get out of the studio by one o'clock and go down to *The Village Voice* and get the pictures there before the 2 a.m. deadline. Like that was my evening. And my doorman called up and asked if I had a radio or TV on and I said, 'No. Why?' And he knew that I knew John Lennon. And he said, 'Well I just heard on the radio that John Lennon was shot.' And I remember my first thought was that, because he said he was recording and he left the studio and he got shot, I thought he had walked out on Forty-fourth and Eighth Avenue. Times Square in those days was kind of a seedy neighborhood and it was easy to get mugged, and I thought maybe he had walked around the corner or something, and John usually didn't have cash in his pocket. Around those times, anyway, Yoko took care of the business end. And he just sometimes wouldn't have a five-dollar bill. I thought maybe somebody tried to rob him and he didn't have money and they shot him in the arm or the leg or something. A shot isn't dead, you know. And then my phone just started ringing like mad. And I got a phone call from a friend of mine who was watching TV in California. And it was actually the first publicist that was involved with *The Elephant's Memory* and we had been involved with John and Yoko a lot together. And he said, 'What's happening?' And I said, 'I don't know. I'm here in New York and I didn't have the TV on yet.' And he said, 'Well, I have the TV on.' And I said, 'Well, what are they saying?' And I remember him saying, 'There's blood everywhere. John Lennon's dead.'

"You know, Phil Spector once said that the most obscene four-letter word—he was talking about obscenity and he said it's not obscene talking about making love to your loved ones. He said, 'The most obscene four-letter word is *dead.*' And I heard that word that night and I just kind of sank down on the floor and just started thinking of all the ways I could change it. How could you change it? What can you do? What can you do? And there's nothing you can do when somebody's dead. I felt real hopeless, helpless."

❖

At the moment that Bob Gruen was sifting through the reality of it all, award-winning international photojournalist Allan Tannenbaum was working in his darkroom when the phone rang. After getting the word, Allan raced uptown to the Dakota. Tannenbaum, whose intriguing photo of John Lennon graces the cover of this book, was one of the last people to photograph John and Yoko. His thoughts turned to the couple:

"It was such a shock. Only ten days earlier, we had walked in Central Park. They were holding hands, enjoying the rebirth of music in their lives. They seemed very much in love and so very much alive."

❖

May Pang was dining out in New York City. It was just an ordinary night, or so she thought. May, who had worked for John and Yoko for years, was still dealing with the crisis of the end of her relationship with John and the loss of connection with the man she had reluctantly fallen in love with. May's friend David Bowie was at his New York apartment. Out of a sense of caring, Bowie and his associates would make sure that May had a warm place to be as the events unfolded late that evening and into the morning. May tearfully remembers the night:

"I happened to be on the Upper West Side as well and at dinner with a girlfriend of mine. And I just heard this radio announcer saying some man, supposedly John Lennon, has been shot. But the guy took it so nonchalant. I sat there—I freaked. I said, 'Why's he being so nonchalant? It could be or not. I don't know.' So I picked up the phone to call a friend of mine, Mario. So I called him up. I said, 'Did you hear?' He goes, 'Yes. I don't know.' And then just as I'm saying, 'Do you think. . .' and just at that moment the radio man came back on. He goes, 'The man was John Lennon. He just died.' I just totally freaked, ran out the door. I called another girlfriend of mine in the neighborhood. She said, 'I'm gonna return you home.' I ran home, and my phone was ringing off the hook, and there's messages already and it turned out it was Ringo's assistant, and she says, 'We need the name of the hospital.' I said, 'Forget it. He just died.' And she just screamed, 'What's wrong with your bloody country! I have to get off the phone and tell every-one now.' I was just totally, totally freaked and then I called up David Bowie because we had met Bowie together and he was in town. His assistant said, 'Well, he's out on a date. But come here now. You should not be alone. Come here.' I went over to see him. They found him and we were all sitting around. His assistant, me, David—we were all sitting around. And then I stayed there until the next morning because they just didn't want to see me leave."

❖

Ernie Anastos was a young anchorman at WABC-TV, and on the night of John Lennon's murder, he was getting ready for the eleven o'clock news as usual. Anastos worked just six blocks from the Dakota in the studios on Sixty-sixth Street just off Columbus Avenue. At that time, Anastos was two years into his job and doing very well. Earlier in the evening he had an appointment for dinner with Charles Grigas, a high school classmate from Nashua, New Hampshire. Following the meal, Anastos and his guest went for a walk through the Upper West Side neighborhood.

"There we were, standing in front of the Dakota on Seventy-second Street. I was such a big Beatles fan, and especially an admirer of John Lennon. I've always wondered to this day what prompted me on that cold night to do what I did. I took Charles to see the Dakota. I pointed up and said, 'That's where John Lennon lives, right up there.' And so there we were just standing there looking up, and wondering what it was like inside. We walked the six blocks back to work. It was just another Monday night in New York City."

Anastos returned to the studios to begin preparing the eleven o'clock broadcast. When the call came in from his colleague, Alan Weiss, at Roosevelt Hospital, Anastos dashed to the studio, his pulse racing, adrenaline flowing, and moisture welling up in his eyes. It was arguably the most difficult piece of news he has ever had to report.

"John Lennon has been shot and killed outside of the Dakota Apartments on Seventy-second Street tonight."

As the story unfolded, Ernie Anastos brought in live reports from the hospital and the Dakota, and through it all, on the surface of things, he held back the emotions that were churning inside. Anastos recalls that painful night:

"I responded emotionally. This was my generation that was attacked. I loved the Beatles, and especially John. Sometimes, on the air while you are broadcasting, you don't have the time to really reach down and express your feelings. But it all came out as I started my drove home. I drove by the Dakota and a crowd, maybe a couple of hundred, was already there. Some were holding candles. Others were staring up at the apartment building. It was a sight I'll never forget. It was a depressing evening. I mean, what were the odds of me traveling to the Dakota earlier, on the same night that an idol of mine was murdered?"

While Ernie broadcast the report to New York, I was performing the same grim duty at WCAU-TV Channel Ten in Philadelphia, where I served as 6 p.m. and 11 p.m. news anchorman. It was approximately 11:50 p.m. when I ran to the set, my hands trembling as I grasped the wire copy that brought the news. It was painful for me to speak the words. I shook as I said them:

"This is Larry Kane with a News Ten Bulletin: John Lennon, the former Beatle, has been shot and killed outside his home, the Dakota Apartments, on the West Side of Manhattan. Details are limited, but we know this much: Lennon was hit by multiple gunshots in the chest, and was pronounced dead at Roosevelt Hospital. John Lennon was forty years old."

In a special tribute broadcast some days later, I would remember the man. Even today, I get welled up when I watch and listen to the tape of that tribute show, pictures of John walking through the park, tucked under the covers at the famous "bed-ins" in Amsterdam and Montreal, smiling devilishly in photos from his teenage years and beyond. There was John descending from the Pan Am Clipper on the Beatles' first trip to America. There were photos of the young art student and the hell-bent rocker in the first city the Beatles captured: Hamburg, Germany. There were pictures with Cynthia Lennon and, of course, Yoko. Our salute was broadcast in prime time. It ended with the following words:

"John Lennon's legacy was the music and the message, but the music and the message will live on."

Words on television could hardly define the emotions inside of me and the flashbacks of the times in the sixties when I stood side-by-side with John, interviewing, arguing, laughing, and serving as the recipient of some of his sharp-witted and often hilarious humor. John's death was a precursor to other brutal events, but I didn't know it at the time. Within months, assassination became a political standard in 1981. Efforts were made to kill President Ronald Reagan, and Pope John Paul II. In Egypt, Anwar Sadat, who took the road to peace and carried his country with him, was gunned down in public. John's murder seemed to begin a vicious cycle.

Biographies emerged as fast as the event occurred. But the real tribute came from the people.

Within one hour of the report of John Lennon's death, over 750 people had gathered outside the Dakota. Some wore housecoats and pajamas. Cars were double-parked and traffic stood still. One hundred and five miles away in Philadelphia, a small group lit candles on the famous steps of the Philadelphia Museum of Art. Similar vigils convened and continued late into the night in Chicago, Los Angeles, and points across the country, but the Dakota was the world's focus. Central Park West became a parking lot. One bystander said what so many people were thinking, "It's like I lost a member of the family."

Some of the crowd started singing Beatles songs and John Lennon songs. The words, sung softly, whispered in the cold night air. There was sobbing and weeping, and just stares into the black night. Police officers didn't have it any easier, as many of them had a special fondness for John. Once declared a radical by the Nixon White House, and literally spied on by FBI agents, John had become a proud citizen of New York, raising thousands of dollars on one occasion to buy bulletproof vests for the men and women in uniform.

The normal reactions of shock and outrage were expected in the United States, the United Kingdom, Germany, and other places where John Lennon had touched the people directly. What was surprising in the aftermath of John's murder was the spontaneous public gatherings and outpouring of support for this freewheeling musician and artist in lands where doing so was tantamount to seeking a prison term. Thousands of young people filled the streets of Moscow and Leningrad in what is now the former Soviet Union. Beatles songs and especially the songs of John Lennon were prizes indeed in such places, products of a black market that would finally come to an end with the fall of the Soviet Union later in the decade.

Individuals across the earth gathered to cry and commiserate, and some, in the face of danger, mirrored John Lennon's public courage to do so. Perhaps the most gutsy display of affection took place at a wall in Prague, capital of what would become the independent Czech Republic. It began at the recess of a garden wall in a churchyard that dates back to the fourteenth century. There, in the days after John's death and under the eyes of agents of the Soviet puppet state, young people created what became known as the "Lennon Wall."

Originally, the wall began as an ersatz grave and memorial to John, but it evolved into a symbol of protest against the regime. Over a nine-year period until the Velvet Revolution brought freedom to the Czech Republic, the wall would be the scene of a continuing battle between the activists and the government. Anti-government slogans were painted on the Lennon Wall. Within days, they were literally whitewashed away. But the government whitewashers would cover the messages only to find them repainted days later. This cat-and-mouse game continued for years. Most of the messages were lyrics from John's songs speaking to peace and freedom. Even surveillance cameras didn't stop the gutsy painters and poets from expressing their thoughts through John's music. Some of the early protesters were jailed and sometimes physically beaten. But their spirit, and the spirit of the man they came to exalt, would not be figuratively beaten. Even in a closed society, the whitewashers will lose in the end.

These days, in an era of freedom in Prague, the John Lennon Peace Wall stands proudly at its original location, and is visited annually by thousands of people from all over the globe. John Lennon never visited Prague, but the small monument stands as testimony to the power of his message and the magnetism of his personality. It remains just another poignant example of John's iconic influence. He never lived to see the revolution in Prague, but as he would have liked it, it was "velvet," peaceful. Not a shot was fired. John would have been proud that in the final years of the communist regime, young people would risk their lives to fight for their own freedom while paying homage to the man and his music of liberation. He was, in music and words, a guide to these young revolutionaries' dreams of free expression and liberation.

Over the course of the next few days, candles were lit for John in every capital of the world. In Rio de Janeiro and in Belgrade, radio stations abandoned their formats and played continuous Beatles music. In Liverpool, England, where it all began, the people gathered for numerous memorials and church services. George Harrison, Paul McCartney, and Ringo Starr all remained in seclusion. Harrison expressed his sorrow, then told reporters, "It is an outrage that people can take other people's lives when they obviously haven't got their own lives in order." In Madrid, the weekly newspaper *Cambio 16* put it all in perspective, declaring, "An imbecile extinguished forever a voice of intelligence." London newspapers used the occasion to blast American gun laws. One writer called America "the eternal land of meaningless crime." But whatever the reaction, wherever it came from, one thing was certain: the tragedy brought a shared sense of not only grief, but unity behind what John stood for.

World leaders publicly expressed their sorrow. Former British Prime Minister Sir Harold Wilson declared the killing a "great tragedy" and recalled the time he awarded the Beatles medals as members of the Order of the British Empire. He failed to add, as almost every politician would, that John had returned his in an act of protest, the kind of public declaration that had marked his life from childhood to death. President Jimmy Carter expressed his sorrow, and President-elect Ronald Reagan, who would survive an assassination attempt a few months later, offered his condolences and regrets.

And as the great wave of public and silent mourning continued around the globe, many of the disbelievers, shocked by the loss, searched for more information and for meaning.

So who was this man, John Lennon? Quite ordinary at birth, he was deprived of the love of his mother and father. Viewed as a screwball and rebel by his teachers, he was a rare wit who provoked laughter and sometimes rage. He was a champion of women who had his fill of them. He was a man of peace who could be at war with himself; an artist who sketched the world and its people quite openly; an author who defied the normal levels of literary gravity; a composer who joined with a young friend named Paul to compose the greatest assembly of pop music in the history of modern man. Lennon was a poet whose passion for people less-talented was matched by an intolerance for people less-tolerant. He was a strong-willed man who became weak from abused substances. His defiance of authority, finessed as a child, would make him grow into a man of principle who rarely compromised his position or his passion. He could be very funny, harshly cruel, and would use his sharp wit and temper to scare the living daylights out of paranoid politicians who had him followed in the night. John Lennon was a rich man who felt for the poor, a father who felt that he faltered, a husband confused. He made love to many women, but he loved only three. His life was constantly reinvented, his genius sometimes sapped by his own demons. In life, he was a creator and inventor. In death, he became an icon. I was proud to have known him. Millions of others felt close to him in their own way. Here now is his story—the story of a man who carried one single passport, but was always, without doubt, in life and death, a citizen of the world.

TWO:
All You Need Is Love

"The great thing about love is that you always get a second chance."
—*John Lennon, Rishikesh, India, February 1968*

Who was John Lennon? What shaped his life? It is all about love.

In the course of a life, love is gained and love is lost. Love—the lack of it, the search for it, the excesses of its sensations—charts out the roadmap along which we live our lives. In the case of John Lennon, the love he pursued and received, along with the joy and disappointment surrounding it, guided both his life and career. The loves in his life were as varied as the times of his life. The man who founded the Beatles and blazed a decisive course in cultural history became who he became because of the conflicting waves of love that enveloped him.

First, of course, were the early influences—an absentee mother, a vanished father, a loving aunt and uncle, and the resulting air of anxiety and uncertainty that persisted throughout his formative years.

And then, there was romance. There were many women in John Lennon's romantic life, but only three that he loved back. They included a high school sweetheart, an avant-garde intellectual with a burning obsession for excellence, and a young woman who came into his life at a time when his path was filled with danger and uncertainty. There was a significant fourth person, a fellow artist who was truly his best friend and confidante. That young man, a beautiful being blessed with enormous talent, was the only man John Lennon truly loved and one who may have haunted him for the rest of his life.

For a man who always seemed cocksure and defiant, the search for true love and lasting friendship was tenuous and often elusive. Those four people helped guide the way. Three women. One man. Four love stories that helped mold the brilliant and conflicted psyche of John Lennon. This is their story and, ultimately, his.

SETTING THE STAGE

Few infants born on October 9, 1940, entered the world with such a tentative grip on life. The birth of John Winston Lennon to Julia and Alfred Lennon was greeted with great joy. That elation didn't last long. Julia Lennon was a free spirit and her husband was absent for most of John's early years. By 1945, the couple had formally separated, a state in which they had existed for most of their marriage anyway.

From the age of five until he was a young adult, John followed a familiar pattern, shuttling between the women who represented the things he needed most—order and affection—and rarely finding both. His father was missing. His real mother, indulging completely in her own social life, would make only occasional sorties into his. Julia Stanley Lennon, while not abandoning John altogether, left him in the care of her sister Mimi Smith and her quiet husband George.

Perhaps guided by the guilt of her absences, Julia allowed John to do anything on a whim, spoiling him to the point of excess. Left with his Aunt Mimi, the young John discovered a woman who provided discipline and organization, which he feared but tried to ignore. Mimi, whose real name was Mary Elizabeth Smith, and her husband were not the parents of record, but they were the parents of genuine love and respect. Their organized but tender loving care provided a substantial foundation for a lifetime of growth, including an emphasis on reading and writing. George Smith was especially sensitive. He adored his wife Mimi and, although she could be dominating, the doting husband was always sweet and cooperative. And according to Yoko Ono, the sweet John, the less-caustic embracing man, was influenced heavily by the relationship of Mimi and George:

"Uncle George was a very gentle and kind husband to Mimi. John grew up seeing that. So John was very sweet and gentle at home."

The road to George and Mimi's house on Menlove Avenue in a lush suburb of Liverpool was littered with emotional potholes. John's father Alfred, known as Freddy, had all but abandoned the family. Mother Julia was independent and footloose. Casual relationships were quite common. At one point, she gave birth to a daughter by a serviceman who disappeared. The daughter was adopted and taken to Norway. In the postwar period, Julia fell in love with a waiter, John Dykins. Conditions were so poor in their one-room apartment that Julia's sister, spurred along by a recommendation from child-service officials, convinced Julia to relinquish control of John to Mimi and George.

And so it was that John became the only child of Mimi and George, and called their residence, known as Mendips, his home until he was twenty-three years old. John stayed in contact with Julia, who subsequently gave birth to two daughters with Dykins. John would visit his mother's home, but *home* was really at Mimi's. This unstable shuttling in John's life caused insecurity and led to naughty behavior at school, but at the end of the day, Mimi was there to check his school work and George was on hand to read books to him as he drifted off to sleep. John viewed Mimi as his mother, and her influence was never questioned. In 1956, Mimi bought John the gift of a lifetime: his first Spanish guitar. When they arrived home, an elated John began playing, but Mimi was cautious, warning him that he could never make a career out of music. A short time later John would create his own band, the Quarrymen. Mimi could never have known what she was unleashing with that thoughtful gift.

Life with Mimi and George was idyllic in many ways. Discipline was provided by Mimi, comfort by the low-key George. His birth mother would occasionally visit and listen to music with him. But Mimi was the queen of the house and John was forever indebted to her sense of caring, the love and comfort that she and George offered, and the dimension of structure that he needed badly.

The peace that entered John Lennon's life was briefly shattered when his father Freddy returned home and, in a foul shouting match witnessed by John, Mimi, and George, demanded that Julia give custody of John to him. John, torn apart by the bitter scene, agreed to go off with Freddy, but later ran screaming to his mother. It was decided then that he would stay with Aunt Mimi, and that was that.

❖

The period from 1946 to 1955 saw the usual growth spurts of youth. John entered into his teenage years a bright and rebellious student at the Quarry Bank School. But once more, his pleasant life was shattered by a sequence of events, this time tragic.

George died of a brain hemorrhage in 1955. The loss to Mimi was devastating, and John's primary male role model was gone. If that wasn't jarring enough, in the summer of 1958, Julia Stanley Lennon was struck and killed by a police car. John's reaction to his birth mother's death was a grim silence. That would become a familiar pattern in his dealing with death. But two months after the accident his quiet sadness turned to an outward bitterness. With his birth father missing in action, Aunt Mimi widowed by the premature death of George, and his mother killed in the accident, John Lennon appeared to be a lonely and bitter teenager. There were vacancies inside of his emotional core, with precious little in his life to soothe the pain. In the early seventies John would finally talk about the loss of his birth mother:

"She was killed after visiting my auntie's house, where I lived, by an off-duty cop who was drunk. I wasn't there at the time. She was just at a bus stop. The copper came to the door to tell us about the accident. It was just like it's supposed to be, the way it is in the films. Asking if I was her son and all that. Then he told us, and we both went white. It was the worse thing that ever happened to me. I thought, I've no responsibilities to anyone now. I was sixteen. That was another big trauma for me. I lost her twice. When I was five and I moved in with my auntie, and then when she physically died. That made me more bitter; the chip I had on my shoulder as a youth got really big then. I was just reestablishing the relationship with her and she was killed."

On the 1964 and 1965 Beatles tours of North America, John and I related to the shared experience of losing a mother at a young age. His was dead for six years; the memories of my mother's death in the summer of 1964 were still fresh. He talked about how long it took to get over it:

"I was in a sort of blind rage for two years. I was either drunk or fighting. . . . There was something the matter with me. Because of my attitude, all the other boys' parents, including Paul's father, would say, 'Keep away from him.'"

There was one young man who would not "keep away from him." Nine months before the death of his mother, fate would introduce John to Stuart Sutcliffe. Stuart became John's sole mate as well as his *soul* mate. Ultimately, Stuart would become perhaps the most important man in Lennon's life.

STUART

Beatles fans the world over revel at the 1957 meeting of John Lennon and Paul McCartney during John's performance at the St. Peter's Church in Woolton, England. Shortly thereafter, Paul joined John's band, the Quarrymen, and the rest is history. While the musical collaboration of

Lennon and McCartney is the most celebrated in rock and roll, there was a second chance meeting in 1957 that, in a number of crucial ways, had an even greater effect on the life of John Lennon. This pairing didn't make headlines at the time, nor was it fully exposed until decades later, but its impact was monumental.

The name Stuart Sutcliffe summons up predictable images in the minds of ardent Beatles fans—the "fifth Beatle," an accomplished painter, and, oh, yes, the guy who died young. But there was much more. Stu Sutcliffe was an exquisite and talented man, a prolific artist, and the closest friend that John Lennon ever had. He was also John's most powerful influence, the unfortunate target of a regrettable and oft-forgotten beating by John, and his death was unexplained, if not controversial.

Stuart's life was filled with curiosity, wonderment, and discovery. He was an artist first, but was also a musician, and, in fact, one of the original members of the Beatles. His sister Pauline Sutcliffe even credits him with finding the name for the greatest band on earth:

"Contrary to popular mythology . . . it is actually from the girl gang in the Marlon Brando movie *The Wild Ones*, and there's a girl gang called the Beatles, and that's where Stuart got it from."

Stuart Sutcliffe and John Lennon shared a passion: a wider search for the real meaning of life, a joint exploration that filled four years of experimentation and discovery. At the end, they discovered themselves. Their time together would be short, and Stuart's end would be painful and haunting, especially for John. In the formative years of John's march to eternal greatness, Stu Sutcliffe was a colossal figure. His sense of style, quest for artistic excellence, and provocative manner affected John Lennon's thoughts and visions for the rest of his life.

Stuart, in essence, was the depository of John's joy, anger, and hope. Pauline Sutcliffe, today a professional psychotherapist, looks back with a deeper understanding. In her analysis, the man in John's life may have been more important than the women:

"Isn't it interesting that the childhood pattern was repeated with the women he loved? Cynthia, the lovely, caring girlfriend and wife, aiming to please. Yoko, controlling, motivated, challenging him to do better, even questioning his success. May Pang, the young lover dedicated to making his every day special and nourishing. With my brother Stuart, it was quite different altogether. They were kindred spirits from the beginning, and there was something so special about their friendship and love for each other."

Tony Bramwell, the Liverpool music icon and lifetime friend of the Beatles, has a heavy heart when he remembers the two young men. "Stuart Sutcliffe was his closest friend. They shared secrets, women, and their influence on each other was incalculable."

Stuart's sense of daring and sensual good looks were a large part of his appeal. What he gave to others as a human being was the heart of his magnetism. Even today, his kid sister Pauline marvels at and respects his influence:

"He was a man, a young boy, of huge integrity, and I also remembered the quote John Lennon said about him: that he looked up to him, he trusted him, he respected him because he always told him the truth, and that he was like a brother, as well. So it echoes to me in the same way that it did—it has the same authenticity when John Lennon said that—because he was like that with everybody."

Stuart's artistic acumen rubbed off on John in more ways than one. Yoko Ono smiles warmly when she talks about John's recollections of Stu Sutcliffe. In some ways, she tells me, it was Stu's influence as an artist that led John to her:

"John told me that Stu was a friend he really cared for and respected. Stu was an artist, and John was, too. Later, John fell in love with rock and roll, and became a rocker, but part of him was always that artist who had artistic conversation with Stu. When he came to Indica Gallery and saw me doing an art show, well, it touched the artistic side of him, I guess.

"Stu was an artist, I was an artist. You see an obvious connection there. But

I was also very much like his mother, too, in John's mind. His mother was tiny. I am tiny. I have a bit of Mimi in me, too. I'm just amazed how everything fit together on a very complex level."

The friendship between John and Stu began and grew in art class. Best friends usually find their bond in mutual interests and in a certain reliance on each other. In short order, John and Stu were embedded in each other's lives, trading gossip, sharing dreams (and sometimes girls), and exuding a feeling of togetherness that others can sense without a single word spoken. Every day, they laughed and commiserated, debated the issues of the times, conspired in their devilish plans to disrupt the school, and made music. John was becoming dependent on Stu, who had the intuition of a mentor and the strong qualities of a leader. For his part, the teenage Lennon encouraged and inspired Stuart to paint while listening to music. So it was music and art that pulled them together, combined with long talks about how to integrate their art forms with their search for the truth of the human condition, a common pursuit for young people, but in the case of John and Stuart, an outright passion. John's artistic talent—which would later become almost as famous as his music—grew under the tutelage of his best friend. Pauline Sutcliffe thinks that, above all, John longed to be an artist:

"I can remember having a very long lunch with Cynthia [Lennon] even just a few years ago because we both had homes in France. And she was telling me this fabulous story about the life classes at art school, because she was at art school as well, and how after hours, after John had run riot through the art school during the daytime, John, Stuart, and she would go down into the life classroom. Cynthia used to have to sit quietly in a corner somewhere and Stuart would teach John how to draw. And that for me was wonderful because John...was truly interested in fine arts and really did want to be that kind of artist as opposed to a recording artist, although he wanted to be this as well."

Stuart, a year ahead of John at the Liverpool Art School, was a teenager with flair and daring, nurtured by his parents and sisters to appreciate the arts, especially music in the form of an acoustic guitar. He and John would while away the hours and do what best friends do: dream, connive, and create together, all the while providing that thick emotional security net, the mutual reliance that makes friends more than friends, but honest soul mates. The relationship intensified when, much to the chagrin of Aunt Mimi, John decided to make a move. The *soul mates* became roommates. Pauline remembers it as a major break:

"John came to live in Stuart's studio at 9 Percy Street. At the time, Stuart shared [the studio] with Rod Murray, who was Stuart's best friend before John came on the scene, because Stuart was at art school before John. Rod Murray tells wonderful stories about how they used to jam—you know, they had acoustic guitars and they would write music and poetry. There was an awful lot of fun, enjoyment and creativity between them. They were having a good time and as inseparable as people could be."

Inseparable, cohesive, married to each other in spirit, the pair continued the daily pursuits of their art and music. Contrary to revisionist history, it was not John who introduced Stuart to music; Sutcliffe had been schooled at home on the acoustic guitar. But it was Stuart who honed and sharpened John's instincts as an artist. And that led to even more development of both John's art and being. Pauline remembers:

"Stuart was a star. When John arrived at art school, Stuart was the most talked about student in the art school. That, in and of itself, attracted John, and you would need to let that ripple through—the drive and motivation, the desire to become more famous than Elvis. So with that as a backdrop, he [John] did have some kind of heat-seeking missile of a nose. He knew how to spot stuff."

And in the natural way of things, Pauline says, that collaboration of creativity, the reciprocated reliance on each other, and the quality of time spent together, led to a deep mutual respect. Stuart Sutcliffe, in his art and heart, was anti-establishment. He inspired and challenged John to become a better artist, and, in return, John fanned the flames of dissent against all forms of authority. Eventually, the respect built into a deep affection and love. They told each other the truth, sometimes painfully. And Pauline Sutcliffe witnessed it up close:

"I think they both absolutely loved one another for very obvious reasons, you know, and we're not talking about same-sex relationships now. More about that later. We're talking about intimacy between men. Stuart was the personification of everything John wanted to be, and John was the personification of that part of my brother that he was uncomfortable with. My brother was a very, very sophisticated anarchist as a painter. He had anti-authority issues that came out in the most effectible way—like when he was told that art students can only produce work from thirty-by-sixteen-inch canvases, he would paint on six-feet-by-five-feet canvases. That's a form of anarchist. That's not going with the rules. It's clear from [Stuart's personal writings about John] that he also found John's way of expressing his anarchy, worrying, puzzling, not particularly acceptable. And when you read on in it, you can see that [Stu] is trying to channel him into using his creative energy in a creative way, rather than a destructive way."

And in that regard, recognizing John's failure to target energy in a positive way is where Stuart Sutcliffe played such an influential role in his development. As Stuart's writings confirm, Pauline says, he was upset that John was tremendously flawed in his negativity towards other human beings, which often flared up with a biting acidity. Pauline explains:

"[Stu] would challenge him and say, 'Why do you behave like that? Why do you not reach out to people? Why do you make such cutting comments to them?' Now I don't think at that age John had a single person in this universe who would even *dare* challenge him—who had the skills to do it in a sensitive and loving way, but in an honest and open way. Stuart did."

Stu's writings show a best friend clearly at odds with the temperament of a young man he loved, and deeply upset by the side of John that would internalize some of his innermost feelings. Still, Stuart tried hard to temper John's anger and his tone. Pauline says he abhorred the idea of John going over the edge, even while understanding that it was John's anger and creative aggression that was helping to develop Stu's own artistry. At the end of the day, what they had in common overshadowed some of their philosophical differences. So, together, as brothers in bond if not in blood, they marched toward an undeniable date with destiny.

Daily life at 9 Percy Street was a maze of exploration. Stuart painted to the music of Elvis, Gene Vincent, the Everly Brothers, and other popular American groups. John and Stuart, sometimes joined by Paul McCartney, would pull all-nighters, indulging in creative jam sessions and invigorating conversation. At John's suggestion and influence, Pauline says, Stu took one of the first major steps in the boys' musical development:

"Stuart was on the social committee at the Liverpool Art School, which means he could book bands for their Saturday night performances at school. He had the power to decide if the bands needed repairs and new equipment. It gave John Lennon's Quarrymen a chance to get newer and better equipment."

The amplifiers used by the group when they first made a splash in Hamburg, Germany, in August of 1960 were financed by the Student Union of the Liverpool Art School.

For the next two years, on Percy Street and at other locations, John and Stuart got even closer. Not even the arrival of Cynthia Powell, the young beauty in John's life, would obstruct the intensity of their friendship. The team and its spirit, aided and abetted by Paul, George Harrison, and Pete Best, moved progressively ahead. The group changed its name from The Quarrymen to Johnny and the Moondogs, and then to the Beatals, the Silver Beetles, the Silver Beats, and the Silver Beatles, eventually sticking with the Beatles.

Over a period of two-and-a-half years, John continued pursuing his passion for music while Stuart painted. The seminal moment for the two and the group was August 16, 1960, when the Beatles left for the decadent streets of Hamburg's infamous red-light district. It was there in the grit of cheap nightclubs, surrounded by deviates of every variety, that John Lennon and Stuart Sutcliffe found the apex of their friendship, as well as the dismal depths of outright despair. There, they would share the kind of new and powerful experiences that create intense and lasting bonds, as well as experience the first incidence of separation.

The strains in their relationship began shortly after Stuart fell deeply in love with German photographer Astrid Kirchherr. Astrid and her former boyfriend, Klaus Voorman, would play a major role in photographing the Beatles and creating a more modern imagery for the band through fashion and branding. The Beatles' famous hairdo, in fact, was actually a creation of Astrid Kirchherr. And her photographs of them comprise a classic collection that captures a seminal moment in their development.

Even as Stuart and Astrid feel deeper in love, John and Stuart grew closer in the shared experience of Hamburg adventures, including non-stop performances, assorted drug use, and sexual experimentation. Some would suggest (including former Beatles' press secretary Derek Taylor, whom I spent much time with throughout the Beatles' North American tours of 1964 and '65) that John and Stuart had a physical relationship. Pauline Sutcliffe wonders:

"No one really knows, but it was entirely likely because of all the strange things they were experiencing. Derek Taylor told a friend that John talked in 1968 about a physical thing with Stuart during a drug tryst. The bottom line is that Stuart was driving John to become a better performance artist even as Stuart was developing his skills on canvas. Did they mix all that painting and playing with panting for each other? Quite possibly."

There were two aspects of Stuart's life that came between John and him: oil on canvas and the fire of love. It was Sutcliffe's overwhelming talent as an artist and his studies with famed painter Eduardo Paolozzi that eventually brought him to a fateful decision. As the three journeys to Hamburg neared their end in 1962, and as the Beatles were beginning to become the stuff of legend, John Lennon again faced loss. His best and dearest friend was in love and engaged to a woman. But it was more complicated than that. Pauline Sutcliffe sees it as a triangle of love:

"Stuart, Astrid, John. You can walk any side of the triangle that you wish. John's jealous of Stuart in relation to Astrid. John's jealous of Astrid in relation to Stuart. John is increasingly competing with Stuart not for the rock-and-roll crown, but with his work as an artist."

For all of Stu Sutcliffe's total belief that the Beatles were destined for greatness, the brilliant young artist became more interested in his own painting than in developing the portrait of the sexy and stirring stage performer he was becoming. His decision to leave the group in the spring of 1961 left John shattered and depressed. Paul and George actually played a role in Stu's departure, pressuring Stu for not being up to the task musically. Obviously, there were numerous factors that led to Stuart's exit, but whatever the reason, that decision apparently led to an act of violence that would have repercussions for the rest of John Lennon's life.

Stuart Sutcliffe died of a cerebral hemorrhage in the right ventricle of the brain on April 10, 1962. At the hour of death, he was on the way to the hospital in Hamburg. His death followed months of disabling pain, weakened motor skills, and enough courage for an entire army of artists as he continued his painting while death approached. The exact reason for his physical demise was never quite established, and the death itself remains one of the great controversies in the life of John Lennon.

Stuart's problems began on the night of January 30, 1961. The group was playing at Lathom Hall in Liverpool when a group of toughs attacked Stuart as he helped load equipment at the rear of the hall. He was kicked and punched so hard in the stomach and head that he was covered with blood by the time Pete Best and John Lennon arrived to battle the roughnecks. It was not uncommon for the band to face the wrath of so-called "Teddy Boys," the slick blue-collar street toughs who made it their business to threaten artists and performers, especially the good-looking ones who vied for the attention of the girls. This beating was especially brutal.

A few months later, Stu suffered another beating, this time at the hands and feet of the man he respected most. It was a late night in Hamburg. John was extremely frustrated by demands by George and Paul that Stuart leave the group. He was also feeling the pressure of Stuart's developing obsession with Astrid and his disenchantment with performing. In a drunken rage, John Lennon beat Stuart Sutcliffe to a pulp, punching and flailing at him and kicking him repeatedly in the head until he lay there in pain, bloodied and beaten. Paul McCartney tried but failed to break it up, but then did manage to get him home after John ran from the scene. The description of the beating was relayed from Stuart to his sister Pauline, who notes that doctors later said Stuart's death was caused by an indent in his skull, the result of a trauma like a knock or a kick. To this day, Pauline Sutcliffe still wonders about the role of the beating in Stuart's death:

"I did say it [the beating] didn't help, but that's a long way from saying he was responsible. A writer once challenged me on whether John would beat up Stuart because he loved him so much, and I suggested to the writer that he didn't understand love and that you can love someone and still beat them up. . . . The beating was all about Stuart telling John he was leaving the group."

The death of Stuart Sutcliffe, just two months shy of his twenty-second birthday in 1962, was an intense shock for John. He learned of Stu's death upon the Beatles' arrival in Hamburg to headline at the world-famous Star Club, and wept inconsolably at the news. That emotional outburst was short-lived, though, and John retreated into virtual silence. As was his pattern, John Lennon submerged his innermost feelings about the loss throughout his life, preferring to analyze his depression in song and writing. John—along with George, Paul, and Pete—was there in Hamburg when Stuart's mother arrived to pick up her son's body. But the Beatles, playing a big and anticipated date in Hamburg, did not attend the funeral in Liverpool. Pauline Sutcliffe still retains a memory of bitterness. When I asked her if there was any guilt on John's part, she replied with a sullen look and subdued tone:

"We don't know [how he felt]. Astrid did send letters to my mother describing how much John missed him and grieved him and this and that, and how he would pay tribute to him night and day and play his favorite songs ... but he didn't show any of that in the months that followed... he didn't even send a bunch of flowers to his funeral. I heard through friends of Yoko Ono that John never stopped talking about Stuart."

According to Yoko, during their fourteen years together, hardly a week passed when John didn't refer to Stuart as an almost alter ego, a spirit in his world, a guiding force. But in the days after the tragedy, much like the days after his mother's death, there was a grim silence.

John did pay a visit to the Sutcliffe family a year later. It was a strained affair and may have added to any guilt he was feeling. The visit was not received warmly by the Sutcliffes.

Stuart had always believed more in the Beatles than the Beatles did in themselves, declaring to anyone who would listen that their potential was unlimited. He never lived to see what the Beatles would become, but his imprint was all over them. For a man panned as a musician by George and Paul, Stuart Sutcliffe left an undeniable mark on the Beatles' performance style, if not their musical substance.

Stuart Sutcliffe left behind a fiancé, mother, father, and two sisters. But it was John Lennon who was beneficiary of the sensitivity, hard work, and desire to find the truth of life, a mission that he began with Stu. Lennon's own work on canvass took off in the early seventies, and the Sutcliffes see a genuine similarity to Stuart's art, which has been feted around the world in its own right. His influence on John is as unquestionable as it is prolific and ubiquitous. Stuart's face appears on the *Sgt. Pepper* album cover; it is said that John insisted it be there. John's subdued reaction to Stuart's death belied his inner turmoil, much as he remained silent and tortured over the deaths of his birth mother Julia and his Uncle George. But in the aftermath of death, Stuart lived on in the spirit of John. John talked about him regularly with Cynthia and Yoko, and in my meeting with Yoko at the Dakota in 2004, Yoko again declared that John respected and loved Stuart and never stopped loving what he was about.

When it came to death, John, who was never afraid to expose his other frailties to the rest of the world, kept it all inside. But for the eighteen years that he survived all of life's tortuous temptations after the death of Stuart and before his own demise, John lived up to Stuart's expectations and his fears. He became a superstar, fought against war and injustice, and regularly taunted the establishment. He never did conquer his natural tendency to be edgy and mean, but then again, that negative and sometimes twisted energy fueled his genius in music, words, and art.

And as Stuart knew and Pauline remembers, John Lennon was not a saint and wouldn't want to be remembered that way. Would a real fan want to know the truth? Pauline says no:

"It's their truth, and behold the person who tries to dismantle that. The people who really want to know all the facets of this man . . . it's about whether they can tolerate knowing about the underbelly, about the other side of people, because nobody is perfect and I get concerned about the hero worship. I just wonder if people can accept him for who really was, not who they need to believe he was. Truth. Raw truth. That's one of the things that really mattered to him, even as a young man. That's why he loved my brother, because my brother knew every single aspect of him."

If the truth is what John Lennon sought, the truth is what he got from his best friend, possibly more than from any other soul in his life besides Yoko. But what Sutcliffe left behind would prove even more significant for years to come. John Lennon learned the craft of the higher arts, conceptualizing and painting provocative art of his own style, but always with Stu's influence in spirit. John's instincts about superficial people were sharpened by Stuart's uncanny ability to read what's behind a person's persona. John's own growth as a rebellious anarchist was reinforced by Stuart's constant questioning of authority. And although Stu Sutcliffe was only partially successful in challenging John to look inward at the dark side of his being, for the rest of his life John was inspired to question his own motives. Stuart died young, but his creativity, nerve, and defiance lived on in John.

CYNTHIA

During the years he knew Stuart Sutcliffe, John developed romantic love for a beautiful young woman with the face of an angel, the patience of a saint, and a heart that would be broken more than once.

John Lennon was sexually active from his early teens. But falling in love was quite another story. Cynthia Powell was no doubt the first woman that John loved in the romantic sense.

During the Beatles' 1964 tour of North America, John was on the phone almost daily talking to Cynthia and making baby talk with his one-year-old son, Julian. As the only married Beatle, John often turned to family to resolve the early conflicts of stardom versus fatherhood. His first romantic love had influence on John's thinking, and had little use, in the words of John, for his antics. John explained this to me during the '64 tour:

> KANE: *Does Cynthia ever give you any critiques?*
> LENNON: *She would come around . . . and say, 'You were lousy tonight. You're pulling those faces.' She doesn't like me clowning around. She says, 'Well, you are always pulling them stupid faces on TV.' I usually pull some kind of face [he smiles and makes a face]. She doesn't like that. She wants me to be straight, you know.*

The romance between Cynthia Powell and John Lennon, somewhat forgotten in the modern era of Lennon remembrances—and often ignored even while it was in full bloom—is a significant one in the life of the young artist. Although the marriage was prematurely instigated by the pregnancy that brought Julian to life, there is no question that Cynthia was John's first real and intense romantic love, and her role in his early days of creativity with the Beatles cannot be discounted. Tony Bramwell, John's young Liverpool mate who followed the Beatles' early rise, remembers it well:

"Cynthia was beautiful, physically and on the inside. Although she knew he was apt to find love on the road, she was totally dedicated to his success, and I might add, extremely influential. He was insecure and Cynthia was there to pump him up, to buttress, sort of, his weak side. She was a wonderful mother who loved John deeply."

After their first meeting at art school, the relationship quickly became passionate, with a mutual understanding of joy and pain. Cynthia Powell learned quickly that her John was obsessed and possessed by the misfortunes of his upbringing, and there were so many. But like her boyfriend, she was no stranger to grief. In fact, Cynthia likely learned to hate the number seventeen. Her father died when she was seventeen. John's mother was killed when he was seventeen, and at the time of John's death in 1980, Julian was seventeen years old.

Cynthia was stunning. Part of her sensual appeal was her shyness and coquettish insecurity. There were many suitors, but only one man who brought her to heights of happiness that even a teenager couldn't imagine. Against her parents' wishes, Cynthia fell deeply in love with John. Both lives would be changed forever—and another life created—on the night John returned from Hamburg in 1962. That night of loving, on the eve of Cynthia's final exams, brought about two significant results—Cynthia failed her final and, in a matter of weeks, she learned that she was pregnant. Social mores of the time would dictate an almost immediate marriage, to which John quickly agreed.

Despite the strains that surrounded the birth of Julian, Cynthia Lennon was a wonderful and devoted wife, dedicated to John and supportive at all steps of the Beatles' meteoric rise. Despite John's late-night rehearsals and his bizarre hours and forms of entertaining, Cynthia Lennon, in her own unassuming way, became an enormous source of strength for John.

There was also a realization, as Cynthia once said, that women were attracted to him "like moths to flame." As she nursed the infant Julian, she provided a level of stability in the most critical time of John Lennon's life, the helter-skelter year between the summer of 1963 and the Beatles' great North American tour of 1964. John, as always unpredictable, was beginning to adjust to the glare of a spotlight so bright and wide that it blurred the senses and distorted the important things of life. Although his stage presence was commanding, the quiet times in the life of John Lennon were marked by brooding, dramatic mood changes, and a high level of insecurity. It was as though all the fame and money could never fill the holes burrowed into his memory during his early years.

During my first travels with the Beatles in 1964, John was eager to talk about his family of three. When the subject turned to Cynthia, his eyes—always mysterious and rarely revealing of his mood—would sparkle and dance. Still, he was rarely chaste on the road. In fact, he was *chased*. But despite his sexual exploits, the conversation would always come back to Cynthia and little Julian, as it did in this characteristic conversation we had in 1964:

KANE: *So have you been in touch with the people at home?*
LENNON: *I talk to Cyn almost every night.*
KANE: *What is she like?*
LENNON: *Well, she's beautiful, you know, and what people don't know is how smart she is. No matter what's happening, you know, she's always there for me.*
KANE: *Does she like the notoriety of being your wife?*
LENNON: *She prefers to just stay in the background as long as the people know that I am married. She just wants to be a normal housewife as much she can be, married to a Beatle, mind you.*

Being there meant standing by her man, playing out the subservient role of wife and mother to a man whose real world was distorted by a success so swift and so public that no normal human being could sustain it without experiencing an intense transformation. Former Beatles press officer Tony Barrow remembers seeing Cynthia's supportive nature come through at all hours of the day and night:

"After rehearsals or a gig, we would go to a bar in the West End. We would drink and talk. It would be late at night, but Cynthia was always waiting for him, always there to embrace him. She was sweetly sensitive, and I do believe most people have no idea what a central figure she was in terms of keeping him somewhat stable during that hard phase when no one knew if the boys were a passing fad or the real thing. I mean, John was the leader, but he was also scared all the time. People forget what a rock she was for him."

After the initial shock of marriage, John settled into a loving routine. But the public, beginning to heat up to the Beatles in ever increasing numbers, was left largely in the dark about the marriage, a fact which was no accident. Brian Epstein saw the marriage as a threat to John's appeal, and the press complied with his wishes to keep it under wraps. Such a fact is almost impossible to believe from a twenty-first century perspective, but Tony Barrow remembers it as a sign of the journalism of the times:

"The press generally was very much kinder to celebrities in the sixties. In John's case, for instance, they went along because we asked them to do so, and the newspapers kept John's marriage out of print. They kept his fatherhood out of print. There was John, well-married to Cynthia, and with child, and with Julian carted around the streets of Liverpool in a pram . . . but that didn't get into the national press because the media generally respected celebrity wishes much more than they would today."

Perhaps this sort of scripted and intentional forsaking of Cynthia is what led to the marriage's bumpy times and eventual demise. But Barrow, who observed the marriage from its early years, has his own blunt assessment of what happened:

"John didn't deserve Cynthia and, in quite a different way, she didn't deserve him. Cyn was a lovely person, at the opposite end of the personality spectrum from John. She spoke softly and was intelligent, genuine, sincere, well-meaning. I never saw her lose her temper or scream and shout. She was the ideal counterbalance to John's noisy, aggressive attitude. She was deeply in love with John, still is I believe, where, in my view, John was never truly in love with her and quite probably would not have married her but for the fact that Julian was on the way and in those days that was the surefire trigger for a trip to the altar. After the marriage was over, Cyn said she did not feel she had lost John because she realized she had never really had him, which summed up their artificial marriage of mutual convenience."

❖

As the traveling reporter with the Beatles in '64 and '65, I never underestimated John Lennon's ability to get his way with women. It is inconceivable that John could walk away from temptation, especially when temptation was waiting around each staircase and every corridor and lurking near the limos and the dressing rooms. Fame and fortune never erased John Lennon's own real view of himself, but the insane tide of emotions surrounding the Beatles' rise to the top easily served as a numbing effect on any guilty feelings that John may have had about his infidelities. As Barrow suggests, Cynthia was not the great love of John Lennon's life, but in a time of chaos, she was a source of great stability. While not faithful in the physical sense, Lennon remained faithful to the romance and stability of the marriage, until he met Yoko Ono.

The music began to die for John and Cynthia after John and Yoko started spending more time with each other in the winter of 1966-67. Finally, the marriage came to an end during the Beatles' famous passage to India where, as fate would have it, a young Canadian named Paul Saltzman would become a surprise observer and documenter of Lennon's transgressions.

Fate. Is it real, or just part of our imagination? The question of fate can be a haunting aspect of our lives. It's that "one thing leads to another" factor that in retrospect seems to shape us. John Lennon's trip to Rishikesh, India with the other Beatles in early 1968 was less than perfect and, for that reason, it is one of the most important and misunderstood events of Lennon's lifetime. For it was on the banks of the Ganges River, in the midst of meditation, away from the maddening crowds, seeking rest and recuperation, that John came to know that he and Cynthia would soon break up.

Was it fate, then, that brought young Paul Saltzman to his date with destiny? The Toronto native, heartbroken and lost in a life transition, sought and found a lifetime of personal philosophy in India. He also made memories that are kept alive by the pictures he took and the images that remain in his mind.

Saltzman, much like John and the Beatles, was aggressively open to new avenues of knowledge. At the age of twenty-four, he was already immersed in a film career and wanted desperately to find himself. He managed to secure a job that would at least pay for his passage to India. In December of 1967, Saltzman journeyed to his film job. A few weeks later, while working on the film in India, the girlfriend that he left behind wrote that she had found another man. Lost in the depths of a heartsick depression, Saltzman finished his film assignment and, already far from home, bewildered and desolate, he decided to journey to find his truth.

"I was in great pain," Saltzman said, ruefully recalling his state of mind at the time. "It hurt so much I was ready to try anything. So, backpack in hand, I traveled to Rishikesh in hopes of connecting with the Maharishi Mahesh Yogi, whose Transcendental Meditation had become the rage of the new age."

When Paul Saltzman arrived in Rishikesh at the gates of the Maharishi's ashram, he was advised by the gatekeeper, "I'm sorry there is no room . . . the Beatles and their wives are here." Less interested in the Beatles, and determined to meditate, Saltzman was given a sleeping place just outside the Ashram where he lived for eight days, and waited. Finally, he came in, joined the community, engaged in classes and casually encountered the Beatles.

Saltzman, lovesick and totally alone, soon took comfort in the band of travelers. One day, he walked over to the edge of a cliff where John Lennon was sitting. Nervously, Saltzman said, "Mind if I join you?" Lennon answered, "Sure, pull up a chair, why don't you? You're from America, oh, that's right, Canada—one of the colonies." Saltzman laughed. John said, "So, I see they still have a sense of humor."

"Why are you here, Paul?" John asked.

Saltzman says the ensuing conversation was healing and surprising:

"I don't know why, but [John Lennon's] openness made me comfortable and eager to tell my story, so I poured it out, detail by detail. To be very honest, I was a little embarrassed, but I'll never forget what he told me. In a soothing voice, spoken like a master, he said, 'Paul, the great thing about love is you always get a second chance. Remember that, you always get a second chance.'

"Looking back at the conversation, there is no doubt he was talking to me, but reminding himself. I observed the Beatles and their wives or girlfriends carefully. The only tension existed between John and Cynthia. There was a real vacuum there. She looked unhappy. He did, too. What surprised me about John Lennon was how effusive he was. Not always a welcoming man to all the people there, he seemed very open to me. We had more philosophical chats and he would ask me if I was okay and all that. He liked TM [Transcendental Meditation]. Remember, he and George stayed there the longest: eight weeks. It was apparent to everybody, on the surface anyway, that the bond with him and Cynthia was evaporating. Of course, I didn't know about Yoko at the time, but considering what we know now, the moments I observed were telling."

There were other tensions, as well. John, as always, was fearful of exploitation. The trusty Mal Evans, the Beatles' road manager and congenial brother figure, told Paul Saltzman that the Maharishi had asked John and Paul for 25 percent of their next recorded work. As Evans reported, John replied,

"Over my dead body." The Beatles, especially John, took trust very seriously. When cash became a priority to others, trust vanished.

As a reporter who traveled with the Beatles through two massive summer tours, I can assure you that it was always difficult for journalists to climb over the "trust gap." I've seen many try and many fail; some had good intentions, others had bad intentions. Paul Saltzman, however, was immediately accepted, so much so that the Beatles and their entourage encouraged him to take photos, which are now part of a fascinating photo diary book called *The Beatles in Rishikesh.*

The photographs of John and Cynthia Lennon are perhaps the book's most intense. They show a man in heavy thought. Cynthia, meanwhile, has a look of strain. No one can say what was in John's mind, but after experiencing scores of art shows where he displayed his photos around North America, Saltzman talks about the effect of the Lennon photographs:

"I've shown these photographs in so many locations. The same thing happens everywhere. There is a shot of John looking rather pensive, sort of a thousand-yard state. And it never fails. At every show, a few people walk in, look at that photograph, and break into tears. There's something about him that makes people cry. I guess it is the tears of mourning, but it might be tears of joy about his life, and the range of emotions he left behind. I don't know. I do know that, as a person, to me, he was a sweetheart."

Paul Saltzman, currently a film producer in Canada, remembers fondly the time he spent with John. Only years later would he discover that, even before Rishikesh, there was a significant other woman in Lennon's life.

During my meeting with John and Paul during their brief trip to New York to announce the formation of Apple (captured on film and included on the DVD in this book), I asked John and Paul about the Maharishi. They both answered curtly, just a night after Paul had called the association a "public mistake."

I asked John, "Was he [the Maharishi] on the level?" Quickly, he answered, "I don't know what level he was on."

What the world didn't know was that fourteen months before Rishikesh, John Lennon was making another passage into the arms of a woman who would dramatically alter the course of his life.

YOKO: PART ONE
THE MEETING

November 9, 1966. John Lennon, the curious artist, was visiting the Indica gallery in London that was exhibiting the work of a young artist named Yoko Ono. John slowly climbed a ladder and glanced at a large magnifying glass. The piece of artwork hanging from the ceiling had one word on it: "YES." John would later say that the word and the art "made me stay" and want to meet the artist. Beatles mystics no doubt view the word "YES" as a sign. The meeting with the artist sparked one of the twentieth century's most famous love affairs and resulted in marriage on Gibraltar three years later. It was a marriage greeted with joy and controversy, and one that forever changed the path of John Lennon. It may have been a spiritual connection at first sight, but the love and friendship took months to develop.

During that first meeting at the gallery, the artist, a major-league attention-getter, gently introduced the superstar Beatle to her work. To this day—to others and in our conversations—Yoko Ono vehemently denies that she knew who John Lennon was or that she had any interest in rock and roll. She was interested enough, though, to send him a book and maintain casual contact. What Yoko didn't know, however, was that at the time of their meeting, the wandering, searching, and inquisitive Mr. Lennon had another affair going on: a growing love for mind-altering drugs. The LSD and marijuana that were becoming a part of his life's routine had already helped to fracture the tenuous marriage with Cynthia. The drugs were an apparent sign that he was looking for something new. While he altered his mind, he appeared, as always, to be looking for other alternatives, much as the flirtation with meditation that would capture his mind for a few months later on.

❖

Our story moves from an art gallery in London in the late sixties to the inside of the Dakota apartment building in autumn of 2004.

The living space always tells the story, doesn't it? In the home of Yoko Ono, there are two depositories of knowledge and creativity—books and art. Further, the high ceilings and expansive dimensions of her Dakota apartment create the sensation that, if it weren't for the elevators inside and the traffic outside, one could easily be in a country garden house surrounded by plush foliage. This feeling merges in the view of Central Park and the European elegance of the stark and defined dimensions of the Dakota.

The huge apartment is bright in color, and with the exception of a formal dining room, it is filled with the furnishings of a warm household. There are portraits of John, posters reminding the visitor of the peace movement and the many causes of John and Yoko, and of course, family photos. In contrast to the dark wood finish of the Dakota's interiors, the household is bright and rich with color. Yoko Ono, now in her eighth decade of life, moves around with the nervous energy of a teenager, and the physical appearance of someone half her age. She is diminutive. There is nary a wrinkle in her skin. The woman is physically fit and animated.

After the handshakes and small talk, we sit down at the kitchen table, her back facing a dramatic window. She clasps her hands, a bit nervously, and says to me, "You look like a Republican."

I reply, "What do you mean?" She answers, "Well you're wearing a bright red tie and a black suit. You look like a Republican!"

"No," I answer, "you've got it wrong. I'm here to *cover* the Republican National Convention and talk to you."

"Oh, now I understand."

Yoko Ono has reason to fear Republicans. After all, it was two Republican administrations that tried to deport her husband. Her demeanor toward conservatives and the establishment, as it were, hasn't changed. As the 2004

Republican National Convention began, she took out a full page ad in the *New York Times* that read: "IMAGINE PEACE Yoko Ono 2004." John may be gone, but Yoko is still lighting the candle for him on special occasions. She knows, as he did, that words can be powerful.

It is late morning as the summer sun shines in from the kitchen window. Yoko sits down at the head of the kitchen table ready to tell her story. She is surrounded by the memories and artifacts of the man who changed her life. Yoko is in her seventies, but her body is trim and her complexion is fair. With her dark hair falling onto her shoulders and her eyes darting around the room, she moves through the apartment in a hurry, a tiny bundle of high-octane energy. There is an air of certainty about her, even though it is rare that she sits for interviews. Today, she is the official keeper of the flame, the proprietor of the musical, political, and spiritual legend that is John Lennon. Her own career as an artist shines brightly, but she is determined that, through new music releases and productions, John's sound will continue to reverberate for years to come. It is a passion to her, as well as a sacred responsibility to John and what he stood for. She is more concerned about perpetuity, and less concerned that observers in far corners of the world view her in a complex light. After all, this is her destiny. After all, she is Yoko Ono.

Yoko Ono. The name connects instantly to John Lennon. It conjures up thoughts of partnership, bitterness, love, and kindness. The majority of writers and pundits have blamed her for the breakup of the Beatles and for John's abysmal fall into drunken obscurity in the early seventies. Others give her high praise and admiration for a keen business sense, a devoted partnership, and for serving as a wonderful wife and mother. She has been celebrated, vilified, honored, chastised, and respected.

The unanswered question about John Lennon and Yoko Ono is the secret to a relationship that weathered a storm of trouble and stayed intact. And, of course, the starting point is the simple question: what *was* the attraction? From Yoko Ono's view it was a union of opposites seeking a way out of their worlds:

"John was a guy from Liverpool. I was a woman from Tokyo. We were so different in that sense. But still, we immediately recognized each other. Understood each other totally from the beginning. All I can say is that we were soul mates. We were both rebels, too. If John wasn't a rebel, he could not have come out of Liverpool. I, too, was a rebel in my own way. I could not have been at the Indica Gallery in London that year, that day, unless I was a rebel."

Their first encounter at the Indica Gallery was an eye opener. Yoko insists that she didn't know who he was but, as she excitedly recalls, his behavior was suspect and enticing. In fact, when she began explaining the scene, she gave me a virtual reenactment:

"I thought John was a very attractive and elegant man. Elegant is not exactly the kind of word you expect to describe a working class hero/rocker like John. But that was how he was. Then suddenly, he grabbed the apple displayed on a beautiful stand built of transparent Perspex, and took a bite out of it. I thought, 'Oh, no! What is going on here?! It's a bit out of line, isn't it?' I probably showed my displeasure, even though I didn't say anything. So John laughed sheepishly and put back the apple on the stand. You know. He took a bite out of my artwork!"

At this point of our conversation, Yoko gets up from the chair and mimics John's action, moving her face close to mine and breathing in about a quarter of an inch from my skin. She continued:

"John then said he heard that there was supposed to be an event or a happening or something. I said, 'This is today's event,' and raised a card in front of him that said 'Breathe' in tiny letters, in my own handwriting. John came very close, right up to my face, and said, 'Like this?' and breathed very strongly. I was a bit taken back, but said, 'Yes' calmly."

Despite this close encounter, Yoko resisted communications with him, until a few weeks later when they exchanged letters. The connection was strained because, unlike most normal men courting a woman, John Lennon had two problems: he was married and he was John Lennon. Although she won't go into specifics on how he did it, John did reach out to her, and that is when, Yoko believes, she almost blew it:

"I started to have some feelings for him, but I was too busy. One time he showed what he was . . . thinking of me and I didn't like the way he showed it."

She didn't like the way he showed it, but as time moved on, through coincidence and schedule, they began to see each other more.

"We started to bump into each other in places. Liverpool Art School asked me to come to lecture and do a performance. I told that to John, when I met him. He thought that was great. 'So you're going to Liverpool?' He moved his eyebrows up and down a couple of times—like Groucho Marx—and looked at me warmly."

The relationship flourished in the months after the art gallery meeting. It is interesting, though, that Yoko was so afraid of her initial feelings that she wanted to stay in seclusion in Paris where she had traveled to after attending a film festival in Belgium. But soon love and understanding were joined in the rhythm of the friendship. It had been building for some time. She recalls:

"I started to have some feelings for him. He had a very funny accent, and that was sweet, too. He, in return, said he was amused that I was an Asian with an American accent. Sometimes he started laughing when I was talking to him. "Your accent!" he would say in his heavy Liverpool accent.

"Then one day, he kind of expressed his feelings for me. I was a bit scared. So I closed the door on him, almost literally. I went to Paris. In Paris, I thought, 'Okay, what did I do? I'm never going to see him again. I messed it up, totally!' It was so painful to think about that, so I decided that I would never go back to London. Never. I'm going to start a new life in Paris.

"Fate would have it that soon, I was invited to go back to London for a performance at the Albert Hall. Of course, I took it, and went back. I opened the door to my apartment, and there were piles of letters from John, just on the floor."

In a person's lifetime, there are moments of decision or indecision that can change one's direction for years. And so it was with Yoko Ono, who was beginning to understand that John's pursuit was not so trivial, nor were her deepening feelings. Yet something was holding her back, and for a short time Yoko found herself on the bridge, taking only short baby steps and getting more and more afraid to cross. By the winter months of 1967, Yoko crossed the threshold and the love affair was in full bloom.

The couple dated from the winter of 1966—secretly, at first—until early spring of 1969 when they were married. In the early days of 1967, John and Yoko began to appear in public together, although secrecy surrounded the nature of the relationship. In March of 1967, the first inklings arrived in the British press about the emergence of the new woman in John Lennon's life. The press reports became so scattered that it caused Cynthia great emotional turmoil, and for a while, John tried in vain to keep a lid on the growing friendship, out of respect for his first love. Eventually the leaks became a torrent of information that couldn't be stopped. By the time of the trip to India, Cynthia knew the end was near. The marriage, followed by the honeymoon peace protests—their famous "bed-in" at the Amsterdam Hilton—became big news around the world. Beatles fans, however, became concerned that their Fab Four would be threatened by the union. For John and Yoko, it was a time of testing. Yoko insists the relationship was strong because of the total honesty that both of them brought to it:

"We know there's no hiding of anything because we're so always together, you know. And my feeling was that . . . I felt that in the beginning when we were nuts about each other . . . the whole world hated us. Well, you have to grab what this is . . . such a beautiful magical miracle, miraculous thing."

Even beautiful and miraculous things sometimes fade under the pressures of everyday life. In the four years after the Gibraltar wedding, John Lennon had learned that musical life on his own and away from the Beatles was lonely and vacuous. With the exception of a glorious album, *Plastic Ono Band,* released in 1970, John found success wanting. That undermining insecurity that is a constant thread of his adult life would again haunt him, this time in his second marriage. And so it happened that the identity crisis of John Lennon's life was again realized through a crisis in his marriage. Was he husband or lover, rogue rocker or rebellious crusader? The truth would come out, but first there would be pain.

Complicating the early marital years for John and Yoko were two separate bands of public opinion that grew into one global mindset. Beatles fans, through their vaunted fan clubs, magazines, and letter-writing adventures, spread the notion that Yoko was responsible for frictions inside the group. When the band's split-up became public, the wrath of those fans, in many cases unfairly, was targeted at Yoko. The press was even worse, portraying the couple as a runaway train wreck, and as people ignoring conventional standards of behavior. The reader should remember that despite the social revolution of the sixties, society in general—and especially in Britain—was much more prurient than it is today. With his mile-high profile, John Lennon was prime fodder for the tabloid media.

Publicity considerations aside, the Lennon-Ono marriage eventually imploded with John's departure into another woman's arms. Yoko Ono says it was the climax to a period of growing tension in the marriage, which paralleled the government's campaign against them:

"In the United States, John and I started to have all sorts of trouble because of our stand for peace when the country was at war in Vietnam. Immigration was trying to kick us out. We were followed by men in dark suits and black cars. Our phones were tapped. The tension was mounting."

It all came to a head on election night, 1972, Ono remembers:

"On the evening when we found out that McGovern lost to Nixon, John and I were in the studio mixing some songs. John was very upset. Then [political activist] Jerry Rubin called and told us that he was giving a party at his apartment in the Village and we should come. So we did. By the time Jerry opened the door to let us in, John was so high, his words were slurring.

"The party was a gathering of New York intellectuals, writers, and journalists. John grabbed a girl, went into the next room and they started to make love noisily. Somebody put a record on, with the intent to cover the noise. But the walls were paper-thin and the music hardly covered the noise. All the coats were in that room, too. So all of us felt like we were stuck, just sitting there, facing the wall to the next room. Finally, some girl bravely went into the next room, took her coat and left. One by one, people did that. I was frozen. I had no idea how long I was sitting like that. At one point, I noticed through the window that it was getting light outside. So I looked around and noticed that everybody left except our assistant Peter.

"After that night, I started thinking: the world hated us for being together. Still, it made sense to be together if we were in love, so desperately as we were. But if it's like this, there's no excuse to stay together. That's what I thought.

"We were together all the time, so it's natural that one gets a bit antsy. Why not? It still took some time before I suggested to John that we should split for awhile. So we did. That was the beginning of the 'lost weekend.' John said, 'But I don't want to lose you.' I said, 'But we'd lose each other anyway if we stayed together.' It was sad. But I felt that we didn't have much choice. So I told him to go."

According to Yoko, John was afraid to be alone. But she insisted that he move out:

"I just said, 'Look we're both still young, sexy, beautiful, and intelligent (laughs). What are we doing?' John said he couldn't move around by himself. He never had to for the longest time. In the Beatles' days, he had a lot of people around him—the entourage—and by going with me, and by announcing to the world that this was the love of his life, or something, he lost everybody. He burnt his bridge, major. So I felt very responsible of that."

By the fall of 1973, Yoko Ono realized that their love affair had hit a wall, so to speak, prompting her to take action—a bold and almost unfathomable action. She actually suggested that John take a lover. And not just any lover. Yoko proposed that John go off with May Pang, a young, Asian-American woman who had served as John and Yoko's assistant for several years. She recalls:

"John said, 'I can't go by myself.' So I said, 'How about so and so, so and so?' I threw out a few names. When I said how about May, he said, 'Oh, no, no, not her!' May was a beautiful girl. I thought, 'You protest too much.' She's the one, I thought. She should go with him. I would do that for this man, who lost everything for his love for me."

When Yoko proposed May as a companion, John reacted aggressively, angrily denying that he would ever be interested in May. He was so vigorous and outspoken in his alleged disinterest that Yoko, a master of reading emotions, was convinced that his protestations were actually a cover-up for a manifestation of genuine interest.

Yoko says she never reckoned that the affair would last as long as it did, or that it would cause so much pain:

"Well, it turned out that it was a very difficult situation for all three of us. There was a time when May called me from L.A. She called me regularly, just friendly, but this was a very different call. She was crying because John was not being very nice. So I said she could come to the Dakota and stay with me. I thought I'd console her because I felt very responsible about her situation, too. May was attractive, young, and hip. She deserved better. So I thought."

I asked Yoko if she ever felt like picking up the phone and saying, "John, let's get back together."

"It was the other way around," she says. "John was always saying, 'Let me come back.' But I didn't think it was a good idea. I don't think you understand what it's like to be hated and humiliated by the whole world. Now, you can say I was proud. My pride was hurt, yes. But it was not good for John, either. We were like those classic doomed lovers that even made gods and goddesses jealous and angry.

"I thought love was everything. Love will conquer everything. I thought I could sacrifice everything I have for this love of ours. But it was getting very dangerous. Lovers like that could be destroyed. The writing was on the wall,

I thought."

The Yoko-John separation is a matter of great conjecture. But in a strange way, John, on a collision course with his dark side, was seeking some form of release. He found it in the arms of the woman Yoko chose for him. And as his career and life headed for rock bottom, John Lennon had found release in the embrace of the young secretary. May Pang, the reluctant lover, couldn't imagine what she was getting herself into. And Yoko Ono would have to put her marriage on pause until the truth in John Lennon came out.

MAY PANG:
THE "LOST WEEKEND"

Society has always had a vague picture of the so-called "other woman." In fiction and in public perspective, lovers and companions do not fare well, especially if their story of love and caring has an unhappy ending. Beatles historians the world over have treated the story of John Lennon and May Pang in different ways. Some give her a slight mention. Others have written her completely out of John's life, bowing to external pressures from friends and associates of Yoko. This is so ironic because it was Yoko who played matchmaker to the coupling of John and May. Even the late author Ray Coleman, in his magnificent book *Lennon: The Definitive Biography,* dismisses the relationship and never even bothers to interview May Pang.

The truth is that in the final years of John Lennon's life, a second woman had a share of influence, and her story shapes his life in different ways. To ignore that friendship and their time together would be a gross attempt at revising history. After all, this friendship and romance lasted ten years.

From first impressions, you would never imagine that the attractive yet reserved lady in her mid-fifties today is the same curious, bright, and effervescent young woman who swept John Lennon off of his feet and played such an important part, privately and publicly, in the final decade of his life.

May Pang is an unlikely heroine in the story of John Lennon's life. In the kitchen of her suburban New York home, her son arrives home from school, warmly embracing his mother who is, at the time of our meeting in the spring of 2004, taking special care of her aging mother. On the walls of this house are pictures of John Lennon. In the den, there are books by and about John, signed and otherwise. In private storage, May Pang has extraordinary sketches of John, including a self-portrait. John, in spirit, is an invisible member of the household. May's children, fifteen and thirteen, celebrate his life and are fully aware of the relationship that their mother had with John.

That relationship and its nourishing influence on a troubled genius has been the subject of whispers and reports for a quarter of a century. Few observers have really understood the joy and pain surrounding it. Many of the writers who have approached the May Pang-John Lennon relationship have treated it as a sideshow. It was not.

Many observers, Beatles insiders, and others have expressed to me that John was happier during his time with May Pang than at any other time in the seventies. That assertion, however, can be disputed by examining the changes in his life from 1975 to 1980. But there was no question that, at the time, he was happy with May. John himself told me in 1975 that his time with May was both joyous and revealing. There is no question that the young May Pang had great influence on his music. How much will be debated. But the tenure of the relationship was more than eighteen months. Theirs was a relationship that began professionally in 1970, became personal in 1973, and continued quietly until his death in 1980.

May Pang, born in Spanish Harlem, educated and influenced in the Catholic school system, was a self-described "good girl" when circumstance and pressure placed her in the arms of one of the most famous people in the world.

Unlike most love affairs, it was not an accident. Although the nature of the situation foretold the abbreviated length of partnership, there is no denying the depth of the union.

Beatles insiders and Lennon friends consistently have a deep affection for

May, while at the same time respecting the bond between Yoko and John. Tony Bramwell, the Liverpool kid who grew up watching the Beatles and later worked for Brian Epstein and Apple, has a more subjective viewpoint:

"I think Yoko stifled him a lot. I don't think she understood the fun surrounding the Beatles. The seventies were an unhappy time for John with all those weird musical experiments. His *Yokoness* period also included all that avant-garde stuff. May was a good human being . . . he could go back to his roots of being a rock star. She allowed him to enjoy himself. While Yoko cut everybody out of his life, May let him see his friends."

Allan Steckler, the Apple executive who hired May, sees it differently:

"I adored May, and so did John. But Yoko gave John his creative impetus. Yoko is a creative woman who was into a lot of things, especially herself, but over and over again, she did things to create situations that made John think. And when John started thinking, he was the most creative man in the world. On the other hand, May was not challenging but nurturing. John was happy around May. She was a piece of cake in the relationship. She was not challenging but loving and sensitive. And it was a real contrast, a real break from Yoko."

May was a different woman than Yoko, and in some ways, more protective at the most difficult times. One of John's friends, the hard-living performer and composer Harry Nilsson, was almost his undoing, tempting John—no doubt a willing participant—with endless opportunities to take drugs, fool around with women, and generally lose control. Throughout their time together, May had to fight vigorously to save John from the ugly orgy of drinking and drugging that had enveloped his life. But ironically, despite her real and growing love for John, it was she who helped him find his way clear back to the arms of Yoko Ono.

The story begins with May's version of a less-than-modest proposal.

For three years, from late 1969 to the beginning of 1973, May worked for the company owned by Allen Klein, who had become the business manager to the Beatles. Almost immediately after her employment began, May became a regular in the company of John and Yoko. For that entire period the vivacious and energetic woman performed a variety of duties for the couple: moving them to different apartments, accompanying them to England to transport luggage and personal items, and joining John (and sometimes Yoko) in major recording sessions. Her relationship with John in those years was warm, but strictly professional. She recalls:

"John and I talked about music and what I liked about it. We were pals. Yoko was demanding but she seemed to really like me. As tough as she was, it was clear that she trusted me. I thought it was a wonderful career move. I was learning on the job and meeting some fascinating people."

May's job had evolved into eighteen-hour work days. She was a regular in the Lennon world, and things were going well until one morning in the Spring of 1973 when Yoko made a simple and stunning request. May remembers:

"She came into my office, you know. We had already been working on the beginning of *Mind Games*. And I come in one morning and she sits on the opposite side of me. She says, 'May, I gotta talk to you.' And she says, 'You know, John and I are not getting along.' I replied, 'Oh, I'm sorry to hear that.' Now, we all knew that. I mean, it was just obvious in the house. It was just almost painful to be around them. And she says, 'You know, John's gonna start dating other people.' And then all of a sudden she says, 'You don't have a boyfriend.' And I just looked at her and I went, 'What? Me? I'm not looking for a boy.' She says, 'No, no, no. You'd be good for John.' And I said, 'But I don't want your husband.' And she says, 'Oh, I know you're not after him.' She says, 'But I think you'd be good for him.'"

May was in a state of total surprise. Her relationship with John was professional, friendly, buddy-like and had never even experienced traces of flirting or any level of infatuation. Her heart was racing as Yoko continued the hard sell. She recalls:

"[Yoko said,] 'Oh, come on May!' And she talks to you like you're a child. She's seventeen years older than me, first off. And I said, 'Oh my God. I'm not interested.' She says, 'No, no. You don't want to see John going out with somebody that's gonna treat him wrong?' And I said, 'No, of course not.' She says, 'Well I know you're not.' But I said, 'I'm not the one.' She says, 'You are, and you should start immediately.' I said, 'I don't want to.' She answered, 'Oh, yes you are.' And she gets up and she leaves."

Yoko's matchmaking effort continued unabated as she continued to put pressure on both unwilling participants. For two weeks, May and John hardly spoke, but the seeds were planted for a romance that would change John's course in an already bewildering decade. In the office, at the studio, and in transit, there was an unspoken tension between John and May. And then, one day, sparks started flying as they approached the studio.

"We get in the elevator, as the door closes, this man pounces on me and plants me a kiss and I just sort of stood back and I don't know what to do. And I look at him and I go, 'Stand over there. Can you just stand over there? Please stand over there.' And he's going—he looks at me and is like, 'I've been waiting to do that all day.' I said, 'Don't even say it. Please just don't!' And I'm now freaking out again. I'm going, 'What's going on?' He goes, 'Come on.' I said, 'I—can we not talk about this?'

"A few minutes later, in the studio, John was standing in back of me, started giving me back rubs (laughing). You could see everybody going, 'Huh, what's going on here?' The studio atmosphere changed and John was having this little playful grin on him, you know. And we got back in the car that night and we're going home and I said, 'You're going back to the Dakota.' And he goes, 'No, to your place.' [I said] 'No, we're going back to the Dakota. You're going home.' And I shipped him home and I said, 'Go. Just go home (laughing).' And he goes, 'Beware of little green men coming through your window.' And I said, 'Just go.'"

Eventually, the little green man came did come through the window and the affair officially began. Because of May's youth, innocence, and professional work ethic, her co-workers in the Apple office were stunned.

Linda Reig, a young assistant at Apple, worked closely with May, and recalls her working attitude toward John:

"There is no question—May was star struck and they spent a lot of time together. In fact, she was present at almost every recording session. She was the go-to person for both John and Yoko. But it wasn't about romance. There were never sparks between them, that I witnessed anyway. John could be a bastard, crude and insulting. May was a sweetheart. It was an odd match— the relationship surprised everyone."

The untold part of the beginnings of this affair is that in the spring of 1973, Yoko Ono was increasingly intolerant of John's heavy drinking and unpredictability. Feeling closed in and hoping to expand her own professional pursuits, she reached out to May Pang. Yoko liked May, respected her work habits, and certainly viewed her as non-threatening. Pang remembers:

"Although it was unorthodox, to say the least, I think she felt that I was safe, that John would never fall in love with me, that she would get the change she needed, and so would he. But she never counted on what would happen."

But over thirty years later, May also questions the real motives:

"[Yoko] thought of John as not a very bright person, and she could never understand why people admired him. And she used to say this to a lot of musicians, that she's the songwriter in the family. He was . . . crying for help . . . he obviously was having a hard time with Yoko. She was becoming more of a dominant figure. . . . I think she didn't find John stimulating enough for her. [And] he was upset because he wasn't creating like he wanted to."

No one, not even Yoko Ono, could forecast the outcome of the "encounter" she had arranged. The result was more than the diversion Yoko had apparently intended. What actually transpired was a friendship and love that would take John Lennon to the precipice of disaster, back to health and safety, and, in the end, back to Yoko. It took two weeks after Yoko's solicitation for things to start to happen. But it took eighteen months for the public affair to end, and John's death to end it forever. The reasons for the romance had more to do than just the lovers' match that Yoko Ono had apparently hoped for. May feels that Yoko had a definite plan for the affair, but underestimated the potential of the pairing:

"She made it happen because she wanted more freedom for herself to do her thing. She thought that nothing could ever destroy their relationship—John would just come back. She thought . . . it was a sexual thing and that in two weeks after he got his rocks off that he would come back."

At the time, the relationship with May became the stuff of gossip and speculation, but John's New York buddy, photographer Bob Gruen, saw it close up. Gruen understood what was happening and why it was happening, and knew that timing and John's circumstances played a role in the affair. The public knew little at the time. Gruen says:

"In the 1972 to '73 period when he's in New York, where there's a lot of drinking and a lot of staying up late, he had kind of a rough Lower-East-Side-kind-of look and he was kind of sensitive about his weight. When he went to L.A., it's easier to look better out in L.A. Especially when you get your hair cut, you got a swimming pool, you're clean every day, you get that L.A. tan. Some of the sickest people look beautiful out there. I know that emotionally he was pretty depressed here in New York and that was part of the reason of the split up. He was drinking and, you know, being angry and depressed every day and Yoko didn't want any part of that. She wanted to move ahead; she was getting sober and moving ahead with her work. And she kind of said at one point with John, 'I'm not going to live with a drunkard, an angry drunk all the time.' That's when he started moving toward May, and she was very comforting to him and he appreciated that. She would take care of him."

And she did, although there were enormous obstacles, especially the drinking and drug use. May tried to set a normal course for him, and even planned special family time together. Shortly after the romance blossomed in New York, John and May left for California. During their time in California—November of 1973 through March of 1974—May tried to bring a sense of normalcy to John's life. In what became a seminal moment for a man whose own father abandoned him, John was reunited with his ten-year-old son Julian in California. May helped make the arrangements and even scheduled a trip to Disneyland for John and Julian. In one of the more uncomfortable moments of the first of three trips to America, Julian, by necessity, was accompanied by Cynthia. John virtually ignored Cynthia on the trip to Disneyland, and May, the ever-sensitive family woman, scolded him for it. As a result of Julian's visit, Cynthia and May became friends with a common adversary, Yoko, and a common love for John. May believes her sense of family was something that John had missed for most of his life, and it brought him closer to her, and to his son:

"He loved the fact that I was stable. I wasn't trying to push away the family. I was trying to *make* the family. Every weekend we made sure we called Julian. I made sure that he was in constant contact with Julian. And he said, 'This is good, you know.'"

Arlene Reckson, manager of the Record Plant, a top recording studio in the seventies, and later a trusted employee of John and Yoko, became close friends with May; it's a friendship that remains intact today. During a visit to see John and May in the Los Angeles days, Arlene knew her friend was in a tough spot:

"It was difficult for May. Yoko was calling all the time. [May] was in love with John, and he, it seemed, with her. May is so giving that it was a heartbreak to watch what was happening. She had familial instincts, and was trying her best to make him happy. And the pressure was amazing, but she's a woman who is sensitive and caring and she eventually pulled him out of it."

May's challenge in California to keep John clean and sober was frustrating and an uphill battle. California was both a nightmare and a reckoning for John. The drinking and drugs brought erratic behavior and abuse. In one horrible moment, at the ugly crescendo of an alcohol-soaked night, John threw her across a room. May believes it was the same pattern witnessed in the beating of Stuart Sutcliffe—violence, a letdown, a plea for forgiveness, and ultimately, regret:

"I think he grew up in that time period that he was abusive, and he was trying to control that. He wanted to understand himself. And that's why all that [primal therapy] was going on. And I remember when he, whenever he was abusive to me, he came back and all he did, he just cried and said, 'May, I'd never want to hurt you.' And I saw that, that child in him. He goes, 'I just don't want to hurt you. I just want to be with you.' There were times he just didn't know how to act out."

Within months of their arrival in L.A., the couple returned to New York City and settled in a small East Side apartment near the United Nations, where they would live for the remainder of their eighteen months together. May, assuming the combination role of lover, friend, and key organizer, was now deeply in love with John. She introduced him to outings on Long Island Sound, visits to museums and, following the ribald Los Angeles escapades, a much quieter existence. But there was always the reality that Yoko was still his wife, and she remained in almost daily contact. The source of the contact remains the subject of an historical, and almost hysterical, debate.

May says that Yoko never stopped calling. Yoko insists in my conversation with her that it was John who called her almost every day. Photographer Bob Gruen concurs with Yoko and says that John was the one who kept in touch. May says that Yoko would send friends like Elliott Mintz, the longtime press spokesman for Yoko and John, and others to keep an eye on the pair. The unfiltered truth is hard to come by, but the clear fact remains: eventually, John came home. Around the weekend of February 1, 1975, May knew that the beginning of the end was near:

"It wasn't intended to be a break. Yoko had called on a Friday. She said, 'John, you have to come today. I've got the guy coming today to help me quit smoking. I got this message and it's got to be today. The stars are right.' I was very uneasy about it and I could feel [John] couldn't handle me pacing and we almost got into an argument. And he turned around, he said, 'Look, it's in the afternoon right now. Well, I'll be back by dinner. Yoko promised me I'd be back by dinner and we can go out for a nice meal somewhere, wherever you want to go.' And he said, 'Let's go down to see Paul and Linda. They're gonna be in New Orleans. I wanna go.' And I said, 'Okay.' He walked out. That was it. I knew it."

That may have been "it" as far as the public perception of the relationship was concerned, but it wasn't the end. The friendship between John Lennon and May Pang continued secretly until his death. There were phone calls and secret encounters, even during the four years that John mainly stayed home and took care of his and Yoko's infant-toddler son Sean. Over the remaining years, John was critical of the men May dated, warning her, as she recalls, that it wouldn't be easy. May describes a sly smile in John's voice as he boldly made such statements:

"Yeah, he was asking me had I seen anybody. And he said, you know, 'You're gonna have a hard time finding a boyfriend.' And I said, 'Why?' He said, 'Because they're all going to compare themselves to me!' And he was right; there's no two ways about it. And that has affected my life. He met one guy that I was dating and he said to me, 'I wish you weren't going out with him.' I said, 'Why?' He goes, 'He's not for you.' He was generally concerned at all times."

As the years went on, even during May's unsuccessful marriage to Tony Visconti, the famed producer for David Bowie, the ghost of John Lennon's love was always in the house. May is remembered as John Lennon's girlfriend, but unlike many of the "other women" in history, she has accepted that moniker with grace, class, and a sense of deep affection.

Although John had found his place again with Yoko, May was never far from his thoughts. And he had a convenient messenger to convey those thoughts.

Mario Casciano, the teenager who had befriended May and John, was asked by John to communicate, send messages, and relay information to May. He did so faithfully right up until early December of 1980. One of the last packages he delivered to May Pang was several copies of John's last recording, *Double Fantasy*. It was just a few days before the murder.

Mario is still enraptured by the life of the star he came to know. He is also convinced that John's time with May was hardly a fling:

"I think he truly loved her. I think when Sean was born, he took a more inner look at his life. But he never stopped loving May. Remember that during his time with her, he became healthy . . . he saw his friends again . . . his music blossomed. He seemed really happy. He always wanted to know what she was doing and if she was okay. They communicated regularly, but when circumstances prevented them from seeing each other, he would seek me out to relay messages to her."

The story of May Pang and John Lennon from May's perspective is contradicted by Yoko. Love is all in the eye of the lover, isn't it? But there is simply no question that John's return to Yoko was more than a reflection on his life with May. It was apparently a reaction to his own needs. Only John can tell us why he came back to the Dakota. But most Lennon experts, including longtime radio host and Lennon watcher Joe Johnson, see his decision based on a search for order:

"Lennon needed to be guided with structure. Alone and unbridled, he tended to spiral out of control, like a jet airplane that has no control flaps. He had the ability to soar and achieve greatness, but without structure and order, he could wander off the page and get into trouble, as witnessed during the so-called 'lost weekend,' which on several occasions landed him in the press for his self-admitted drunken fits in the local nightlife. Though he was with May Pang during the period, and she supported him during one of his most successful creative times, she wasn't strong enough to hold him. That's what Yoko's great strength was with John. She had the ability to reel him in, yet make him feel that he was in control. And though we lost Lennon at too-early an age, Yoko should be given credit for saving his life up to that point. The Beatles and John were surely on the path to self-destruction as witnessed by the *Let It Be* tapes and, perhaps, it was Yoko's grasp of pulling him to safety that allowed him to give us some of the world's most-remembered music."

If John was indeed looking for a lifeboat, Yoko was ready, as she always had been since that first fateful meeting in the London art gallery.

Yoko: Part Two
The Return

From the beginning, when their love affair went public, to the end of their life together, there was a constant stream of sarcasm and skepticism in the worldwide media directed toward Yoko and her intentions. Through it all, even during the separation, John remained a sensitive earpiece for Yoko. He was defensive about negative press and, she says, extremely comforting:

"I felt like my blood was just gushing down . . . he would say [about the press] 'Oh, it's just horrible!' And we'd just share that in the middle of the night. And he'd say, 'Oh honey are you okay?' And then, 'I'm going to make some pizza.' He would make me some food. It was just that gentle side."

When John returned to the Dakota, and to Yoko, the couple communicated more openly. John, free of the addiction that had tortured his life, was now high on the thing he did best—talking. The intimacy that Yoko describes in their reignited relationship was illuminated by the art of conversation. From my perspective, the most memorable and invigorating part of knowing John Lennon was engaging him in any kind of debate or verbal joust. In their marriage, Yoko describes, conversation was actively consensual and constant:

"It was in the Dakota elevator and we were talking like crazy and we forgot to push the button. So the elevator was not moving and we didn't know it and this woman was saying she thought it was great after so many years that we were still so enthusiastic about chatting with each other."

Through eleven years of marriage, a public separation, the birth of their son, Sean, and a marriage to one of the world's most famous men, Yoko Ono declares that the love never stopped being intense:

"I guess the most heightened moment was after we came back together again. We were both ecstatic from then on. The most heightened moment was the day Sean was born, it was John's birthday, too, and we got the notice on the same day that John was allowed to stay in the United States. It was a triple whammy!

"Another heightened moment I remember was the last month, the last weekend, the last day. On the last day, at the studio when we were waiting for the engineers to prepare the board in the next room, John said something to me that was incredibly intense and sweet. I just said, 'Oh,' like I didn't get it, looking at the wall or something. But in my heart, I thought, I'm over forty, and my husband is saying something like this. I'm a lucky woman. Afterwards, we were driven home, and what was waiting for us was the worst disaster that we never thought would happen to anybody."

Yoko says that, close to the end, the two of them were more romantic than ever, and that John was very loving:

"John was known for being a macho cynic. But actually, he was an incredibly passionate romantic. We were both romantics. *Wuthering Heights* was our story. We thought he was Heathcliff, and I, Cathy.

"Towards the end, I was starting to think the pain I went through for being with John was all worth it. I thought, 'Look at us. We are so close now.' Life is what happens while we are busy making other plans, as John said."

Unaware that the end was near, reconciled to what they hoped to be a new kind of relationship, Yoko says that the final days were intensely warm:

"We were so sweet to each other. It was coming to a point where I went out and I was shopping and I said, 'Oh, I better get some chocolates for John because John likes chocolate.' So I bought him chocolate, brought it home, and as soon as I came out of the elevator, the door opens and John says, 'Hi.' I said, 'How did you know that I was coming back just then?' He said, 'I just knew it.' And so I said, 'Okay, well, I got some chocolates for you.' [And he said] 'You shouldn't have. You shouldn't have,' because he doesn't want to gain weight or something, but he loves it! And I was, at the time I was thinking, 'What is this?' It's so beautiful that he even knew when I'm gonna come back that moment and he opened the door. So we were like that and it was getting intensely sweet about a month or so just before he died."

And so it appeared that the famed relationship of John and Yoko had matured into a real friendship, a marriage of understanding. But Yoko is quick to point out that it was still passionate:

"Well, we were still making it. I mean, if it's friendship, you don't make it. So, of course, in the end, there was that sort of gentle but cuddly 'we accomplished this' kind of feeling."

In the end. The words that Yoko Ono never thought she would be saying. In the end, as it was at the beginning, the world blamed Yoko for everything and anything.

The news media, of which I have been a proud member for forty-six years, sometimes runs in packs. Whether it is a presidential campaign or the hunt for celebrity gossip, some reporters are bent on proliferating stereotypical images of well-known people. Therefore it became casual and easy for authors and others to portray Yoko Ono as a tough and unfeeling woman. But beware the image makers! There is no question that Yoko Ono is a strong-willed creative force. Some of her excesses and failures in judgment have been detailed in this book. But there is no questioning her impact on John Lennon's life and her commitment to the man. There is also clear evidence that in the final years of John's life, the love she gave to her soul mate was deep and convincing.

Photojournalist Allan Tannenbaum has covered the first uprising in the West Bank and Gaza, the first Gulf War, and other critical events in modern history. He was also there near the end of John Lennon's life. Tannenbaum remembers his photo sessions with the couple in Central Park in late November 1980. Photojournalists are trained to notice and react. What he noticed was something that he admired:

"They had begun to trust me after my initial photo shoot [with them] for the *Soho Weekly News*. So we went to Central Park. We walked and talked and every once in a while we would stop to take a picture or two. They were very warm with each other and were holding hands, looking very much in love. A few days later I showed John some of the proofs. He said to me, 'You know why I like your pictures? Because you make Yoko look so beautiful.'"

Tannenbaum's work went over so well with the couple that he was invited to shoot stills of them, naked, as they settled in at a New York studio to film a video to promote the song "(Just Like) Starting Over" on the *Double Fantasy* album. Tannenbaum stood behind the film cameras as the couple simulated sex for the cameras.

"It was a surreal scene," Tannenbaum recalls, "a little odd but I really enjoyed watching them enjoy each other's company. There was a real glow between them. Sometimes she would give orders and John would answer with a smile: 'Okay, Mother. Whatever you say.' There was no sense of dominance, just a really happy couple."

Today, those who regularly deal with Yoko are extremely affectionate. Mark Lapidos, creator of the annual "Fest for Beatles Fans"—the popular Beatles fan gatherings near New York and Chicago—calls her a "doll" who every year contributes to the fan conventions and offers her best wishes. "Not a year passes," Lapidos says, "when she doesn't acknowledge John's life with gifts to auction off and messages of pure kindness."

That kindness over a long period of time has been felt by the Lennon's former West Village neighbor, and sometimes family photographer, Bob Gruen:

"I like Yoko a lot. I think she's a fascinating person. She's very intelligent. She's very giving, very generous. A very strong person who is very loyal to her friends. When people ask me, 'What kind of woman is Yoko Ono?' I always answer, 'She's the kind of woman that John Lennon could marry.' You know that so many people, they hear about Yoko Ono in the press and particularly the English press. You know, in England, if you can't say something bad about somebody, they don't write about you at all."

Considering Gruen's praise, a reporter would wonder why Yoko Ono has been so reluctant to allow people to see her as she is. Gruen has a theory:

"Well, in some ways she has tried to let people know. She's always been open. It's just people misinterpret what's going on. For one thing, early on—and I have had this discussion with her—she always looked very serious and severe in her pictures. I was trying to get her to lighten up and smile once in a while 'cause backstage and, you know, at home, she smiles a lot, she laughs. She's a wonderful, open, happy person, you know. But it's a Japanese custom not to smile in photos. And they grew up that way. Whenever you see pictures of Japanese people, you know, portraits of them and so on, it's always a very straight face. They feel that life is not funny. Life is serious and it's not something to laugh about."

The relationship between John and Yoko, one of the most famous pairings in the world, will always be the subject for analysis, dissection, and inspection. The people close to them have perhaps the finest perspective. Bob Gruen, for one, feels that John Lennon needed the strength of Yoko, understood it, and had a deepening respect for her:

"She was open to his feelings and he was the kind of person who realized that, if she's making you feel this so strongly, she's damn good. It is a big plus side to her personality, that she's strong . . . but not to say overbearing, not 'mean' strong, you know. She's a tough girl. You know, a good New Yorker can take care of herself and she doesn't get pushed around too easily. And I think that helped John 'cause John would have more of a tendency to be nice to somebody or you know, say, 'Okay,' when he didn't really mean 'Okay,' because he didn't want to piss somebody off. You know, whereas, Yoko would be much more pragmatic. If the answer was 'No,' she'd just say 'No' and say, 'Next question.'"

Having people offer pragmatic advice during troubled times was critical in the life of John Lennon, and Yoko Ono had plenty of it to give. Shortly after John's release of *Some Time in New York City*, performed with the band Elephant's Memory, there was a concert at Madison Square Garden. It would, as Gruen remembers, become a devastating experience for all the players, but mostly for John:

"During recording sessions, there was a lot of drinking, and chemical additives to aid the drinking and, you know, help you stay awake longer and feel better and whatever. When the *Some Time in New York City* album came out, it got miserably panned in the press. Around that time, we played Madison Square Garden. We thought it was fantastic; the press hated it. They thought it was raunchy and loose and rock and roll and they hated the fact the Yoko got to sing. They wanted to see John do a Beatles' song. I mean, he did a couple, but not enough. And they thought this new raunchy rock and roll was terrible, especially the political stuff.

"He got very depressed and he drank a lot more and he really kind of sank into a deep depression for a while. It was that the reviews of the concert, the lack of sales of the album. She was less affected and helped him get through it."

Some Time in New York City was released in 1972. The U.S. government had John under surveillance. The new music was not well-received. The man was suddenly being maligned by the same media that had been so positive about his work with the Beatles. It was a dark and troubled time and, by all accounts, Yoko helped him deal with it day-by-day. The marriage was developing into the pattern of most marriages, maturing into a period of mutual dependency, but John seemed to be the most dependent of the two.

May Pang provided the support in late 1973 and through most of 1974. But once John returned to Yoko—and after years of self-imposed silence and playing at-home dad throughout most of the seventies—John was, according to Beatles historian Denny Somach, encouraged by Yoko to get moving again:

"I think he felt, and I think this has been documented, that he was sort of drying up, and that's when he credits Yoko with revitalizing him and getting him excited, 'cause you know, after he put out the *Rock 'n' Roll* album in '75, he didn't record for five years, 'til '80. She encouraged him, while he was nesting Sean, to start writing at home, to energize that talent inside of him."

❖

If, indeed, "all you need is love," then John Lennon had his share. But his conflicts were created by his choices. For her part, Pauline Sutcliffe, a great student of John's life, again sees a parallel between his early development and his adult loves:

"Stuart was so influential. So were the women. Just look at it. May Pang is the nurturing, loving, selfless love. Yoko is the competitive, challenging one, opening up new ideas . . . which would have been very appealing because I think he was bored and depressed about his life when he first met Yoko. And she was like a shot in the ass. But if you go back to Aunt Mimi, this was the woman with discipline while his natural mother Julia was real warm and loving. I still have questions about why he became hermetic and withdrawn when he went back with Yoko because there was so much in him that needed to come out."

Whatever their respective influences, the three women who shaped John Lennon's adult and romantic life are worlds apart. May Pang speaks openly about the man she describes as a "man I loved and respected." Cynthia, who today lives in southern Europe, has refused to talk about her life with John. Yoko, who runs the Lennon empire, has had no contact with May since 1975, and has managed minimal contact with Cynthia, although in public comments she has been respectful to both of them.

There are still signs, though, of the competition for his affections.

May Pang was the primary studio coordinator on three of John's early seventies albums—*Mind Games, Rock 'n' Roll,* and *Walls and Bridges.* One of the hit songs from *Walls and Bridges* was "#9 Dream," written for May and featuring her voice whispering John's name. At the time the song was released, in September of 1974, there were no music videos. Yet a video was produced in 2003 featuring, among other songs, "#9 Dream," part of Yoko's ongoing productions updating and visualizing John's music. Yoko is seen in the video mouthing John's name, but the voice is May Pang's.

Yoko, who now coordinates all productions and recordings of John's music, could have placed anyone in that role. She decided to cast herself and to lip-synch the words. It is both a telling moment and a fitting tribute to her lasting affections, and perhaps to her feelings relating to the eighteen-month separation from John.

Imagine: two of the women who loved John joined in song, evoking his name, competing for his affections—or the perception of it—a quarter of a century after his death.

The loves of John Lennon all had abiding faith in the man through times of pleasure and pain. But in the grand scheme of things, John's return to Yoko was a determining moment in his life. Emerging from the fog of drugs, brought back to passion with the caring of May Pang, John began to see what he needed. And what he needed was his own re-creation of the art that defined his life to that point. Coming back to Yoko was also a drive for a sense of direction, helping him ascend to a dimension of living that he had failed to achieve before—genuine fathering and a new view of the meaning of reproduction. Also underway was the attempt to find the peace and the truth that would come before his death, and a final attempt to bring light to the dangerous darkness in his life.

THREE:
Danger in the Shadows

"My mother told me to stay away from that lad. He was trouble, she
said, but who could avoid his charm and his charisma."
—*Tony Bramwell, boyhood friend of John Lennon and British musical icon*

"He always liked playing the role of tough guy. He was tough, but he
was real and he could cry in private like anyone else.
—*Tony Barrow, Beatles Press Officer*

All the people closest to John Lennon shared one frustration about the man
they loved and admired: they could not keep him out of trouble.

But trouble was central to John's life as an artist and as a person. Causing
trouble was a way for him to push limits and explore new frontiers as a
child, teenager, adult, and artist—sometimes for the better and sometimes
for the worse.

The greatest trouble in John's life probably stemmed from his willingness
to speak his mind about important issues such as the Vietnam War. He possessed an uncanny talent to articulate these issues and force people to see
them in new ways and act to bring about positive changes. In that regard,
John's ability to cause trouble ended up making the world a better place.

But John also possessed an uncanny talent to cause unnecessary trouble for himself and those closest to him through reckless and sometimes downright boorish behavior. That brand of behavior and the trouble it brought almost ended John Lennon's career just as it got underway, and continued to make his world a less desirable place for most of his life.

John's lifelong friend and fellow Liverpool native Tony Bramwell remembers John's talent for trouble well:

"John had this wicked sense of humor. He saw things differently from everyone else. At times, he would play tricks. He would take chances. He was what they called in the fifties somewhat of a 'juvenile delinquent.' But he was charming at the same time, except when he had a drink in his hand."

Bramwell was involved in the birth of the Beatles and the evolution of their record company Apple. From the beginnings in Liverpool to what he calls the "Yokoness" phase of John's life, Bramwell watched John Lennon grow. He was not surprised when John became his generation's leading voice and social critic.

"He was always different and he was always daring people. I guess you could say that his acts of outrage as a teenager would manifest later in his protests as an adult. There was a fire in his belly and anger in his heart. He was an amazing person, but he had a deep and mysterious personality. So if you wanted to be with John, which I did, you had to take the whole parcel: the good and the bad. But there's no question that he would stimulate you, make you wonder about things."

John's development as a social critic began during his attendance at the Quarry Bank School in Liverpool, where his art flourished along with his satire and cynicism. His sketches there poked fun at two groups: teachers and the disabled. John became famous for poetry and art portraying educators with sexual themes. He also had a penchant for depicting disabled people, especially those with deformities, in a harsh light. The source of this obsession remains a mystery. Perhaps his work reflected his own fear of being disabled. It should be pointed out that John spent many hours in his adult life supporting charities for the less fortunate. His mockery of people with physical disabilities would seem the stuff of an immature teenager. Fortunately, he abandoned that pattern of behavior before he entered adulthood, except for certain moments onstage when he would twist his body and hunch up his arms and make the faces of the disturbed.

His ridicule of establishment figures and his talent for creating trouble for them and himself, on the other hand, only escalated as he grew older. Many wrote off Lennon's troublemaking as the work of a bad boy wannabe or callous delinquent. Those close to him understood that his intentions and personality ran deeper.

Tony Barrow, the Beatles' press officer who spent many late nights trying to gloss over or make amends for Lennon's troublemaking, still remembers John with fondness and respect:

"He always liked playing the role of tough guy. He was tough, but he was real and he could cry in private like anyone else. When he made the 'Jesus Christ' statements in 1966 before the tour, and when he realized that he screwed up and let the other boys down, he broke down uncontrollably. He was beside himself. But when he appeared at the press conference, he tried hard to temper his apology. He was John Lennon, but he was as insecure as the rest of us."

May Pang, who was as close to John Lennon as almost anyone in the world, thinks that some of it was playacting:

"John would have liked you to believe that he was capable of misadventure. He loved people thinking that he was tougher and more unpredictable than he really was. He was quite nervous about public reactions to his own actions, but he never wanted anyone to know that he felt vulnerable."

The greatest damage from John's relentless risk-taking probably resulted not from the celebrated incidents and outrageous public comments, but those episodes that occurred in the shadows—incidents dangerous enough to destroy his life and works just as they were beginning to bloom. Luck would have it that he managed, sometimes barely, to escape the slings and arrows and the decisive consequences that often accompany such daring.

❖

The Beatles' tour of 1964 was filled with late-night trysts and all-night parties. Unwritten rules of the day prevented journalists from reporting on these private affairs, let alone asking the participants any questions about them. It is unthinkable what would have happened in today's media environment. Scandalous tales that have been uncovered about President John F. Kennedy, for example, and the private lives of other famous world figures were taboo material for reporters back in the sixties. I watched many women go into the Beatles' hotel rooms, a scene that most people would expect to see, but I avoided giving play-by-play accounts of those adventures.

John Lennon would later recall those crazy Beatle nights in a 1975 interview, saying, "The Beatles tours were like the Fellini film *Satyricon*. We had that image. Man, our tours were like something else, if you could get on our tours, you were in. They were *Satyricon*, all right. Wherever we went, there was always a whole scene going. I could never sleep, such a heavy scene it was."

A heavy scene it was indeed. For this reporter, it was beyond *Satyricon*. It was, for an American like me who came of age in the fifties, a cross between watching the ultimate sexual fantasy play out and witnessing a world of barbaric adventure that I never knew could be real. In his ultimate realness, John was unafraid to share those vivid memories years later with Yoko. When we met at the Dakota in September 2004, Yoko hinted at possible guilt and perhaps a touch of historical pride in John's need to recount his lurid life on tour.

"Well [Larry], you know the other side of it, maybe (laughing). By the time that he got together with me, he was a different person from when he was touring, you know. He told me a lot of stories about it, what was going on when he was touring. I mean, he was totally honest with me. He said, 'If

I can't be honest with you, what's the point?' So he was."

Although this reporter viewed the late-night activity as irrelevant to the Beatles' history, what *is* relevant in the story of John Lennon was how close he came to career-threatening disaster during some of those nights, sometimes due to his own benevolence.

The Beatles, carefully watched by manager Brian Epstein and fiercely protected by road managers Neil Aspinall and Malcolm Evans, plus traveling press manager Derek Taylor, were usually prudent in their selection of after-hours playmates. I never once saw an underage girl brought to the Beatles' rooms. Except for the leaders of their local fan clubs, who cheerfully greeted them in the dressing rooms in most cities for autographs and pictures, underage girls were never allowed near the Beatles. The band scrupulously avoided situations that might compromise their image and their success. The Beatles, although feared by the older generation, were clean-cut and fabulously well-behaved, in public at least. That was their image, and they were determined to protect it. But on one sultry night, or early morning depending on your own body clock, that strict code of avoiding underage women was violated in a most dangerous way. And John was at the center of it.

The Beatles' triumphs and dreams of even greater achievement almost came crashing down when John took his edgy life to a bad place in the early hours of August 20, 1964. Politicians caught in scandal will always tell you that the *appearance of impropriety* is just as bad as a real impropriety. That was the problem that early and scary morning at the Sahara Hotel in Las Vegas. The episode tells you what happens to a sensitive guy who makes the mistake of inviting the wrong people to the wrong place, but it also displays the naiveté of a man with good intentions. Those already jaded with stereotyped imagery of the dark and daring life of rock and roll stars may find this hard to accept. But it happened. It is the truth.

The night before the episode was a whirlwind: the first concert in the Cow Palace in San Francisco; a flight to Las Vegas; entry into the hotel past an out-of-control crowd in the lobby; and finally, rest in my room on the twenty-third floor, the heavily secured Beatles' floor. The hotel was noisy and chaotic—from the crowds outside to the kids trying unsuccessfully to climb the fire stairwells to get to the band. Despite the distractions, I drifted off to sleep, excited to be there, but apprehensive about what might come next. What would happen in the following hours would actually make the insanity of the first twenty-four hours of the 1964 tour seem like a day at the beach.

A heavy knock sounded on my door around 5 a.m., startling me out of sleep. The face in the doorway was that of Malcolm Evans, a face that would cheer anyone up, even in the middle of the night. But his eyes showed concern, and his features were contorted in anguish. I will never forget his words:

"We need you down in the lobby. There's been a spot of trouble with John. Can you put on a tie and jacket?"

I had known Malcolm Evans for less than forty-eight hours, but I knew he was worried about something. He waited outside while I got myself together. What could it be? I couldn't figure it out, but I knew that whatever it was, the stakes were high. It turned out that the stakes on the table were the rest of the Beatles' tour and perhaps even the rest of their careers.

In the hallway, Evans was joined by Derek Taylor and Neil Aspinall. Taylor served as the group's able spokesperson, a stylish, seasoned professional who fancied himself an older and more mature Beatle. Aspinall was an early friend of the band, quiet and suave, but close to the vest. They explained that a dangerous situation was afoot. Twin sisters were in John Lennon's room, catching autographs and posing for pictures with Lennon. They were part of a group of fans that had penetrated security. Most of the visitors had left, but these girls were sleeping on the second bed in John's room.

"It's all quite proper," Derek Taylor said. "Not a damn thing happened in there."

I scrutinized his face for hidden meanings and to gauge his sincerity.

Derek added, "Their mother is in the lobby, demanding to know what they're doing up there, and we need you to go and tell her everything is proper."

"Where are the girls?" I asked. Malcolm winced. Neil said nothing. Derek gave me the answer with a finger that pointed down the hallway.

The door to John's room was not locked. Derek opened it. John was dozing on the bed, his eyes half-open. The twin sisters rested on the edge of the second bed, their eyes glazing at the TV on the bureau. It was strange seeing underage fans inside one of the Beatles' rooms.

It was then that I understood the magnitude of the potential problem.

"Why me? I'm not going to be part of any lying," I said.

"There's nothing to lie about. They just came in to visit," Derek insisted.

I turned and asked, "Why me?"

Derek answered, "You're a reporter. You look trustworthy."

I made it clear that I would trust his word, but refused to play any part in a whitewash.

Mal Evans and I took the elevator to the lobby. The decorative entrance to the casino was nearly empty—just a few stragglers holding their cups of coins from the one-armed bandits. We approached a woman in her mid-thirties who appeared to be shaken with worry. Where had she been while her daughters were sneaking past security to join a party with a rock-and-roll band upstairs? The casino chips in her hand provided the most likely answer. Still, this woman also held in her hands the power to destroy the good-guy image of the Beatles. In the wholesome climate of 1964 America, even the appearance of hosting two underage girls in a hotel room could have quickly ended their careers. Instead of standing for one of the most powerful and positive explosions of feeling and music in modern history, Beatlemania would have deteriorated into an ugly word representing the worst type of people and behavior.

Taking Taylor's word, I identified myself to the mother and explained the girls' visit as an innocent quest for pictures and autographs. Even though I declared my independence as a journalist, she wasn't convinced. But when the elevators opened a minute later, a police officer emerged with her daughters, both of them smiling broadly and chatting excitedly about the details of John's kindness. I was convinced. After all, how could two young girls look so innocent if a sexual encounter had taken place?

Still, there was an oddity to this episode. How did the police officer get to the room? The role of that officer has always been a mystery to me. But I do know this—a brief investigation into the matter was launched by the Las Vegas police department. There was no follow-up. Some journalists speculated that lawyers in Los Angeles had, months later, arranged a settlement with the mother. That would have been a travesty because John invited those girls just to, as he would say the next day, "watch a little telly with me." His judgment was flawed, but from my perspective, his intentions were forthright. It was entirely consistent with the John Lennon I came to know.

As dawn was breaking, mother and daughters left the premises. Malcolm Evans grinned. Derek Taylor called up Brian Epstein with a status report, and then Derek and Malcolm thanked me warmly. Epstein was furious about the incident. And I still didn't feel good about it.

"Was John messing with those kids?" I asked.

Derek said, "No."

Was I naïve or uncaring? Neither. I just couldn't believe that a Beatle would risk his future by getting involved with young girls in that way. But then again, John sometimes walked a fine line between earnest friendship and deceptive debauchery. Still, I was convinced this was a case of mistaken intentions.

Lennon, who originally wasn't aware of my involvement, professed his innocence when he learned about my early morning wake-up call. To this day, I don't know exactly what happened in that hotel room. My instincts tell me it was pure innocence. The real story will never be known, but the incident was an intensely close call for the boys that placed their careers in serious jeopardy.

What is more telling about the episode is how it illustrates the tightrope

John walked in the after-hours life of the touring Beatles.

John, however, seemed oblivious to the dangers surrounding the episode. When I approached him on the plane the next day, he said, "Thanks. It was nothing, you know. Just some sweet kids."

As I grew to know John better, I discovered a paradox deep within him: John was a very sexual person; but beneath his complex exterior, he was also a very friendly, guileless human being, just the kind of man who would invite two kids into his room to watch some late-night TV. He also sympathized with Beatles fans who wanted to get close to him for a little while and was seemingly unaware of how dangerous that proximity could be.

John continued to walk the tightrope between his tendency toward outrageous behavior and his desire to appease the norms of an adoring public for most of the rest of his life. During one particularly troubling period—his eighteen-month "lost weekend"—he fell off it several times.

That dark period was heavily influenced by his relationships with two fellow musical giants: singer-songwriter Harry Nilsson and infamous producer/mad-genius Phil Spector.

May Pang, who was by John's side throughout the period, was especially wary of Nilsson. She says:

"John loved Harry. He loved his energy; he loved his writing. What he loved in Harry was the beauty of his friendship and relaxed personality. That's what he saw. Harry drank, a lot. But Harry was the type of guy that if you go out drinking with him, he'd be sure at the end of the night that there would be a big brawl and that you are the one who's in trouble, even though he started it. Harry would keep feeding John drinks until it was too late."

Mark Lapidos, has a different perspective on Nilsson:

"Outside of the drugs, Harry was a great friend to John. Like John, he didn't suffer fools lightly. He would rather share time with friends, real friends, than hang out with superficial entertainers. He was genuine, no b.s. My wife Carol and I enjoyed his company and the time he spent at our conventions.

But we never saw the destructive side that people talk about."

John loved Nilsson, but Nilsson's friendship was beginning to wear thin, even early on during the Los Angeles days segment of the "lost weekend." Music arranger and producer Mark Hudson, for one, saw the bad side of Nilsson's influence on John:

"Harry was a great guy. I really had affection for him. The two were very tight, but John was beginning to notice that Harry might be bringing him down."

That destructive side was a nightmare to May Pang, John's lover and unofficial guardian in Los Angeles. Pang was also fearful of Spector, the legendary and mercurial rock producer who invented the famous "Wall of Sound" in the early sixties and was producing Lennon's latest solo album. The demons surrounded John in Malibu, Hollywood, and Beverly Hills, and May felt helpless. So, at times, did John.

"When he did work, John had a great work ethic," May recalls. "He liked to be on time and work, work, and work. Phil Spector was different. At times he would come into a session two or three hours late, dressed in some costume. One night he was a doctor, the next night a karate expert. He drank heavily. He drank a bottle of Vodka every night and held everybody at bay by screaming at them. I hated when he popped those nitrates. They smelled like dirty socks and he would pop them under everyone's noses.

"The worst scene happened one night when Phil was playing his 'I am God' routine. He took away John's glasses, so John had no idea where he was. He literally was frothing at the mouth. John was screaming and he thought that he was being put into this sexual gay thing because Phil's bodyguard George was trying to tie him up. He thought he was going to do something. He was kicking and screaming. Nothing happened, but it was terrifying to John."

Spector's musical talents had always impressed John, but there was always that air of danger surrounding Phil Spector. Hudson vividly remembers it:

"I was at the A&M studios with my brothers (The Hudson Brothers) and everyone knew that Lennon was in the big studio with Phil Spector, and through the walls you could hear Spector just going off on John. One time, Spector pulled out a large gun and started chasing John through the hallways. John was trying to laugh it off, but it was horrible. I mean Spector's reputation had preceded him. I was scared to death."

Away from home, passionate for a new woman who allowed space for his insecurity and unevenness, and influenced by friends who played the role of social wrecking crew, John Lennon was sinking into the abyss. And then came the nights at the Troubador.

The Troubador was a popular West Los Angeles nightclub. For John and his friends, visits there could be either memorable or despicable. One night, John, May Pang, and legendary guitarist Jesse Ed Davis got together for an early evening dinner at a restaurant in Santa Monica, where John got famously drunk before disappearing into the bathroom.

"He returned from the bathroom with a Kotex on his forehead," May recalls. "I pleaded with him to take it off. He just smiled."

The trio headed to the Troubador where John continued to drink and ignore the pleas of May Pang. This episode ended unceremoniously when John said to the waitress, "Don't you know who I am?" The waitress, in one of the more direct retorts in John Lennon's life, said, "Yeah, you're some asshole with a Kotex on his forehead." The "Kotex Incident" passed with little fanfare. But what happened a few days later, on March 13, rocked John's life.

John and Harry Nilsson had decided to catch the Smothers Brothers act during their engagement at the Troubador. Tommy Smothers, after all, had joined the chorus for the recording of "Give Peace A Chance" during John and Yoko's Toronto bed-in a few years earlier.

As they so often did together, John and Harry quickly became drunk. On an empty stomach, smoking like a steam engine and egged on by Nilsson, John began heckling the Smothers Brothers. Heckling a band is one thing. Interrupting the timing of a comedy act is overtly destructive. The language was foul and so was the action. Actor Peter Lawford, accompanied by a young lady, was seated nearby. He repeatedly yelled at John to stop the tirade. But Lennon continued. Ken Fritz, manager of the Smothers Brothers, came over to make a personal appeal. Fritz raised his arm. Lennon raised his right fist and took a swing at Fritz, and then lobbed a glass full of liquor in Fritz's direction. As the club's bouncers forcibly removed Lennon and Nilsson, May watched in horror. John would later, with embarrassment, describe the scene for me:

"We started yelling at Tommy and his brother. I think we almost screwed up the act. A few weeks before I was in the same place, I found a tampon machine or something in a restaurant, wore one on my head. Heckled some more. And I don't remember how it happened, but they threw my ass out."

John was contrite. He seemed humiliated by the incident.

May Pang also remembers the incident with a great deal of chagrin:

"I realized that I had to work harder to clean him up. There were bad influences there and, at times, I was losing the battle. But underneath was such a caring guy. The drinking was drying him up emotionally, and that night was the worst."

Unfortunately, "that night" didn't end with the inglorious exit. Even as the trio left for the car, an even more potentially damaging event occurred. A fifty-year-old freelance photographer tried to immortalize the moment by pointing her camera at John. The photographer, Brenda Mary Perkins, claimed Lennon slapped her over her right eye in response.

Proclaiming his innocence, John saw a darker side to the photographer's intentions, when he declared, "Well, I was not in the best frame of mind. I was wildly drunk. But I was nowhere near this chick, she's got no photographs of me near her. It was my first night on Brandy Alexanders, and they tasted like milkshakes. The first thing I knew I was out of me gourd.

"Of course, Harry Nilsson was no help feeding them to me, saying 'Go ahead, John.' It is true I was wildly obnoxious, but I definitely didn't hit this woman who just wanted to get her name in the papers and a few dollars."

Ms. Perkins filed a complaint with the Los Angeles Police Department.

After a two-week investigation, the district attorney proclaimed there was not enough evidence to support criminal charges. John was lucky. A criminal indictment would have cemented the Nixon administration's relentless efforts to deport John based on his marijuana conviction a few years before in the United Kingdom.

In any person's life, grim and ugly moments can lead to precipitous decline or a realization that it's time to change. As it turns out, the humiliating bender at the Troubadour was simply the moment of truth for John. The nightclub embarrassment seemed unbearable for him. John sent letters of apology to the comedians, their manager, and the management at the club.

The Troubadour mess ended up serving a purpose. It shocked Yoko back home in New York. In Los Angeles, May Pang was beside herself. But most of all, the publicity surrounding the incident and the public outrage it caused chastened John. It ended up inspiring not just that typical morning-after apology, but weeks of self-analysis and extreme remorse. It was the beginning of the end of the bouts of drinking that had beleaguered his body, mind, and soul.

Tony Bramwell, whose love and respect for John was never in question, remembers that alcohol had always brought out the worst in Lennon:

"John was on creative edge all the time, but he was a bad drunk—a bad drunk as a teen, a bad drunk as an adult."

Jeffrey Michelson, who eventually ran Apple's ad agency in New York, saw John's nose for misadventure as an inevitable companion to his genius:

"From my personal experiences, John was a genius because the nature of his work changed the field. He set a new bar and went beyond the outer limits. He had a different level of mental function, but that could go in the other direction.

"I've only met two real geniuses in my life: Norman Mailer and John Lennon. Both men had genius and both had the ability in one direction to be smarter than you and, in the other direction, to be more stupid in their excesses. The size of John's mental factory was huge. He had the ability to be insightful and brilliant. He was very kind, but he could also use his wit and mental capacity to be very cruel and take dangerous risks. I think all geniuses take their mental capacities to highs and lows."

And as with many artistic geniuses, John's highs and lows were often inspired by his substance abuse. He said it was a pattern that began in his teens and escalated from there:

"I started on pills when I was fifteen, maybe seventeen. When I became a musician in Hamburg, the only way to play eight hours every night was to take pills. The waiters gave you them—the pills and drink. I was a fucking dropped-down drunk in art school. *Help!* was where we turned on to pot and we dropped drink, simple as that. I've always needed a drug to survive. The others, too, but I always had more, more pills, more of everything because I'm more crazy probably."

One thing is clear: John was a risk taker from childhood, but without the cover of drugs and alcohol, he could be as realistic and practical as anyone. In our Dallas stop in 1964, all four Beatles were tantalized by the "bunnies" who worked as cocktail waitresses in the private club of our hotel, the Cabana Motor Inn. Paul McCartney was especially curious, and I thought John's eyeballs were leaving their sockets when one of them brushed by him. I chuckled at the reaction, but Lennon, fearful after the close call with the teenagers in Los Angeles, yelled out, "None of that rubbish here! This is Dallas. We're almost at the end. Be careful lads." And with that, Brian Epstein looked like the weight of the world had been lifted from his shoulders.

But that capacity for restraint seemed to be absent during his days in Los Angeles with Harry Nilsson. Was John aware that his life was out of control, that his behavior was pushing him over the edge? But, more importantly, why wasn't the intense and sometimes controlling wife, Yoko Ono, taking a more active role in helping him deal with his excesses and depression? Or was her pushing him out the door with May Pang really her way of showing him the dangers of life without her and, ultimately, of bringing him back?

In an interview three months before his death, John analyzed his behavior during that era with *Newsweek* reporter Barbara Graustark. He called the post-Beatles period "an extension of my craziness with the Beatles. But when I freaked out, Paul or Epstein would be there to contain my personality and cover up. Suddenly I was adrift at sea, and for the first time there was nobody there to protect me from myself."

Lennon found his way out of his "lost weekend" period and back home—figuratively and literally.

But during this period, other people were watching John Lennon—and not with an eye to protecting him. They wanted to send him back to his original home, England, by deporting him from America.

FOUR:
Give Peace a Chance

"Lennon's four-year battle to stay in our country is testimony
to his faith in the American dream."
—*Irving R. Kaufman, Chief Judge of the
United States Court of Appeals, Second Circuit, October 7, 1975*

Today, it seems almost inconceivable that someone could be openly
targeted for deportation by the U.S. government just for expressing his
desire for peace and justice in the world. But John Lennon lived in different
times, and he became the target of just such a campaign from the late sixties
to the early seventies.

Lennon had strong opinions on a variety of troublesome topics, and was
never afraid to express them. He had the power of poetry, lyrics, and art to
make his case, and used his great passion and fame to proclaim it.

From his childhood on, John utilized his own bully pulpit to promote
social and political causes, many of them unpopular when he began to
champion them. Anti-war buttons and protests of racial inequality adorned
all of his berets and other hats on the Beatles' tour in 1965, a year in which
the Vietnam War was escalating and the racial divide was growing even wider
in the United States. When we sat for an interview and posed for a snapshot

in Chicago in '65, John held up a copy of *Ebony* magazine with the head-line, "The White Problem in America." My bosses back at WFUN radio were shocked by his public protest.

Beatles manager Brian Epstein was even more appalled by John's political theatrics, which he felt could jeopardize the band's popularity. Epstein did his best to stifle Lennon, but there was no stopping John. Protest was woven into the very fabric of his being.

Whether you agree or not with John's views, one thing remains certain: he was the first superstar celebrity to use his fame—and to risk it—to endorse political causes. He cleared the way for hundreds of other celebrities to chan-nel their energy and money to causes. And as he wove his web of protest, the man seemed fearless.

Where did it begin? Was his indignation and fury over war and injustice the result of the seeds sown in his troubled youth? Or was it just an attempt to tap into the social discontents of the times to increase his influence and fame? No way. One of the most remarkable aspects of John Lennon's life is his consistency on social and political matters. Before and after he became one of the world's most famous people, John was virtually the same man: a hard-line cynic, an individual who never failed to ask serious questions, an intellectual warrior whose queries about injustice forced others to think and act. In his own way, John Lennon was a courageous and extraordinary inves-tigative journalist.

Pauline Sutcliffe, the sister of original Beatle Stuart Sutcliffe, believes that John's social crusading was a manifestation of something that had been inside him all along:

"All the political stuff in the seventies that John became involved in seemed to me just a another form of the anarchic spirit that would manifest [itself] as an adolescent. I mean, he found another outlet and a more accept-able way of expressing his attitude, whatever. And he was clearly anti-estab-lishment from the very beginning."

John Lennon's bad-boy image began resonating early and, as he neared his thirtieth birthday, more often. His lifelong battle with the establishment escalated dramatically in 1969, reaching a turning point in the fall of that year. And although his actions may seem tame by today's standards, many reacted with shock, apprehension, and anger towards him.

On September 1, 1969, John Lennon returned the Member of the British Empire (MBE) medal that he had received along with the other Beatles in recognition of their worldwide success. John simply wrapped the medal in a brown paper package and sent it back to the Queen of England, along with the following note:

"I am returning this MBE in protest against Britain's involvement in the Nigeria-Biafra thing, against our support of America in Vietnam, and against 'Cold Turkey' slipping down the charts. With love. John Lennon."

John's Aunt Mimi was furious over his action, as were many others in England. The irony, never lost on John Lennon, was that the original awarding of the medals to the Beatles spawned protests from war veterans and others who thought it was wrong to honor a musical group with the same distinction granted to military heroes.

When John mailed the note and package to Buckingham Palace, he thumbed his nose at the ultimate symbol of British tradition and authority. Not content with just shocking the Queen, he also sent the same note to the Prime Minister.

Despite his own penchant for explosions of brief violence, John Lennon was a true pacifist. He understood the difficult nature of personal relationships, but clearly abhorred the notion of young men and women going to war because of political decisions they had no control over. That hatred of all kinds of war, from the carnage in Biafra to the war in Vietnam, was further fueled by his relationship with artist Yoko Ono.

John was mesmerized by Yoko's art the moment he first laid eyes on it at a 1966 exhibit in London. He was fascinated by her ability to use art to force people to see the world— and their role in it—in a new light. In recent years, Asian art critics have embraced her work, especially a piece called, "Play It

By Trust." The work consists of a game board with playing pieces. It is monochromatic, and precipitates confusion. Observers or 'players' can never figure out where they are within the actual game. The net result: competition becomes impossible, and so, in effect, does conflict.

John's instinct for protest and Yoko Ono's more intellectual approach made for a potent combination. Stuart Sutcliffe taught John how to draw and paint. Yoko Ono tutored him on the power and meaning of symbols and how to express his beliefs without words.

Throughout all three Beatles tours of North America, Beatles manager Brian Epstein tried to muzzle John and the other band members on political matters to avoid any controversy, which was not part of the Epstein game plan for mainstream success. Every time I asked John about the war in Vietnam, Epstein would become visibly upset. But John would grow excited, eager to engage in debate, hardly concerned about consequences.

"What would be your personal solution to stopping war?" I asked John one evening.

"Don't know if there is one except to stop fighting," he said. "If all the power blocs have the same weapons, somebody will still want more. Why fight when you can talk, man? It is so simple."

John would often remind me that I was the first reporter ever to ask him about the war in Vietnam. That first foray into highly charged topics came on August 18, 1964. In 1970, after he had become more heavily involved in organized anti-war activity, he reflected on those earlier years and the beliefs he shared with his fellow Beatle George Harrison.

"Even during the Beatle days, I tried to go against it and so did George. Epstein always tried to waffle on us about saying nothing on Vietnam. So there was a time when George and I said, 'Listen, when they ask next time, we're going to say we don't like that war and we think we should get right out.' That's what we did. At that time, it was a pretty radical thing to do, especially for the 'Fab Four.' You've got to remember that I'd always felt repressed, we were all so pressurized that there was hardly any chance of expressing ourselves. [We were] always kept in a cocoon of myths and dreams. It's pretty hard when you are Caesar and everybody is saying how wonderful you are and they are giving you all the goodies and the girls; it's pretty hard to break out of that and say, 'Well, I don't want to be king, I want to be real.'"

That determination to be "real" was the essence of John Lennon. His union and marriage to Yoko Ono only reinforced the urge, and helped him find new outlets for it. A week after John and Yoko were married in Gibraltar, the happy couple arrived on the seventh floor of the Hilton hotel in Amsterdam. They did not come alone.

The couple invited reporters along for the honeymoon, which would become a "bed-in" for peace. Photos and stories on the bed-in appeared on the front pages of newspapers around the world. In a story meeting at my newsroom, at what was then WFIL-TV in Philadelphia, we decided that we needed to get an interview with John on the air. In an age devoid of satellites, phone interviews were the fastest means available. I reached John at the Amsterdam Hilton on March 27, 1969.

KANE: *Hello*

LENNON: *Hi, Larry, how are you?*

KANE: *Hi, how are you doing?*

LENNON: *Okay.*

KANE: *Listen I wanted to ask a few questions. First of all, how's marriage?*

LENNON: *Beautiful.*

KANE: *Are you putting on the world . . . or are you just having fun or what?*

LENNON: *Look, you know we're putting people on as well. We dedicated [our honeymoon] instead of having it in private, we sort of dedicated it to world peace, you know, and we believe that sincerely. It's like two events. It's like a happening event kind of thing, only the happening is we stay in bed for days and nights or stay in the room mainly. And which is pretty heavy going, really, even for a honeymoon.*

KANE: *Are you trying this as somewhat of an anti-war protest?*

LENNON: *Yeah, sure, it's a protest against violence, you know, and also the other part of the protest is called 'Hair Peace,' which is peace spelled with P-E-A-C-E. It's a pun on P-I-E-C-E, et cetera, et cetera, instead of smashing things up, the people just grow their hair as a form of protest until there's so many hairy people that they carry a continuous sign of their protest, you know.*

LARRY: *This is probably the first attempt of its kind at making a baby in public, isn't it?*

LENNON: *I don't know about making a baby in public, you know. But, I mean, it's not exactly making love, but it's conceptually making love in public, you know.*

KANE: *It's just somewhat of a message to the world, right?*

LENNON: *Yeah, sure. I mean we've dedicated a week of our time. Now, a lot of people, cynics, sort of say, 'Oh well it's easy, rich, staying at the Hilton, you know staying in bed a week.' But just try anywhere, and this isn't because we have time to spare because we don't. This is our first two weeks. I haven't had any time off since India, which is over a year ago and Yoko hasn't taken a holiday in three or four years. So we are sincerely dedicating this time we have to peace, you know.*

KANE: *So to all the cynics who say that it's something dirty or something filthy, you just say that it's a dedication to peace?*

LENNON: *It is, and if the worst that happens is we give somebody a laugh, well, that's okay, too, you know.*

KANE: *Trying to make the world a little happier?*

LENNON: *Yeah. I think everybody is—we both think everybody is getting a little bit serious about it, and although it's serious, you still need laughs, you know, and we're here to provide laughs, as well as some sound and film.*

KANE: *Thanks, John, and best of luck on your marriage.*
LENNON: *Okay, Larry. Nice talking to you.*

A week later, in a brief phone conversation, John, elated and emboldened by the experience, and not faced with a tape recorder on the other end of the line, talked with me about the great tease that he offered to the world press:

"Larry, all these reporters came from London thinking they would see John and Yoko fucking in public. We screwed them, didn't we? We figured, the honeymoon was going to be public anyway, so why not just state our case for peace under the covers and in our nighty shirts. We want to make people laugh, and at the same time, take a look at the world. Some of the peace folks want violence. I may be a violent person inside, but I want peace in the world. I want people to laugh. You gotta remember: the establishment is just another word for evil."

John was enjoying the public spectacle so much that he and Yoko were ready for an encore. A ten-day marathon dubbed "bed peace" began at the elegant Queen Elizabeth Hotel in Montreal on May 26, 1969.

I had a brief conversation with John from his "bridal" suite. "Just the thing to do, Bed for Peace II," John said, "and I promise you, Larry, this one will make me some history."

His beard flowing below his shoulders, John and his bride entertained the media and the public with declarations against war and hunger. But this time, they wanted a permanent record. So they recorded one. John invited Tommy Smothers, Derek Taylor, Montreal Rabbi Abraham Feinberg, members of the Canadian Rhada Krishna Temple, and Petula Clark to record a song with him and Yoko in bed. Clark was the only other professional singer on board, but the song "Give Peace a Chance" would become a hit single. In a sad note of irony, along with the classic "Imagine," it would later become a hymnal refrain of John Lennon's death.

It is difficult to pinpoint exactly when John Lennon became so adamantly and publicly opposed to war. But his opposition was certainly in place by the 1965 tour, where he would perk up and verbally fire away whenever I asked him about the escalating conflict in Vietnam.

"The generation before us fought to save the world from Hitler and the Japanese colonialists. Why not save Southeast Asia from dictatorial communism?" I asked.

"That's rubbish, Larry," John retorted. "How can you compare? Really. Would you serve your country for a war like the one growing over there?"

The answer to that question came in February 1966, when, facing a draft notice, I decided to enter the United States Air Force Reserve. Basic training ended on June 4, 1966, and because of my military obligations, it would be impossible for me to join the Beatles on their 1966 tour. But I did manage to pay a small visit to them during the tour, precipitating a tense moment that would remain memorable for its hostility. I remember it as our "great airborne debate."

I arrived in St. Louis to watch the Beatles' concert at Busch Stadium, and Brian Epstein invited me to join them afterward on the plane from St. Louis to New York. It was on the plane, for almost two hours, that John Lennon and I fought an intense verbal battle over the war in Vietnam. At first, John was thrilled to see me, but when he noticed that my hair was closely cropped, he sensed the implications and roared into a tirade.

"You're fucking with me, Larry. I can't believe you piece of shit. Ya' look like you've been scalped at Custer's Last Stand."

"I'm just doing my thing for my country," I answered.

Taut and angry, he replied, "Your thing sucks."

We were sitting in a rear row of the airplane, drinking and smoking, when John recommended in no uncertain terms that I desert my country. "Why don't you come over to England and we'll find you a good job?"

I answered, "John, no way. This is my obligation, and I was lucky to get into the reserves."

"What the hell is 'lucky'? You're serving a fucked-up cause."

"I'm just doing this thing for my country. I have to do this thing."

"I say it again: your bloody war sucks!"

Head-to-head, jaw-to-jaw, we argued the case for and against war. John was so angry about my voluntarily going into the military that his cheeks flushed as he argued his side. What surprised me, in the heat of the moment, was the passionate force in his feelings. He was so wound up that I thought he was going to jump out of his seat.

In retrospect, which is always clearer than real-time thinking, John was years ahead of his time in his perspective on the war in Vietnam. His view of a mighty power fighting a lost cause for all the wrong reasons would be validated by the succeeding decade. I, on the other hand, was doing at the time what I thought my country needed me to do.

A funny bit of irony resulted from the mid-air debate that was sparked by the sight of my cropped hair. Following the 1966 tour, movie producer Dennis O'Dell and director Richard Lester talked John into playing the role of army private Gripweed in the movie *How I Won the War*. O'Dell, who helped mold the Beatles' first film, *A Hard Day's Night*, says it wasn't easy getting John fully on board:

"It was a natural for him, but he had to change his look. After all, he was playing a soldier, not a musician. He wasn't especially happy about what would happen."

What happened was a haircut. John agreed to have his hair sheared short for the role, but not without trepidation. He was concerned, among other things, that his hair clippings would be sold for profit. So, in true Lennon form, he had the hair clippings burned, reminding me of the time in Seattle at the Edgewater Hotel when he and his Beatle buddies urinated on a carpet they were standing on to prevent people from seizing it and cutting it into pieces to sell as Beatles memorabilia.

The movie, a minor success, had an anti-war theme and provided another opportunity for John Lennon to participate in his most urgent cause. Most of the film was shot in Almeria, Spain, and it was there that he composed the song "Strawberry Fields Forever."

When I saw the film, I had a little personal giggle. Just a few months after my haircut, John got his. Visiting London in 1968, I reminded him of the irony. He was only slightly amused.

Our wartime debate continued over the years. John was so far ahead of the curve. History will show that his aggressive anti-war theme was launched years before other celebrities would jump on the bandwagon. But John's protests against war were only part of his controversial rhetoric in 1966.

❖

Earlier in the year, John had enraged people around the world with comments about Jesus Christ. His comments would be magnified, scrutinized, and criticized in a way that severely endangered the Beatles' popularity. This controversy would make the episode with the teenage girls at the Sahara Hotel in Las Vegas look like kids' stuff, which in reality it was.

Early rock stars like the Beatles, idolized by the young but always regarded with suspicion by their elders, were never expected to speak out about anything, least of all issues as charged as religion and war and race. Even seasoned movie stars during that era remained apolitical in their public pronouncements. After all, only a few years before, many entertainment-industry people who expressed social sympathies saw their careers and lives destroyed by the blacklisting campaign of McCarthyism.

John Lennon broke down those walls of silence. During my initial interviews with John in 1964, I was struck by his willingness to talk about subjects beyond music. It was one of the reasons we hit it off so well. John was an intensely serious man who enjoyed serious questions, and I was a serious journalist who was more interested in world-affecting issues than in haircuts and jellybeans—two topics that 99 percent of reporters focused on when questioning the Beatles.

On the '64 tour, during an official interview that would be syndicated to radio stations across America, I asked John and Paul how they felt about the fact that the audience might be racially segregated at their upcoming concert in Jacksonville. Both became visibly angry and defiant. They vowed that the Beatles would not play to a segregated house. In the end, their resolve paid off—the audience at the concert was not segregated.

In the following two years, John would offer a number of pointed outbursts of concern for the sanctity of the human spirit. But nothing had prepared Epstein and the rest of the Beatles' core for the case of John Lennon and Jesus Christ.

The controversy began innocently during an April 1966 interview with one of John's favorite writers, Maureen Cleave of London's *Evening Standard*.

Cleave's interviews always sought out Lennon's intellectual side. Later in 1966, Cleave would profess to me that the public's delayed-yet-venomous response to the words Lennon spoke during their discussion on world religion took him completely by surprise.

"Christianity will go," John had told Cleave. "It will vanish and shrink. I needn't argue with that—I'm right and I will be proved right. We're more popular than Jesus now; I don't know which will go first, rock and roll or Christianity. Jesus was all right, but his disciples were thick and ordinary. It's them twisting it that ruins it for me."

Four months later, as their third and final American tour was about to get underway, the quote, largely ignored in the British media, became a banner headline in the U.S. magazine *Datebook*. Within hours, wire services across the world reported that John Lennon had claimed that the Beatles were bigger than Jesus Christ.

Reaction was intense. At least forty American radio stations, most in the so-called "Bible Belt" of the Midwest and South, pulled Beatles' records off the air. Others burned the records in public bonfires. At my own radio station, WFUN in Miami, letters and phone calls ran two-to-one against Lennon. The government of South Africa, a bastion of early Beatles support, banned all Beatles songs. John's public opposition to apartheid in South Africa no doubt contributed to the government's decision.

Brian Epstein, fearful of empty seats and frightened promoters, immediately flew to America to try to douse the flames of the controversy. Before he departed, and over a subsequent three-day period, Epstein tried to convince John to apologize. John was holding firm—no apology would be forthcoming.

Press officer Tony Barrow got into the act. Barrow was a stabilizing force for all the Beatles and understood the origins of John's lifetime of daring protest. He also understood the American media and knew that something had to be done. He says:

"His anti-war, anti-establishment views were all part of that pattern originating with the school days of Liverpool. He never really graduated from those days of outrage, and he didn't want to be seen as weak. John felt that what he said was taken out of context. He wasn't trying to insult people's religious beliefs and didn't want to look like he was caving in. He certainly didn't want to backtrack."

After hours of pleading and cajoling, Barrow and Epstein prevailed by appealing to John's team spirit. Fearing he had let down his brothers in the band, John relented and agreed to face the press at a news conference in Chicago.

Looking back, the transcript of that news conference shows a sad and dejected John Lennon pouring his heart out after he had inadvertently threatened the Beatles' careers. It was typical Lennon. There was never room for superficiality or phoniness in his life, and the "confessional" in Chicago, as he would later call it, was thorough and heartfelt.

John began with a simple statement:

"I just happened to be talking to a friend and I used the word Beatles. I just said that they are having more influence on kids and things than anyone else, including Jesus, but I said it in a way that is the wrong way."

Reporters pressed him for more; John obliged:

"I'm not saying that we're better or greater, or comparing us with Jesus Christ as a person or God as a thing or whatever it is. I just said what I said and it is wrong . . . and now it's all this. . . . I'm not anti-God, anti-Christ. I am not anti-religion. . . . I believe in God, but not as an old man in the sky. I believe what people call 'God' is something in all of us.

"I apologize if it will make you happy. I still don't know quite what I've done. I tried to tell you what I will do, but if you want me to apologize, if that will make you happy, then I'm sorry."

Tony Barrow, the devoted press officer, had hoped for more, but this was all he was going to get. He stood by, respectful of John's truth and nervous about the rest of the tour.

A few days later, during our debate over Vietnam on the flight from St. Louis to New York, John reviewed the controversy and told me he was stunned by the reaction. In hindsight, the Christ controversy was caused less by what he said than by adult oblivion and indifference to the liberating outspokenness of young people in the sixties. John had never really said the Beatles were more important than religion, and he wasn't boasting when he stated the undeniable fact that the Beatles were more popular than Jesus. By stating these facts, he was actually commenting on the state of a society that would produce them. His only crime was speaking his truth, and for daring to declare the obvious: that in 1966, rock and roll—brought to new heights by the Beatles—was the most important force in the lives of millions of teenagers.

John and the Beatles survived the Christ controversy of 1966 with an underlying irony. As he often did with my interviews, Lennon used almost every one of the Beatles' news conferences on the 1966 tour to lament America's escalating role in Vietnam. But his rhetoric on the war, so important as a battle cry to anti-war protestors, was largely ignored by the media. Yet in the end, his peace sentiments would have a much more positive and lasting effect on Beatles fans than any negatives from the Jesus remarks.

More than anything, Lennon's maligned quotes about religion once again reaffirmed the core traits of his being—determination, resolve, intellectual curiosity, and an uncompromising commitment to free expression. These traits often led him to a lot of controversy and danger. But in the context of the sixties, they also provided many young people with a refreshing alternative to the age's vapid celebrities and callow political leaders. Those traits allowed John Lennon—artist, songwriter, singer, and poet—to become the voice of his generation.

In 1966, I thought John's views on Vietnam, especially regarding my service, to be the height of naïveté—the uninformed opinions of a young passionate man. Yet many people from his generation took his words very seriously and used them to shape their own views. And, unbeknownst to anyone at the time, many people from the older generation who had risen to powerful positions in the U.S. government took his words even more seriously. So seriously, in fact, that they launched a campaign to silence him. Those views and the government's hidden agenda would become part of an arduous legal struggle in the seventies. On the surface, the battle would appear to be rooted in a simple marijuana-possession conviction. But it was much more than that.

❖

The early activism of John Lennon that I witnessed on the 1964-66 North American tours accelerated along with his relationship with Yoko Ono during the late sixties and early seventies. His increased commitment to ending the Vietnam war did not go unnoticed within the U.S. government, and in fact, it was largely misinterpreted.

The secret intelligence gathered on Lennon's comings and goings was based on faulty premises and an obsessive-compulsive government view on celebrities' influence. Convinced that celebrities like Lennon could undermine public support for the Vietnam War, members of the Nixon Administration and the U.S. intelligence community began a campaign to gather information on Lennon's activities so that he and his friends could be silenced.

During those years, Lennon began to associate with people who were already on the government's enemies list. After he and Yoko moved to Manhattan's West Village, he was drawn into the web of publicity-seeking activists who sought to exploit his fame for their own ends.

Photographer Bob Gruen, who lived in their West Village neighborhood, first saw John and Yoko in the flesh at a protest against the state's murderous rampage at the Attica Prison riots in 1971. He recalls:

"I didn't see them around the streets much at all and then in November of that year I went to the Apollo Theatre for a benefit for the Attica prisoners injured in the riot and I went 'cause I heard Aretha Franklin was going to be there. And when I walked in, I was walking up the side of the theater and I suddenly heard the announcer say, 'John Lennon and Yoko Ono of the Plastic Ono Band,' and I felt like I was hit by lightning."

In that theater, Gruen noted the growing alliances between Lennon, Ono, and some prominent anti-war protestors.

"When they first came to New York, Yoko knew a bunch of people that kind of got in touch with people and a whole bunch of people came to see them and Jerry Rubin and Tom Hayden and Abbie Hoffman, and a couple of those people had come around and started talking about it. That's why the FBI finally started following him and the government wanted to throw him out. It was because the local radicals tried to enlist him to their cause and the government thought that he was going to get involved with them."

Gruen believes that John never considered himself a radical.

"I don't think that he really agreed with the kind of disruptive tactics that the radicals were trying to get him involved in," Gruen explained. "Frankly, all he wanted was just to be here and live a happy life in America.

"As Yoko explained to me one time," Gruen said, "John and Yoko weren't really against anything. They were always in favor of something. They weren't against the war as much as they were for peace. He wasn't against anything. It was always hugely just in favor of peace or in favor of voting. And they tried to keep it positive in that respect—instead, to get people to open their minds and imagine and be real."

Apple's creative director, Allan Steckler, shared many one-on-one conversations about war and peace with John. He recalls:

"I loved talking to him about the state of the world. He had such a purist view. He was a peace poet before Yoko came along. But she played a major role. They were partners in peace and fit very well into the New York antiwar scene. But, believe me, it was very real. No bullshit. They weren't against America. After all, John loved this country. They were just for peace. There were no personal agendas. They just didn't need the publicity, if you know what I mean. The political climate was very much like the mood after the Iraq conflict—partisan, divisive, people going to extremes. The government, or sections of it, displayed tremendous paranoia."

Beatles expert and broadcaster Joe Johnson was impressed by Lennon's courage and integrity in the seventies:

"Though he was worth a reported $235 million when he died, John appeared to live the life of the working class. In the 1970s, John gave the everyman a model. He took to the streets in protest of the mistreated, spoke out against the war and racial injustice, and put the world on with his stunts for peace with Yoko Ono. Most men in his tax bracket would have been more than happy to lay low and not ruffle any feathers. Instead, Lennon always pushed the envelope to the edge, even taking his own U.S. citizenship to the near breaking point."

Just how close did he come to that breaking point, the point where he would have been literally thrown out of the United States?

During John's associations with Jerry Rubin, Abbie Hoffman, and other darlings of the peace movement, forces in the United States government, fearful of Lennon's influence over the country's young, began moving to silence him.

In 1972, the Nixon administration ordered the Immigration and Naturalization Service to begin formal proceedings to deport John Lennon from the United States. The stated reason for the action was John's marijuana conviction in England in the sixties.

But John's attorney, Leon Wildes, broke the sham case wide open when he forced the release of two documents: a letter from Republican Senator Strom Thurmond to William Timmons, assistant to President Richard Nixon, and an accompanying memo from the Senate Internal Security Subcommittee. Dated February 4, 1972, the letter suggested that "many headaches would be avoided if appropriate action was taken." The memo described John as a "member of the former musical group known as the 'Beatles.'"

Its point was clear: that John and Yoko were involved with anti-war groups and that termination of his visa would be a "strategy-countermeasure." The assistant to the President wrote back in March and assured Senator Thurmond that the government had issued direct orders to rescind John's visa. The Justice Department and the Senate subcommittee feared that John and his friends would disrupt the Republican National Convention in Miami, and other events leading up to the 1972 presidential election.

The case finally ended in October of 1975 after fierce legal arguments. Wildes declared in open court: "There is substantial reason to believe that official governmental action was based principally on a desire to silence political opposition squarely protected by the First Amendment."

Chief Judge Irving R. Kaufman, speaking for the majority on the Second Circuit Court of Appeals, emphatically agreed. In his ruling, Kaufman declared that curbing dissent was the primary reason for the case against John. He ruled: "If, in our 200 years of Independence, we have in some measure realized our ideals, it is in large part because we have always found a place for those committed to the spirit of liberty and willing to help implement it. . . . Lennon's four-year battle to remain in our country is testimony to his faith in the American dream."

Judge Kaufman was familiar with high-profile cases. He'd served as a gang-busting prosecutor in the 1930s. In 1951, he presided over the Julius and Ethel Rosenberg espionage case. The Rosenbergs, convicted of giving atomic secrets to the Soviets, were executed upon signed orders from Judge

Kaufman. And a few years before his retirement, the veteran jurist came down against the government's case against John Lennon.

John was thrilled, proclaiming, "It's a great birthday gift from America for me, Yoko, and the baby." The baby, Sean, was born the next day, on John's thirty-fifth birthday. It was a good week for the Lennons.

The victory was clear. But pieces of the strange case were missing, and it would take a long time to put them all together. In 1981, a year after John's death, University of California history professor Jon Wiener began a sixteen-year struggle to unlock the FBI files on John Lennon. His effort, using the Freedom of Information Act, resulted in startling revelations on the extensive FBI surveillance of Lennon. The FBI followed John almost everywhere, even to his TV appearance on the syndicated *Mike Douglas Show*. They even followed his friends.

Release of the FBI files confirmed to John's close friend Bob Gruen what he feared when he and John were neighbors in New York City's West Village. Gruen recalls one unusual night in 1972 when he was traveling from an uptown studio to his downtown apartment:

"I was a little scared when a car followed me home because I live pretty off the side of the city down here. I left the studio and there was a car behind me and we went around three turns together and after the third turn I thought, 'This guy's making all the same turns.' And when I pulled around the corner, just by my house, I pulled kind of really fast. I pulled into a parking space and jumped out of the car and turned to look at him. He looked at me and sped off down the street. It was like two business-looking men. It was more mysterious than scary."

Attorney Leon Wildes didn't know who John Lennon was when he went to work for him. But questions about the Lennon case and its implications for free speech in America still make up the majority of the questions his law school students ask about his storied career. Wildes continues to look back at the Lennon case with admiration for his client:

"The one thing that was so important was his pride in America and the passion to stay here, to be part of our process. Winning that case lifted a veil over his head and gave him new freedoms to create and, as it turns out, to be a wonderful father. The judge in the case, Judge Kaufman, waxed poetic about Lennon, and how his belief in our system prevailed over the attempts to stifle him."

Wildes' victory for Lennon meant that the case was returned to an immigration hearing. A year later, John appeared in court with an all-star cast of supporting characters: TV journalist Geraldo Rivera, actress Gloria Swanson, actor Peter Boyle, and famed author Norman Mailer, who shared with John the courage of his public convictions. One after another, they testified about the good works of Mr. Lennon. Mailer described John as "one of the great artists of the western world." After four years of arduous court battles, John Lennon was given the green light to get the U.S. resident status that he wanted so badly.

The people in the U.S. government who had waged a long, hard struggle to kick John Lennon out of America were wrong about his intentions. John wasn't out to undermine the United States, its government, or the nation's democratic process. More than anything, he wanted to become an American and help America become a stronger, better nation.

But on one issue, the paranoid leaders who launched the campaign against him were actually right on target. John Lennon's pleas for peace did profoundly impact the younger generation.

At high schools across the nation starting in 1972, scores of graduating classes chose John's "Imagine" as their class song. Young people across the country identified with Lennon and his message of peace and hope. And that message endures to this day.

Wally Podrazik, the noted media expert and Beatles historian from Chicago, says Lennon's struggle to become an American endeared him to many people in the U.S.:

"The other Beatles had places in America, but John made it clear through his immigration struggle that America was his choice. He loved the freedoms and so desperately wanted to live here. In the view of many, John had become an American by his dedicated decision to fight to stay here."

Isn't it interesting that a multimillionaire who could have lived anywhere, chose as his final destination—like so many immigrants before him—the United States? Was it the spirit of the people that buoyed him, the vast open spaces, the hard-fought freedom of expression, or a search for obscurity?

Perhaps it was all of the above, but one thing is certain: the city he chose to live in would play a major role in his own cultural revolution.

FIVE:
I Love New York

"It was the strangest thing seeing him all isolated in that room, just smoking away. I thought, 'was that how he was spending his days?'"
—*Linda Reig, Apple employee and Lennon assistant*

East Side, West Side. When it came to the fourth decade of John Lennon's life, he saw the many faces of New York City, and lived a better life for it.

Can living in a particular city change the course of a person's life? As a citizen of the world, John Winston Ono Lennon was welcomed everywhere (except perhaps the White House). But from the time he traveled to America for the first time in 1964, John was both overwhelmed and mystified by New York City. After marrying Yoko Ono in Gibraltar in 1969, his bride was a powerful influence in steering him to the isle of Manhattan, a place that Yoko had considered her home since her experimental art days in the 1950s.

So it was New York City, and he was in love with it. After the first tour of the states, it was apparent that John understood where the action was in America. I asked him his first impressions of America at some point during that tour, and he replied, "I think its marvelous, especially places like New York and Hollywood. I especially like the big places, the big cities, where the people are, where life is."

Throughout his life, John Lennon was a traveling man. During his child-hood in England, Lennon lived in no less than six different homes before his twentieth birthday. In his early adulthood, he followed the instincts of those who were closest to him. Stu Sutcliffe enjoyed the European continent, espe-cially Germany. Although John both loved and hated the times he spent in Hamburg, he was drawn to Europe because of its culture. Cynthia Powell Lennon was content in England, and so was John in the later years of their failed marriage. During his time with May Pang, the young woman encour-aged him to fulfill his longing to be near the sea—their time in Long Island would provide special memories. But Yoko made Seventy-second Street in New York City the most permanent home he ever had.

New York City, its high-rise canyons of power surrounded by gritty neigh-borhoods, was a perfect fit for John Lennon. Throughout his life, John had a fixation with the Roman Empire, and he viewed New York in that context. He once reflected on his decision to live in Manhattan in historic terms. "If I'd lived in Roman times, I would have lived in Rome," he said. "Today America is the Roman Empire and New York is Rome itself. . . . It was Yoko who sold me on New York. . . . She made me walk around the streets and parks and squares and examine every nook and cranny. In fact, you could say that I fell in love with New York on a street corner."

John would tell friends that New York had the same energy as Liverpool, and would talk about how much he enjoyed the 24-hour-a-day access and the spirit of the people. In typical Lennon fashion, he described his com-monalities with New Yorkers when he said, "I like New Yorkers because they have no time for the niceties of life. They're like me in this. They're natural-ly aggressive and they don't believe in wasting time."

So when he arrived in New York with his newlywed in 1969, a path was paved for the musical genius to enjoy the intellectual and cultural sensation that is New York. His infatuation with New York began, of course, during his first view of it in the summer of 1964. There were a few visits in the late sixties on Apple projects, but his marriage to Yoko guaranteed that New York would be his full-time residence. Five months after their wedding, John let New Yorkers know he would be more than a passive resident, appearing at the Apollo Theater to raise money for the families of inmates of riot-scarred Attica prison.

Although they had decided to live in New York, settling in for John and Yoko in 1970 was a complex project. Before deciding on Bank Street in the West Village, John and Yoko were virtual transients, living at times in the Regency, St. Moritz, Park Lane, and finally, the St. Regis hotels. Between the fall of 1969 and late 1971, John Lennon had no sense of permanence in his living style—jetting to and from England, leaving suitcases behind, and showing up in New York in mid-1971, bloated and wearing all black. In fact, John and Yoko were so drastically overweight that Allen Klein, then Apple chief, insisted on a trim-down and bought them new clothes, just in time for a performance with Frank Zappa at the Filmore East.

Their moving patterns in those early days in New York were so disorganized that assistant May Pang, who physically made most of the moves, loaned them some large steamer trunks to get around.

"I was constantly moving them," she recalls. "Until the Dakota came along, they couldn't figure out where to live. It was a sequence of moving and packing, then packing again to move. I think this lack of permanence was bad for John."

Once the couple stopped hotel hopping and settled into the Bank Street home, stability returned. The Bank Street apartment was small and confining, but it was also in a real neighborhood, and allowed the couple its first attempt at understanding the nuances of a community.

The time in the West Village also marked an acceleration in the use of mind-altering substances. Although drug use is often the subject of humor when contemporary fans reflect on John in the seventies, it was no laughing matter for those close to him. Like the cigarettes that filled his lungs for decades, the drugs were becoming a serious addiction. Wary of his previous marijuana conviction in England, John made sure that the Apple office in

Manhattan had a routine to acquire his illicit supplies through a route that would be untraceable. There were weekly deliveries, in fact. Fate would have it that Linda Reig would be the cash courier. Reig, an employee of Allen Klein and Apple, was a young innocent who first set eyes on the Beatles as a twelve-year-old when they arrived at the Idlewild (later to be named John F. Kennedy) Airport in February of 1964. As one of her routine assignments, Reig was entrusted to pick up large amounts of cash and bring it to 105 Bank Street.

"There is no question that I did the drug runs," she recalls. "I would pick up a thousand dollars in cash and deliver it to the Bank Street address. John's driver would pick up the drugs, mostly marijuana. One time, I arrived at Bank Street with the money. The door was open. It was a mostly dark room and John was alone on the bed, smoking grass. His eyes looked glazed. He asked me if I wanted a joint. I didn't know what the hell to do. So I said, 'yes'. And I smoked it. I was stunned. Here I was smoking a joint with John Lennon. It was the strangest thing seeing him all isolated in that room, just smoking away. I thought, 'was that how he was spending his days?'"

In fact, many days were spent in near darkness, and some of the nights were spent at the Record Plant, the Midtown recording studio that John and Yoko favored. Nights could be long, sometimes ending at 4 or 5 a.m. At times, John and Yoko's employees pulled all-nighters as well, especially while working on Yoko's film projects. Always seeking to be different, Yoko Ono fancied herself a great filmmaker. John, according to friends, obliged his wife as she went to seek out various creative forms. He was tickled by Yoko's imagination. He was sometimes proud and sometimes indifferent to her creations, but always extremely respectful of her intentions. Two of the projects Yoko undertook in New York raised eyebrows, and one of them even raised skirts. Linda Reig was assigned to work on several of Yoko's film projects. It was her first and last experience in the film industry. On one of the assignments, her experience included the responsibility of going out to procure and lure insects. She remembers:

"I may have been the first person in the world to call a casting agency to see if there were flies trained as actors. I called farms and zoos and pet stores to find the perfect fly. Yoko produced a film called *The Fly*. Yoko filmed a naked woman covered with honey and a fly who was literally attached to the woman by the honey. The woman, a model, didn't seem to mind that the fly was ravenous and crawling all over her body. I never did find trained flies. We just found one and put it to work. On a second film called *Up Your Legs Forever,* we recruited women to appear naked from the waste down. The movie just showed different women naked from the waste down. We paid the women one dollar [each] for their appearance. John told me, 'You're next.' He wanted me to drop my skirt and appear in the movie. I replied, 'No, I won't. Why don't *you* drop your pants and go naked from the waste down.' He laughed and handed me dollar bills to pay the women."

The Fly and *Up Your Legs Forever* never gained any commercial success, but they validated Yoko's attempts to create new art forms. John seemed confused by the projects, but in 1975, clear of drugs and feeling the optimism of an expectant father, he told me, "Yoko, you know, she is very talented. Takes care of all the business. Her art is not appreciated, but some day it will be. There's a lot of talent there. In some ways, her efforts seemed to be lost in me own spotlight, but I think she gets all that. . . . Some day she'll get her due."

That "some day" never happened in John's lifetime, but in the years 2001 to 2004, Yoko's art gained respect in galleries from New York to London and Tokyo. *The Fly* and *Up Your Legs Forever* are distant memories, but her art is now a big draw.

John and Yoko's life in New York was itself an artistic endeavor of sorts, mostly inspired and manifested by sudden desires. Beginning in December of 1970, May Pang, then a special assistant to John and Yoko, spent many weekends traveling to England to pick up clothing, personal possessions, and even one time a copy of the film *Erection*, a work that John and Yoko directed about the construction of a building.

Despite this highly disorganized transatlantic life, John and Yoko found some semblance of order on the lower West Side of Manhattan. John and Yoko spent most of their time together, and the neighbors in the West Village allowed the Lennons to live in relative peace. But the gregarious John also needed the mental stimulation of talking to people—something that's always available in New York City. I can report from personal experience that John Lennon was a world-class conversationalist. The most difficult thing for his counterpart in any conversation was keeping up with him.

Bank Street was also a home to intellectuals, some of them self-styled, who gratified John and Yoko's constant need for verbal stimulation. On the protest front, there were visits by Jerry Rubin, Abbie Hoffman, Tom Hayden, and poet Allen Ginsberg, all leaders of the anti-war movement. Their musical friends in Manhattan included Ringo and George, Elton John, Frank Zappa, and others.

There was always a wide cast of interesting characters in John and Yoko's New York life, but John never duplicated the intimacy he had with Stuart Sutcliffe with any other man. The close male friends for John Lennon were few and far between. One of them was the successful actor Peter Boyle, most recently a star of TV's *Everybody Loves Raymond.* Boyle and Lennon connected after the actor started dating *Rolling Stone* reporter Loraine Alterman, who was a friend of Yoko's. Lennon and Boyle hit it off right away, sharing similar views on politics and the arts scene. When Boyle married Alterman, John stood in as best man. John and Yoko stayed especially close to Boyle and Alterman during Loraine's pregnancy with the first of their two daughters. The child was born just four days after the murder at the Dakota. Boyle was a perfect companion to John. An accomplished actor, Boyle had found his truth early. Originally a monk in the Christian Brothers, Boyle was one of Hollywood's most versatile actors, who was known off-screen for his virulent opposition to the war in Vietnam. With Peter, John found a man he could really talk to.

Reclusive by nature, and skeptical of long-term bonds, John had few people in his life in New York City who were as important to him as Peter Boyle and Bob Gruen. They were people he could relate to, especially on a political level, and specifically in a city that was the centerpiece platform for liberal debate in America. But more than that, he felt comfortable in their presence.

Gruen, especially, was welcomed warmly. Although he was a photographer whose friendship with John could foster his career, he was careful not to push the envelope in the relationship. John hated being used. So did Yoko, and while others drifted in and out of friendship with Lennon and Ono over the years, Gruen remained a constant. He recalls their sensitivity to people looking for something beyond friendship:

"There were times backstage and in the studio when I could have used the telephoto but I didn't want to intrude, so I didn't take the picture. A couple years later, when Yoko and I were talking about the time, she had mentioned that she was aware of that and that impressed her. [She said] that most people they knew, or most people they'd meet, instantly wanted to get as much as they could from them. Everybody wanted to glom on to John and Yoko. And she was impressed with the fact that I didn't do that, that I seemed to have something going myself and [did] not to have to take from them. I would often leave special pictures for them; I was one of the few who actually gave them something without asking for anything back, you know."

In New York City, as in all venues of John Lennon's life, finding real friends without special agendas was difficult. Still, perhaps building a Rolodex of close friends was not exactly what Lennon desired. What John loved most about New York was its confluence of people, architecture, raw grit, and as Bob Gruen remembers, the level of anonymity it afforded him. He would see this phenomenon in action on occasion, when he would photograph John and Yoko out and about. Gruen's photos of the Lennons are special because of the intimacy they captured. He was so trusted by John and Yoko that he photographed them at more venues than any other photographer. He is also the visual chronicler of sensitive family photos with son Sean.

Perhaps the most famous photograph of John Lennon is the one that Bob Gruen took in which he is wearing a white t-shirt with the words "New York City" emblazoned across the chest. The photo was taken on the roof of the building housing the apartment that John shared with May on Manhattan's East Side. Fitting that the man who loved New York would forever memorialize the now incredibly popular and timeless piece of fashion.

Gruen, a New Yorker who still lives in the West Village, has a clear understanding of the lure of New York to John:

"I think one of the reasons he lived in New York was because, more than other cities, it does tend to give you a level of privacy, even when you're walking around. You know, people will walk down the street and go, 'Oh shit! There's John Lennon!' but they don't really stop and change their day, because they're busy too. So it's kind of live and let live. You see famous people all the time in New York without them necessarily being surrounded by autograph hounds or that kind of thing happening."

Gruen, a shy and soft-spoken man, received a lot in return for his friendship—not the professional luster that you would expect, but the joy of friendship and the fun of being around someone you respect, someone who enjoyed talking and eating and other pleasures of life.

"You'd always have a good time with him and be laughing most of the time, but come away having learned something," he says. "And I always liked the fact that he liked to eat well. And so, he was a lot of fun to hang out with. I usually tried to arrive during meal time!"

John's everyday life in New York City offered new opportunities for an exploration of the real life, not the celebrity existence of pomp and circumstance that he had lived within for most of his time since 1963. Undaunted by security concerns, John Lennon become a neighborhood "regular," first on Bank Street. Although he loved the West Village, there was no question that more space was needed. It was no secret that John and Yoko wanted a child.

On April 1, 1973, the Lennons purchased an apartment in a place that has become the stuff of legends—the Dakota—on Central Park West at Seventy-second Street. John's neighborhood haunts, restaurants, and coffee shops moved uptown. But the interruption of the marriage with the "lost week-end" gave him exposure to another neighborhood. In the space of a decade he lived in Lower Manhattan (Bank Street), the Upper West Side (the Dakota), and in between, with May Pang, on the East Side. Perhaps his most intimate and freewheeling neighborhood environment was the small apartment he shared with girlfriend May, located near the United Nations. John's freedom to move about was at a maximum on the tony East Side.

The East Side experience was especially enticing to John, whose daily routine was virtually unchanged throughout his stay there. In the morning, he would drink a cup of coffee and devour the *New York Times* cover to cover. May Pang remembers that John was so on top of world affairs that he was prepared for a verbal duel with anyone who cared to debate him. New York life, May remembers, was stimulating in other ways, as well, providing a chance for John to accept the "everyman" moniker that he was seeking all of his life:

"I remember the simple moments most of all. We were on an upper floor and he loved sitting on the terrace watching the expanse of the East River. It gave him a sense of wide open spaces. He also loved the neighborhoods of New York. We rarely used cars in the city. I encouraged him to walk in the neighborhoods and he did, window shopping, visiting galleries, eating out, and just being a citizen of the big city. He especially loved going to the movies. After all, he always had this fascination with movie stars. So everything was right there for him within walking distance. How many cities give you the kind of opportunities that John had?"

John had a driver's license but he rarely used it. Often, during their time together, he longed for the open waters of the ocean. On a spur of the moment. John and May would head out to the Hamptons on Long Island, fashionable then but not as popular as they are today. And, May says, they always had company:

"His favorite beach place was at the home of Peter Boyle and his wife. They were gracious hosts, and even though Loraine was close to Yoko, there was never any friction about my relationship with John. That's one thing that was interesting—John's real friends never took sides as long as he appeared happy. He was the happiest I've seen him when he walked into the ocean waters and started swimming or gliding on his back. It was the sense of freedom he enjoyed so much. He tried to teach me how to swim, but he was so good at swimming I nearly drowned trying to keep up with him."

For Lennon's psyche, New York brought what Los Angeles in that wild spring of 1974 could never bring him. On Bank Street with Yoko, on the East Side with May, and returning to Yoko and the Dakota in the last five years of his life, John was able to be part of real neighborhoods. He simply delighted in visiting neighborhood restaurants, walking the streets, and occasionally heading out to the sea. And of course, during his final years at the Dakota on the Upper West Side, John loved to stroll through Central Park, lounge in coffee shops, shuffle down streets, and take a long view of things.

New York is a city where you can have fame in the glare of the big lights, and obscurity in the density of the population. John's "tree man" and regular companion in the latter seventies, Michael Allison, remembers John's love for New York:

"John Lennon viewed New York as the center of the universe. I truly believe that the city inspired him to come out of his loneliness in the late seventies and to find creative energy. John also loved the people of New York, their indistinguishable spirit. I often think of how he would have reacted to September 11, 2001. He would have been outraged and there's no doubt in my mind that he would have been the first to volunteer to bring police and firefighters food and water. Although he was rich and famous, the spirit of his youth, the fight in him for others and their needs, could never be extinguished."

Broadcaster Geraldo Rivera, whose career came of age at ABC just blocks away from John's home, calls it a "marriage made in heaven." Rivera, who befriended John early on, says, "He was a New Yorker tried and true. After all, he spent a full fourth of his life there. And just as he fought so hard to stay in the United States, his primary goal was to make New York his home forever. When he helped me in my fundraising activities for the less fortunate in Central Park in the early seventies, his eyes would open wide as he met people. It seemed that New York, with all its everyday victories and blemishes, reflected his own life. He and Yoko, in a short time, had really made a mark on New Yorkers with their outward love of the city."

John Lennon first came to New York on the Beatles tour of 1964. Perhaps the Beatles greatest concert ever was given in New York—at Shea Stadium, to be exact. And one could argue that it was in America—particularly in New York City—in the heat and insanity of touring, that John Lennon electrified America with a presence so strong, powerful, and controversial that he would set standards for decades to come.

SIX:
Eight Days a Week
(Lennon on Tour)

"Legs wide open. Pelvis forward. Mouth almost swallowing the
microphone. Guitar held high on chest. Eyes darting. Angelic look
on face. Devilish eyes. Turns around. Glances at Ringo. Nude
woman races across field. Head turns. Big smile."
—*Larry Kane, reporter notes from August 20, 1965, Comiskey Park, Chicago*

"Sex is overrated unless you're the one doing it."
—*John Lennon, in flight from Los Angeles to Denver, August 26, 1964*

The first time I laid eyes on John Lennon was on Friday the fourteenth of
February, 1964. Superstitious I'm not, but skeptical I am. That's just a nec-
essary tool in the business of journalism. And my initial skepticism would be
validated when we met face to face a few hours later, as well as at several of
our other early encounters.

While I sweated on the tarmac of Miami International Airport, several
thousand teenagers were packed like sardines behind me inside the National
Air Lines concourse. Fresh from a triumphant appearance on *The Ed*

Sullivan Show, the Beatles and manager Brian Epstein arrived in Miami for a few days rest and a second appearance on *Sullivan* that would take place at the Deauville Hotel in Miami Beach. I was assigned to cover the story of their arrival in Florida for the local radio station for which I was news director, all the while wondering why I wasn't at City Hall and the courthouse covering what I believed to be more important news.

The Beatles descended from the steps of the plane one by one, and it was then that I noticed what I would always refer to as "the squint." Nearsighted and often disoriented by it, John Lennon watched his steps carefully as he descended. He acknowledged the fans with a wave while consistently holding that thousand-yard stare of wondrous curiosity, while Paul McCartney always smiled heartily at crowds and charmingly at individuals.

An hour later, I covered a sparsely attended news conference inside the Deauville Hotel on Miami Beach. The Beatles dutifully and affably answered questions, and then retreated for a few days of sun and surf before performing the second *Sullivan* concert on February 16. They returned to England a few days later with the knowledge that America was ripe for their picking later that year. Beatlemania had been born, and was poised to bloom.

The Beatles officially "invaded" America in August of 1964 to begin the first of their three North America tours, and I would be along for the entire ride. For two summers and part of a third, I followed "The Boys" (as they were called by insiders) around the New World. On airplanes, in hotel rooms, backstage, on film sets, at parties, during press conferences, and through down time, I became the ultimate Lennon watcher. And the story of his touring days is like the rest of his story—unpredictable and revealing. I got to see it all firsthand as part of the Beatles' entourage. Talk about a revelation.

❖

There is no more compartmentalized, intimate experience than the glorious entrapment of air travel. Locked in a cabin for several hours, passengers can engage in fascinating in-depth conversations that speak volumes about fellow travelers. During the thirty-six separate flights that I shared with the Beatles from 1964 to 1966, spanning approximately 32,000 air miles, I was able to converse, laugh, argue, and play with the likes of John, Paul, George, and Ringo with an incredible degree of intimacy.

During most of that time, the aircraft of choice was an American Flyer's Lockheed Electra, a noisy but efficient turbo prop. In the rear was a semi-oval compartment where the Beatles could relax alone. The Beatles' inner circle traveled up front, along with a few reporters and other guests. Although they ventured out at times, Paul, Ringo, and George typically stayed in the rear. John, ever restless and rarely mellow, would spend much of the flight time row hopping, trading cigarettes, downing drinks like a desert trekker discovering a welcome oasis, and, in his own charming way, as he always managed to do, making trouble.

The devil in Mr. Lennon was part of his persona, nurtured at an early age in the guile and savvy of a master artist and satirist. Except, in an airplane, there was no artist's palette, just the mind's creative desire to stir up the passengers. And that, in a myriad of playful and creative ways, is what John Lennon did so well. For most of the stops on our tour, the child in John Lennon came out with gusto and creativity.

I was always targeted as John's special victim, probably because my straight-laced style, as perceived by John, made me appear vulnerable to him. Or perhaps he liked me so much that he thought I would enjoy mashed potatoes and peas being massaged into my hair, or the fascinating sensation of ice cubes dropping down the back of my shirt and nestling just above the waist. Of course, at any time, there was the potential of a Lennon-induced pillow fight, where sometimes the feathers or pieces of foam would fly about the cabin and add to the haze of cigarette smoke and the smell of scotch and bourbon. As juvenile and moronic as these acts sound, they reflect the absolute release displayed by John from the dramatic and sometimes suffocating life of road touring that he hated with a passion. Make no mistake about it—John Lennon was made for the stage, but if he had his way, he would have been parachuted in to the arenas in some sort of magic way, avoiding the rigors of riding, flying, and being chased by what appeared to be life-threatening crowds.

In 1968, during an interview at the St. Regis Hotel in New York, John and Paul McCartney offered some insights on touring:

KANE: *What was the highlight of your American tours?*
LENNON: *Escaping from Memphis! (referring to an airplane-engine backfire that was perceived as a gunshot on the 1966 final American tour.)*
KANE: *Will you tour again?*
McCARTNEY: *Well, anything can happen. . . . We only stopped touring because there was nowhere else to go.*
LENNON: *With all the rifles and the big masks and all that, the clubs frighten me to death.*

Although John forced a smile to accompany his statement about security, there was no question from my viewpoint that John Lennon, of all the Beatles, was the most frightened of touring and of the crowds, even as his charisma brightened up the faces and heated the bodies of thousands of people in those packed arenas. There were only two places where he found solace from the strain: the airplane, high above the melee of madness, and the privacy of his hotel room.

Even though he was frivolous in his airplane antics, John spent many spare moments reading. He was the most well- read of the Beatles, pouring over newspapers, magazines, and, sometimes, a novel. Uncle George's bedtime reading in John's childhood was obviously an inspiration. While on the 1965 tour, I gave John a copy of a haunting novel about life after a nuclear war, entitled *Alas Babylon.* The book clearly had an affect on John. He stayed up all night reading it, and it fueled his anti-war fervor. That wasn't my intention, although our conversations about the novel were scintillating, to say the least, as he envisioned the people of the world trying to crawl their way back from the horrors of a nuclear catastrophe.

It was a near catastrophe that we all experienced in the Electra en route to Portland, Oregon, that exposed the absolute depths of John's fear of flying. In retrospect, it's almost funny, except for the fact that, at the time, it was truly harrowing. Sitting alone in a window seat, I was the first to notice that the right-side engine was on fire. I almost didn't believe it at first, but when the reality of the moment set in, I jumped up and ran to alert the pilots who were in the back chatting up John and Paul. I simply shouted, "There's a fire on the right engine!"

John Lennon jumped up and ran for the exit door, ignoring the pleas of myself and others that sure death would accompany any attempt to exit. But he still tried to get to the door, all the while saying, "It's Buddy Holly man, it's Buddy Holly!"—a not-so-subtle reference to the fifties plane crash that killed Holly, the Big Bopper, and Ritchie Valens. Eventually, cool prevailed, and Lennon, his blood vessels bursting out of his forehead, calmed down and grabbed a cigarette.

It was just another reason to appreciate John Lennon. Most public people—politicians, musicians, and celebrities of every type—would go to extreme lengths to hide their phobias and fears, and especially the manifestation of those frights. Living against the grain, Lennon was never afraid to show that he was a mortal human bring who could feel pain, exhibit fear, and lose control of himself. More than even his magnificent music, it is that sense of affinity with the average person that makes John Lennon, despite all of his frailties and failures, such a vibrant person in life and in the memories of millions.

John's affinity for his fellow humans came out in the way he related to the acts who had the misfortune of opening for the Beatles across the country. John always had a genuine affinity for these fellow musicians. On the aircraft, in both 1964 and 1965, he was the first of the boys to stroll down the aisle and chat with entertainers who made the sacrifice of opening to crowds that didn't listen to them. Thousands upon thousands of fans would go into that nonstop primal Beatlemania scream from the minute they entered the arenas. As a result, stars like the Righteous Brothers, Jackie DeShannon, Brenda Holloway, and King Curtis were virtually ignored. With the sense of a club player just years from his salad days in Hamburg, a sympathetic Lennon made special time to talk music with and frequent the company of these musical professionals. It was spontaneous and respectful, and nary a night went by that he didn't perform this act of grace.

One opening act in particular provided John with an accidental platform to speak out against racial injustice, a social dilemma that he would devote much time and energy to fighting. The Exciters were forerunners of the successful black girl groups of the later sixties and seventies, and they were just what their name implied: superbly sexy and terribly entertaining performers. It was on a brief layover in Key West in 1964 that John—along with the Exciters—made national headlines after John and the ladies were photographed in the swimming pool together. It was a simple act, but complex for the times. When the photos were published across the nation, shock and scorn exploded in the South. The scene of a white man and black women in a pool together outraged the sensibilities of people who thought racial separation was the real law of the land. Lennon did not apologize, and, in fact, used the moment to speak his mind on the topic of racism. Ironically, the photograph was released a day before the Beatles played the Gator Bowl in Jacksonville—a concert that John and Paul had threatened to cancel because of reports that blacks and whites would be segregated. On the night of September 11, 1964, the Gator Bowl was a scene of racial harmony.

❖

There were four things on John Lennon's mind during the 1964 and 1965 tours—the music, the down time and what to do with it, a genuine concern for the fans, and a daily obsession with the life of his infant son Julian, who remained in England with Cynthia. Many who have observed and analyzed John's long absence from Julian Lennon during the beginnings of the Yoko Ono era, may be surprised to learn of his profound concern for Julian. There were daily phone calls back to Cynthia (in the era before direct dial, mind you), and constant talk about fatherhood. The same man who was so freewheeling about taking on-tour risks with women, wouldn't let a day pass without hearing Julian's voice. In 1965, at least, he had grand plans for his son.

> KANE: *Tell me about your son Julian.*
> LENNON: *I'll keep looking at him crawling on the floor, thinking where did he come from?*
> KANE: *How do you feel about your obligations as a father?*
> LENNON: *Well, I just want him to grow up happy, that's the main thing.*
> KANE: *What can you give him?*
> LENNON : *Just love. . . . He's just going to grow up happy and know he's wanted. I'm not having any of that boarding school or sending him away. He's going to be with us all the time.*

As time went by, that wish would not come true. Love, divorce, and remarriage would impede that dream. But on tour in the sixties, John Lennon had a vision for his son of a young man who, unlike himself, would be surrounded by normal parental love and intense feeling during his early years. After all, John's father practically abandoned him, and his biological mother was rarely present throughout his childhood and was killed when he

December 14, 1980. Fans in Central Park mourn the murder of John Lennon.

Beatles George Harrison and John Lennon flank
Stuart Sutcliffe, John's best friend and original Beatle, in Hamburg.

John and the Beatles are greeted by Queen Elizabeth
at the Prince of Wales Theatre, London, November 4, 1963.

Paris, January 16, 1964. John strums the guitar as the Beatles relax with manager Brian Epstein.

Paul McCartney instructs Ed Sullivan on the guitar as John and Ringo look on, February 8, 1964.

August 15th, 1965. A carefree John smiles at Paul and the
biggest crowd in entertainment history at Shea Stadium, New York.

John's comment that the Beatles are "more popular than Jesus" sparks protest at Candlestick Park, San Francisco, 1966.

John and young Julian Lennon pose for the camera in the Lennon's Weybridge home in late 1967.

John and Cynthia Lennon find a moment of peace in Rishikesh, India,
February 1968, even as their marriage was unraveling.

The Beatles at Rishikesh.
Front Row l-r: Ringo, Maureen Starkey, Jane Asher, Paul, Maharishi Mahesh Yogi
(center, back), George, Pattie Boyd Harrison, Cynthia Lennon, and John.

John Lennon and Paul McCartney come to New York in
May, 1968, to announce the formation of Apple Corps, Ltd.

January 30, 1969. His hair flying in the winter wind, John leads the Beatles in a rooftop
concert at the Apple headquarters in London, their final performance together.

March 25, 1969. John and Yoko continue their weeklong Bed-In for Peace at the Amsterdam Hilton.

John with the Plastic Ono Band in Toronto, September 13, 1969.
l-r: Klaus Voorman on bass, Eric Clapton on guitar, Yoko, John, and Alan White on drums.

John, Yoko, New York City Mayor John Lindsay, reporter Geraldo Rivera, and a young New Yorker announce the One-to-One Concert for Willowbrook benefit.

John performs for the benefit of the mentally challenged at the One-to-One concert on August 30, 1972.

March 1974. John shares happy moments with May Pang
on the lawn outside their hotel in Palm Springs.

Atop the apartment building where John lived with May Pang on New York's East Side.

Inseparable and combustible, John and Harry Nilsson share a peaceful 1974 moment.

November 28, 1974. John and Elton John performing at Madison Square Garden in New York.

John and Yoko in the "White Room" of their Dakota residence with infant son
Sean Taro Ono Lennon. Sean was born on John's birthday, October 9, 1975.

July 27, 1976. After
years of legal strug-
gles, John Lennon is
awarded his green
card, allowing him to
stay in the USA.

August 1980. John and Yoko begin work on *Double Fantasy* at the Hit Factory studio in Manhattan.

A pensive John at the control board of the Hit Factory.

Videotaping an amazing sequence of scenes to promote *Double Fantasy*, John and Yoko walk through Central Park, pause in front of the Dakota (left), then make their way to a Soho gallery where they enter a white bedroom (above), change into kimonos, disrobe, and make love. Photographer Allan Tannenbaum's dramatic photo on the cover of this book was taken during that historic photo session.

A mosaic of memories. The Strawberry Fields memorial to John Lennon in Central Park.

was seventeen. On the 1964 and 1965 tours, I was witness to an obsessed father, a man determined to be a father not only in name, but in real time, real life. While reality and career obligations never allowed John to succeed in this endeavor—and the world knows many of the details of that particular failure—it's important to understand that the desire was there to be a doting father.

Art Schreiber, national correspondent for Westinghouse Broadcasting, who covered part of the 1964 North American tour, has fond memories of John doing "baby talk" on the phone:

"This was serious business for him . . . and he seemed determined that whatever was happening around him, there would be time in his life for Julian. And there was also an intense regard for his wife, Cynthia. I mean, this was a young father who seemed determined to make sure that things were right. I know John was preoccupied by the insanity of the tour, but he was insistent there be time to make the call home and connect, connect with his wife and his son."

❖

A common thread that runs through the story of John on tour is his sense of caring about the fans and the average person, and his hatred for the wealthy and those with authority. In all of music history, there is probably no more fan-friendly group than the Beatles. Lennon and McCartney would launch into daily tirades to their handlers over the fact that thousands of fans would not even get as much as a glimpse of them. Local police and security personnel, often with the compliance of the Beatles' management, saw to it that there was "safe" separation between the fans and the boys. But the Beatles and John Lennon, despite his natural fear of crowds, never wanted it that way. They wanted to enjoy firsthand contact with their fans almost as much as the fans wanted to get close to them. As a result, the Beatles were deeply concerned about the perception that overzealous security was their own fault. And often, their fears would come true as the media and fans portrayed the musicians as being distanced or unapproachable. The desire to reach out to fans would develop into a theme that would continue into John's solo career.

It was an interesting conflict: the member of the band who feared the risks of touring the most, demanding that fans have greater access. It was a conflict that required facing his own public demons while at the same time fostering that ever-present role of champion of the people. This was a man whose face turned ghostlike on stage at the Montreal Forum as he saw machine-gun-toting policemen line up to protect the stage against potential attacks on the English lads in the strongly anti-British Quebec province. It would be the same man who walked toward the Dakota on that December night in 1980, concerned about his personal security, but always appearing to be open and approachable.

John and the boys were more than approachable on the sunny afternoon of August 26, 1965, as the Beatles enjoyed their rented house in the posh Benedict Canyon neighborhood of Los Angeles. I was lounging by the pool with them when we all heard a scream. Suddenly, a small body lunged over the retaining wall and fell not far from Ringo's feet. Somehow or other, the little girl, mud and blood caked on her face, had managed to climb a steep hill in order to invade Beatlesville. Instead of dispatching her, which road managers Mal Evans and Neil Aspinall wanted to do, John calmly put his hand on her shoulder, whispered something in her ear, and used a towel and water to clean up her face. What happened in the next few minutes will remain one of my most priceless visual memories of John Lennon. He talked to her quietly, one-on-one, with an obvious sense of sincerity and true caring. I never heard a word he said, but this teenage stalker, humbled by gravity and a retaining wall, hurt inside and outside, broke into a toothy smile that would melt an ice cube on the spot. This was where John Lennon showed me the man inside the man. The same man capable of savaging a reporter with an icy stare or humiliating a millionaire with his direct and acerbic wit, would shine brilliantly when confronted by the fears, frustrations, and yearnings of youth. Maybe, I thought, he was seeing himself in that little girl. Maybe he remembered the days when he was on the outside looking in.

No situation revealed Lennon's anti-authority streak and outright scorn for the rich and powerful more than an incident in the beautiful, fountain-laden city of Kansas City, Missouri. Lennon's one-man protest was launched on the flight to Kansas City when he rejected a powerful plea from Brian Epstein to offer a special compromise to the wealthy promoter. Kansas City was a late entry on the Beatles' 1964 tour agenda; added after they received a large cash offer from the eccentric millionaire owner of the Kansas City Athletics baseball team, Charles O. Finley. Finley had offered Brian Epstein $150,000 for the concert, an outrageous sum by the day's standards. Epstein accepted on behalf of the band, but Finley later decided he wanted more for his money.

I stood in the entranceway to the boys' suite in the Muehlebach Hotel and watched Finley try to negotiate a sweeter deal with the Beatles. He was negotiating with Brian Epstein, hoping that the boys would play longer than their usual 35-minute concert, and he offered more cash to make it happen. Finley made the offer, and as Epstein watched with his eyes wide open, Lennon, speaking for the group, shook his head "no." Finley made a larger cash offer; Lennon again shook his head. The promoter, visibly upset, raised the offer a third time; Lennon again rejected it out of hand. Finley, in a rage, stormed out of the room. Later on at the stadium, on the way out of the dressing room, I heard John yell out to Finley, "Chuck, you shouldn't have spent so much money on us!"

In a rare concession, the Beatles played an extra song: Wilbert Harrison's hit "Kansas City." The local fans went wild. But for me, the most remarkable memory of the evening was of the brazen Lennon confronting a powerful millionaire. It was part of the pattern: John staring down the establishment, speaking for the group, bypassing Epstein, and willing to serve as the "front man" for controversy, even though he was doing it with the blessing of Paul and the others. Lennon's disdain of the establishment had begun in school, continued all of his life, and manifested itself in this moment of confrontation with the American millionaire. In John's face, I could see him gloating at his power, the ability to stare a rich man in the eye and say, "No."

This same brand of nervy independence was displayed by all four Beatles, but especially John, at a fundraising garden party in Brentwood, California, hosted by Alan Livingston, the chief of Capitol Records, a few weeks before the Kansas City incident. To generate money that would go to the Hemophilia Foundation, the four Beatles stood in the rear of the mansion's backyard signing autographs for Hollywood stars like Jack Palance, Jack Lemmon, Shelley Winters, Dean Martin, Lloyd Bridges, Edward G. Robinson, and others. John played the role well, but later was disgusted that "real fans" couldn't be there.

"It was all potty," Lennon told me of the garden party. "It does bother me that real fans don't get to see us, but people with money can. It was a fake, ya' know, that party. It was a fake Larry, you know it was!"

The highlight of the lawn party for me was when John leaned over to Brian Epstein and said, "Who's the old bag with the funny hat?" It turned out to be Hedda Hopper, one of the most influential Hollywood columnists of her time. In Cincinnati, a few days later, John chased the mayor of that city out of the Beatles' dressing room. He simply wanted no part of officialdom. It was rude and rudimentary behavior, to be sure, but it was John—a man who was sickened by superficiality and who longed for the presence of less-shallow human beings. I always noticed such a startling contrast between John's negative reaction to celebrity meetings and the positive chemistry that would brew when he met ordinary people, such as the countless fan-club encounters in the dressing rooms. For John, the rich and powerful were just a distraction. And so was the press.

In most cities, there was a formal news conference set up for the Beatles, and Lennon was incensed by the predictable sameness of the questions. Even today, American journalists like to follow the pack, armed with little more than buzzwords and stereotypes. In the early days of the Beatles in America, the boys were annoyed by the same old questions in every city, as well as descriptions of them that were less than pleasant: "mop tops," "ants," "insects," etc.

LENNON: *Mop Top!*
KANE: *Does [the expression] ever get to you?*
LENNON: *We just break up whenever we see it. Along with the use of 'Yeah, yeah, yeah.'*
KANE: *Which is only in one of your songs.*
LENNON: *Well we didn't mind [when] it got into the international password, 'yeah, yeah, yeah,' but it's been flogged to death along with 'mop top' and 'mop-haired foursome.' Do I look like a mop top to you?*

❖

To those who had the pleasure of watching him in person, the memories still bring flashbacks of a level of performance that was electrifying. With John Lennon, there was never a need for the accessories that accompanied many artists. He had the ultimate garnishing—his own mind and body.

Watching sixty-one concerts over a three-year period was a memorable and educational experience for me—memorable from the standpoint of being an eyewitness to so many strange and unusual happenings, and educational from the perspective of learning the habits and social relationships of the individual Beatles.

Paul McCartney was a man who never met a stage he didn't like. He would pace in the dressing room, comb his hair it seemed like a hundred times, and always looked like a tiger waiting in the grass, ready to explode with emotion. When McCartney finally appeared on stage, he flirted more than any-

165

thing else. He made love to the audience with his eyes. Ringo was jovial but distanced from the crowd by his rear position, and George was rarely animated, but his upper torso moved up and down with the finely tuned rhythms of his guitar. With George, there was almost a sensation that he was playing for his ears only.

John Lennon was a different performer altogether. His presence, so powerful and enriching, was preceded by a pre-concert routine that was both methodical and, at the same time, baffling. The truth is that no one is really born to get up on a stage and entertain before thousands without feeling some sort of malady of the brain or stomach. Vulnerability, like it or not, is part of our human picture. With all the courage and sometimes false bravado of his public utterances, John Lennon the performer was much more vulnerable than most people would imagine. Of course, we can all relate to such vulnerability, but we don't expect the people we adore to be less than perfect. Fortunately for the world, John's imperfections made him even more lovable and captivating.

During many episodes on the 1964 and 1965 tours, I witnessed, up close and with some trepidation, the emotions that overwhelmed John prior to live performances. His fears could result in sweating, trembling, and sometimes erratic behavior that went far beyond the common physical symptoms of stage fright.

The afternoon and night of August 14, 1965, comes to mind. The odd scene took place on that Saturday in CBS Studio 50 in New York City, which is today known as the Ed Sullivan Theater at Fifty-third and Broadway. The Beatles had arrived back in New York twenty-four hours earlier. The weekend would be busy: a rehearsal at 2 p.m. Saturday and then a full *Ed Sullivan Show* taping that evening which would be used for the show's September 12 fall season premiere.

The Beatles arrived at the stage door on Fifty-third street for what would become a three-hour rehearsal. When Malcolm Evans, their trusted road manager, walked the band into the side entrance, he looked dour and almost depressed. Road managers, by nature, always looked concerned, especially in transit, when their sense of security is on heightened alert. But this was a much different Mal Evans than the jovial, happy-go-lucky man that I spent so much time with on the 1964 tour. His eyes squinted through his signature plain glass-frame glasses, and a cigarette dangled between two shaking fingers. Concern was written all over his face as he trailed the Beatles into the compact dressing rooms.

A few minutes later, Evans emerged. I said, "Mal, what's going on?" He answered, "He (John) is sweating, shaking, looks like too many pills and shit." I responded, "Pills?"

Mal, still with that frown on his face, said, "Yeah, uppers, downers, pain stuff, I think, ya' know."

I had seen John take pills before. But until the point of the *Sullivan* rehearsal, my mind had never connected drugs with the shakes he always seemed to experience just prior to a concert.

Years hence, biographers and friends would verify that John's body was heavily invested in medications, but the legends of John's pill popping in his twenties were grossly exaggerated, according to Beatles' press officer Tony Barrow:

"All of them took pills in Hamburg where they learned that the drugs could help them stay up with enhanced energy until all hours. In Liverpool, they would sometimes do a gig at lunch, another at night, and John, especially, needed a little help from his little friends to just stay up. I did see mood changes many times from him, but pills or not, he was always crazy nervous before performances. And he was unpredictable. "

That is an understatement. The same act of performing on stage that gave Paul McCartney such unbridled joy, seemed to rip at the nerves of John— not always, but enough for this reporter to notice. Mal Evans had always said that the Beatles as a group were nervous before shows. "It shows that they are real stars. But that's what it's all about, ya' know. It's a good thing, being nervous; it's a sign of a star to me."

On that afternoon, backstage at Studio 50, Evans was pacing around the dressing room area, clearly disturbed. "Do the boys know that he is not right?" I queried. "No, they think he's just nervous about 'Help!,'" Evans replied. Tony Barrow had mentioned that Paul was revved up and anxious about singing "Yesterday," but I had no idea that "Help!" would be a problem for John. "It's not the song," Malcolm Evans said, "it's just a mood. He's in a bad mood."

After a few minutes, the Beatles emerged from the dressing room. John brushed by me with no acknowledgment, not even a nod of the head. He stared straight ahead, his eyes seemed fixed and angry. He walked toward the stage like no one was there, as if no one existed, even as those invited to the warm-up and rehearsal screamed with excitement.

The sound check took several hours. The Beatles, always excellent and demanding perfection, took almost three hours to get comfortable. When John sang "Help!," he still had that thousand-yard stare and showed little emotion during the dress rehearsal. Through the entire rehearsal John was looking stoic and determined. Vince Calandra, a producer on the *Sullivan* show, was stunned that the Beatles wanted to go over the engineer's sound equipment. Calandra, now a talent producer for the American Film Institute, remembers the scene:

"It was just unbelievable. Lennon was nervous, no question about it. But he used that nervous energy to prod the technicians to improve the sound. McCartney and Harrison were more polite about it, but John was direct and to the point. He scared one of the techs so much that he ran out to a store and bought some sound gear to enhance what was there. But the engineers respected the involvement. Lennon and the guys were in a way validating how important they were."

It was during the rehearsal that I noticed the continuation of a habit that had begun on the 1964 tour: John Lennon could sing and chew gum at the same time, a particularly interesting performance quirk. How could John manage the sticky stuff bouncing around the inside of his cheeks while he played guitar and sang? During the rehearsal hours, Brian Epstein joined me near the curtain, gazing at his subjects with pride but also pacing back and forth like a caged animal. We exchanged pleasantries even as the boys passed by us on the way back to the dressing room. Paul looked perfectly happy, but John was grim.

Just before curtain time, John led the Beatles toward the stage. Sweat was soaking through the top of his shirt. He glanced over and suddenly his eyebrows arched upward, the visual sign that things were okay. Mal Evans and Neil Aspinall looked nervous, then somewhat relieved.

The Beatles fourth and final appearance on the *Sullivan Show* that night (although it was not live, but taped for later broadcast), was a triumph of entertainment genius. McCartney's rendition of "Yesterday," requiring extraordinary range, was dead on. John's lead vocal on "Help!" was so perfect that if you closed your eyes you could have been listening to the recording of it. When the *Sullivan* taping was over, Mal whispered to me, "Now we'll keep our fingers crossed for tomorrow night. To me, it's only another show, but it's really big for them."

The next night—August 15, 1965—would turn out to be an epic moment in the history of contemporary entertainment. Over 55,000 people would jam into Shea Stadium in the largest live concert event ever. Brian Epstein had kept the Beatles out of the largest venues in 1964, fearful of every promoter's nightmare—the photographic image of empty seats. Promoter Sid Bernstein, who earlier brought the Beatles to Carnegie Hall, convinced Epstein that he could fill the baseball stadium. Epstein was reluctant, but trusting Bernstein's entrepreneurial talents, he agreed to stage the Beatles at Shea that fateful Sunday evening.

Following the *Sullivan* taping on Saturday, the Beatles retreated to the Warwick Hotel, where I was waiting for them on a special assignment. Because of my unusual rapport with them, Epstein and the boys (especially John) urged Ed Sullivan Productions to hire me to conduct interviews with the Beatles for a filmed documentary titled *The Beatles at Shea Stadium*. The audiotaped interviews would be conducted before and after the concert, and the first series of conversations was held on Saturday night—less than twenty-four hours before the Shea event.

Entering the suite at the Warwick, I was stunned to find John slumped over the couch with his head in his hands. He looked up at me and had that glare-stare that usually signaled that he was unhappy to see someone.

"What the hell are you doing here?" he asked.

"I'm here to record the Shea interviews," I replied quickly, wanting to reassure him, as I did in most cases on the tour, that I wasn't there to intrude or to invade someone's privacy.

"All right, then, sit the fuck down," he said.

Our interview, the first of a session with all of the boys, moved quickly, with John declaring his glee and excitement about performing before the largest concert crowd in history. But when I pushed the stop button on the recorder, John leaned over to me and, with that famous purse of his lips, whispered, "Tell you the truth, Larry, scared to death, ya' know. Scared to death. How, can you tell me, the police can control those kind of crowds? Sitting ducks, I tell you, sitting ducks. Don't get near us Larry. We're sitting ducks."

Fear stirs our insides during all phases of our lives. For John, the entertainer, fear seemed to play a large part in his outlook toward performances. This seemed to me a contradiction. The same man who yearned to mix with the real people also dreaded large and friendly crowds. This was, after all, the man who chose the busy streets of New York City as his home and enjoyed walking freely among the proletariat. And yet gremlins who stoked fear and borderline panic lived within him. Was it fear of failing? Was it fright about the potential for physical harm? And did medications play a role?

What made this all the more bewildering was the ultimate power and outright joy of his performance on stage. It was the "getting there" that was the problem. But once he arrived, his performance skills shattered the excitement barrier and delivered on all promises. And there was no greater example of John Lennon's powerful presence than that first concert at Shea Stadium on August 15, 1965.

❖

The Beatles arrived at Shea via two modes of transportation. A helicopter took them to a landing site near the World's Fair. Minutes later, a Wells Fargo security truck took them the rest of the way, entering Shea Stadium through the centerfield entrance. The truck stopped near second base, where the concert stage had been set up. The Beatles stepped out of the truck and headed toward the dugout on the third base side of the field, where I was waiting on the steps along with Ed Sullivan, promoter Sid Bernstein, and scores of police. I will never forget Bernstein's wide eyes as the Beatles arrived. Still a legend in Manhattan society, Bernstein remembers the night:

"I had done Sinatra and all the biggies but this was so fabulous. Watching them head past me into the dugout with the roar of the crowd blocking out every other sound of that night was amazing."

The dugout led to a corridor and a group of dressing rooms. In one of those rooms, John, Paul, George, and Ringo got dressed in light khaki military-style uniforms accentuated by six-sided stars given to them by the Wells Fargo drivers. Their walk from the truck to the dugout, which took about sixty seconds, and the screaming that accompanied it, was enough to take your breath away, and the screaming continued unabated while they slipped into their outfits. When Lennon led them up the steps, the "sound barrier" was broken.

The screams were the most intense I had heard at any single concert, and after two minutes of howling, and a cursory introduction by Ed Sullivan, the concert began with a screeching but dynamic performance of "Twist and Shout," the Isley Brothers' hit that the Beatles practically adopted.

The summer night temperature was in the mid-eighties and John Lennon would have none of it, opening the buttons of his jacket as he swiveled and turned on the stage. "Shake it up baby now," he blared. And did he shake it up! It was vintage John Lennon. His mouth, as always, was just an inch away from the microphone. His legs were spread wide, pelvis arching forward. The guitar was held high, and as his midsection lunged toward the crowd, his back stayed erect, almost swaying to and fro.

The body language was pure Lennon, but there was in full effect another aspect of his performance style that is rarely noticed. John's face appeared as if he were in a dream, at times angelic and swooning, at other times intense, but always with that trademark grin, even with stick pins and jellybeans flying in his direction. In a pure and simple observation, I realized the Lennon mystique was informed by the presence of outright joy. The same man who lived in perspiration-enveloped fear, transformed himself into a bundle of sheer ecstasy and elation. On that same stage, in a matter of minutes, he would play the electric piano with his elbows, and utter unintelligible words to the thousands of fans. The words sounded Japanese, but they were a throaty mispronunciation of fake words—another Lennon signature move. He was playing with the crowd and enjoying every minute of it.

At one point during the chaos, Paul booed a police officer who was chasing away a fan who had jumped the barriers and made it close to the infield. Lennon looked over and threw Paul a look of anger. Later, John told me he was afraid that Paul might have incited the crowd to start booing en masse.

Mood differences aside, it was a landmark concert for John and Paul. Both had offered stirring renditions of two popular 1965 songs, Paul's melodic and embracing "Yesterday" and John's signature title song from the movie *Help!*. It was during that song that I witnessed the ultimate Lennon stage talent: the ability to sing the song and turn in so many directions while he was doing it. John Lennon was, all by himself, a theater in the round.

As a veteran observer of the Beatles' live performances, I had never witnessed a concert like the one at Shea—emblazoned by pure emotion, driven by unmatched crowd enthusiasm and momentum, and highlighted by the wonderment of John's eyes as he glanced around the semicircle of screaming fans that filled the baseball stadium on that windy and sweltering summer night.

Once again, the pre-concert nerves and that terrible agonizing look on his face were transformed in a matter of seconds. It wasn't a split personality. It was the ability of John Lennon to block out those fears, something he talked about quite frequently:

"You know, we're in the dressing room. I'm nervous, tired, smoking. I don't even want to put the clothes on. I'm so tired sometimes . . . but then once you get dressed, the stomach stops churning, and you start getting ready."

Nothing, of course, can get a performer ready for technical breakdown, which is exactly what occurred at one point during the Shea concert. The wind was kicking up the dirt from the infield. Amid the screams and the backbeat and the crowd trying to surge, I realized that the boys couldn't hear each other.

Vince Calandra, who was at Studio 50 the day before, and is now a Hollywood producer, was coordinating a one-man crew that was filming the Shea concert for the same *Ed Sullivan* TV special that I was hired to do interviews for. He watched from the first base dugout, and was blown away:

"They just could not hear each other, and they kind of got lost in the mix. But Lennon was amazing. Even though they couldn't hear each other, he forged on. I'll never forget that in one single show, he played guitar, the harmonica, and the keyboard with his elbows. . . . Lennon was quiet in the dressing rooms at the *Sullivan Show*, but there was an animal like magnetism on stage. Even when he blurted out words that you couldn't understand . . . the crowd went berserk."

My notes from the night tell a similar story: "They can't hear each other. Ringo looks puzzled in the back. John's coat is open. He's amazing. Plays guitar, harmonica, and the keyboard with his elbows. Wind kicks up dirt from infield. Nothing seems to faze him. Man is a fanatic. Even McCartney smiling at him. What a show! Got chills from watching them. Can it get any better?"

Along with the Exciters, rocker Del Shannon and the Supremes showed up to toast the Beatles on that glorious night after the Shea concert. In the interview session that followed, John was cocksure and uplifted, convinced like the others that the Beatles had broken a barrier. Like most of his post-concert life, John Lennon was in a good mood. The fear that stalked him would disappear in the glow of victory.

❖

Perhaps no one single concert showed off the ultimate stage talent of John Lennon more than the most controversial one of all. The fans of Cleveland were fun but riotous at the city's Public Auditorium on September 15, 1964. The Cleveland concert was a historical first, though some would say "hysterical"—but not in the humorous sense.

Lennon and his tribe were at their best. As was the usual routine, a portion of the crowd stormed the stage. Suddenly I saw a man enter the stage from the left side, shaking his head up and down. The intruder, it turns out, was a protector. The high-ranking cop quickly and physically pushed the Beatles off the stage, without any explanation, and proceeded to use one of the stage microphones to announce that the concert was being stopped. The Beatles, furious, retreated to the dressing room. It was the first half-concert in Beatles history. No one was angrier that John. He cursed and screamed all the way to the dressing room where he continued his tirade. Later, he would tell me:

"I felt like kicking him off because it's so annoying when they come marching up on stage the way they did, just came in and pushed George and I off the microphone, but they didn't say why. Apparently, somebody was getting hurt, but nothing was really happening wild. He comes on, shoving us off and shouting 'Get off the stage.' I felt like kicking him."

John's defiance of anything close to authority was clearly visible, but he manifested his anger in an unusual war. First threatening not to come back on stage, Lennon led the boys out of the dressing room and all four gave the embattled Cleveland fans the most spirited show (or half of it) that I had witnessed to that point.

My vivid memory of the night is John inhaling air with his nostrils and creating that angry Lennon stare at police officers surrounding the stage. He gave more than a performance. In the space of four songs, he delivered vivid rock and roll, total sexual energy, and a stare that said to the interrupting police officers that the Beatles got the last word.

❖

Despite the chaos surrounding him, and the emotional pressure of performance, John Lennon was ecstatic about that first tour in 1964. On the final night, in a room at the Riviera hotel outside of New York City, John reflected with me:

> KANE: *Is there any particular memory you would like to cherish from this trip?*
> LENNON: *Well, just the whole thing has been fantastic. We will probably never do another tour like it. It could never be the same as this one and it is probably something we will remember for the rest of our days. It's just been marvelous.*

He was right. It was never the same after 1964.

The 1964 tour was a medley of high drama, great music, and back room behavior that was not for the faint of heart. Most people assume that going on the road with a rock band means nightly trysts of sex and drugs. They are not far off in their view, but with the Beatles and their clean-cut imagery, finding temporary love was not as easy as you might expect.

Although married in 1964, John obliged willing participants on a regular basis. Despite his appetite for sex, Lennon did not, as is suggested in the various tell-all books about his life, engage in deviate behavior, nor did he attempt to engage in unusual sexual feats and wake up the next morning to tell about it. He was discreet and used great caution in picking his partners and, as I observed, was respectful to the people he met. Most of the women during the tours were screened by Malcolm Evans and Neil Aspinall, and their "talent scouting" hardly guaranteed a successful night. In both Minneapolis and Portland in 1965, John complained to me that the women he met "didn't want to have a go at it." Even superstars strike out at times, and Lennon was wiser for it. He would take rejection philosophically and move on.

During our first visit to Hollywood in 1964, at parties and in the Whiskey A Go Go nightclub on the Sunset Strip, John had a memorable tryst with movie star Jayne Mansfield that never got much newspaper ink at the time. Although they were deeply engrossed in each other on a couple of occasions, very few photos were taken, no big stories were written, and no one really knows what happened. But after the Los Angeles trip, I jokingly asked John, "So it must be incredible to have all these women wanting you?"

He replied, in one of his most memorable retorts, "Larry, sex is overrated unless you're the one doing it."

Sexual tension was another thing. What amazed me during the tours was the incredible sexual energy that he created on stage. He never flirted with his eyes as well as McCartney did. But there's no doubt that his body language and the confidence in his appearance turned on so many members of the audience.

It was an irony to me that the most sex that occurred between John and his fans was the unsatisfied sexual tension that existed between the performer and the people in the audience. Was part of that attraction the same thing I saw—that the man who looked so cocksure was underneath it all so vulnerable and needy?

Whatever the physical and sexual ramifications, one thing was certain. The sometimes gentle soul with the wicked inner conscience, had one dangerous talent: just being there, just showing himself and launching his breathless passion on stage, he could, inadvertently, on a moment's notice, start a riot—in a concert hall, and inside the body of a fan.

SEVEN:
John and "The Boys"

"I'd been kingpin up to then. Now, I thought, if I take him on, what will happen? But he was good. He also looked like Elvis."
—*John Lennon, on his fateful decision to bring Paul McCartney into his band*

"[John] always felt Paul was more like his equal, that he never had to worry about him. 'I don't worry about Paul. Paul can handle himself,' he goes, 'but I worry about the other two.'"
—*May Pang, on John's view of the other Beatles*

Make no mistake about it. In the beginning, the Quarrymen, Johnny and the Moondogs, the Beatals [*sic*], the Silver Beatles, and the Beatles—by any name—were John Lennon's band. That was in the beginning. Eventually, it became a grand confluence of two flowing talents: John Lennon and Paul McCartney.

The trio of John, Paul, and George—the original core of the Beatles— would sit around in their earliest days and dream like dreamers always do. In the late fifties, the friends kept their music alive by doing what most aspiring musicians do—they played for themselves. John, in a remembrance of the very early days, once said, "There was no point in rehearsing for nonexistent dates. But we went on playing together just for kicks, usually in each other's homes. We kept the record player going a lot of the time playing the latest American hits. We'd try and get the same effects."

The relationship between John Lennon and Paul McCartney, especially, is the stuff of great legend, and even greater misunderstanding. Although there were fractious moments, the musical bond was sealed early on and the heritage of their history remained mostly positive to the end of John Lennon's life. Remember, when John invited Paul to join the band, John was nineteen months his senior. For teenagers, with their dramatic spurts of growth, nineteen months is a significant age gap. So it is notably impressive that John Lennon chose a younger man with exceptional talent to join his group.

Martin Lewis, who has worked on Beatles-related projects since 1967 and is viewed as one of the world's leading Beatles scholars, says Lennon's invitation to the younger McCartney was not only a landmark event, but a decision that showed incredible maturity for a fifteen-year-old:

"First of all, Paul was better-looking, more adept on the guitar. What wisdom [on John's part]! From the beginning, he treated Paul as an equal. When all the sages and experts look at the fractious times in their relationship, they forget the brilliance of that early decision. From the beginning, he showed reverence for Paul and his talents. John basically put his own musical passion ahead of a natural desire to be king. The measure of a man's character are what choices he makes. Lennon deserves enormous credit for his instinctive desire to make the group better. It turned out to be an incredibly healthy sibling rivalry."

During John's reflective period in the late seventies, he remembered that fateful decision:

"There was a friend of mine called Ivan who lived at the back of my house, and he went to the same school as Paul McCartney, the Liverpool Institute High School. It was through Ivan that I first met Paul. Seems that he knew Paul was always dickering around in music, and thought that he would be a good lad to have in the group. So one day, when we were playing at

Woolton, he brought him along. We can both remember it quite well. We've even got the date down. It was June 15, 1955. (John often got dates wrong; the actual date was July 6, 1957.)

"The Quarrymen were playing on a raised platform and there was a good crowd because it was a warm sunny day. I'd been kingpin up to then. Now, I thought, if I take him on, what will happen? But he was good. He also looked like Elvis.

"I had a group, I was the leader. I met Paul and I made a decision whether to—and he made a decision, too—have him in the group. I made a decision to have a better person in the group. It made me stronger. The decision to make the group stronger was mine and mine alone."

Hindsight is one of life's easiest tools to master; it provides you with the ability to judge the past and refine your vision of it. The group did become stronger because of Paul, of course, and the collaboration of the two would make history. But in the early days of the boys' success, there is no doubt that John Lennon's voice, on the basis of quantity and quality, was the lead voice of the Beatles. NPR (National Public Radio) commentator and Beatles historian Walter J. Podrazik, a student of that era, states that "as time went on, it was a dual leadership, but in the beginning, John Lennon was the bandleader. Just listen to the newest release of [the LP] *Beatles '65*. He had the dominant voice and the dominant role. It is the Lennon numbers, like 'Twist and Shout,' that really stand out."

At first, Paul easily accepted his secondary role, perhaps for no other reason than the fact that he was new to the group and John had all the momentum and control. Paul's time would certainly come, too, and John wouldn't do anything to impede his growth.

For scholar Martin Lewis, the early days and subsequent rise to fame would create a bond, a seal of mutual confidence in and respect for each other, that could never really be broken, no matter what would happen later:

"He sensed Paul McCartney [was a] brother. . . . The fact that they started writing songs together showed they had a real relationship. Lennon and

McCartney gained confidence from each other. . . . The heart of the Beatles was their writing. The Beatles would have been a just a great cover band without their writing."

There was more to John's contribution to the band than the special creative collaboration with his co-genius McCartney. During the historic 1964 and 1965 tours, Lennon was the leader for greater reasons than his seniority. At the zany and unruly news conferences, a routine in each city, Lennon was always witty and sharp, but because he was a genuine leader, he also made sure that Paul, George, and Ringo got in their verbal licks. Content with my own daily private interviews that I would tape for national radio syndication, I could stand in the back of the fast-talking news gang and marvel at John's endless wit. One of John's most amazing talents, which slowly sank into my consciousness during these daily junkets, was the way he would always involve his mates. He'd level his classic barbs at the press, mostly in jest, and then naturally turn his head left or right as a physical sign that Paul, Ringo, or George should add to his nonsense or handle the next question outright.

Throughout those watershed North American tours, John was clearly in the lead, especially at all live events and gatherings and public appearances. There was a brilliance to his leadership, a cutting edge to his ad-libbed pronouncements, and although he had massive insecurities, he also had a commanding presence when the band was all together. Whether he knew it or not, or did so consciously or not, John Lennon lived up to the ultimate standards of excellent leadership. He was the leader, and was viewed so even after the breakup.

The man viewed as the world's greatest scholar of the intricacies of the group is Mark Lewisohn of London. Lewisohn has a clear focus on whose band it was.

"I think when I was growing up I favored Paul as a Beatle. Then I had a George spell in the seventies," he says. "The more I studied and talked to people who knew them, the more I realized that John was the heart and soul of the Beatles. I say this with all due respect to Paul McCartney, whose extraordinary talent propelled the group to such success, but, in reality, they were John's group. They said they were equals. . . . Even when they stopped saying they were equals, it was obvious whose band it was."

In light of Lewisohn's keen observation, it was all the more amazing to have a close-up look, as this reporter did, of the interaction of the four. It was fascinating to watch. With all the pressures of touring, and especially with their life inside a controlled cocoon, the sharp sense of humor and performance was more than admirable. John's intuition toward his mates was almost supernatural.

John especially had paternal instincts toward Ringo, who reciprocated with a genuine affection and respect toward the sometimes erratic and unpredictable team leader. Unlike the others, Ringo stayed out of the dissent concerning John's love affair with Yoko Ono, which had famously caused estrangement among the boys in the later Beatles years. Ringo, however, had always been thankful and joyful that John would have him in his band, and he was proud of the association. Also, Ringo was an easygoing sort of character with a surprisingly positive outlook on life, belied as it was by his somewhat droopy face. During the 1965 tour, I asked Ringo if he felt he was "behind the scenes" or living in the shadows of the others:

KANE: *Does it bother you that John and Paul always get the spotlight?*
STARR: *They may be the leaders, but when we travel together and work together I feel like an equal. I'm treated with great respect, you know. I miss these guys when we are not together. When I had me tonsils out, and they traveled for a while without me, I really missed them, you know.*

John's sensitivity to Ringo's plight extended well into the seventies. Considered the fun and sometimes goofy Beatle, there was a side to Ringo Starr that few people noticed. Ringo had an intellectual view of the world that was often concealed by the public imagery of the man in the back beating the drums, his head bobbing and his arms moving vigorously. I noticed early on that Ringo's views about the Vietnam war and race relations in America complimented John's perspective. But John also was well-aware that Ringo was the most sensitive of the boys. Also, Ringo was the last one to join the group and didn't have the grand early history that John, Paul, and George shared, and so he gladly accepted a sort of secondary role.

In the social moments—on the airplane, in news conferences, and while partying—John spent most of his chat time with Ringo. It was no surprise to me that, after the band's breakup, John was more concerned about the solitary life that Ringo was leading in Los Angeles than perhaps any of the other Beatles. At one point, the drummer would even reside for a time in the house that Lennon and May Pang shared in California.

John was kind to Ringo in professional ways, as well. John's support in this sense demonstrates what is typically a glaring omission in many Lennon biographer's description of him: that is, he always demonstrated a creative unselfishness that is rarely seen in the world of music, if not all of art. In addition to providing music for Ringo's first album, John was selfless in assisting the drummer in his rise to solo success.

Bruce Spizer, author of *The Beatles on Apple Records* and *The Beatles Solo on Apple Records*, recalls being impressed by Lennon's creative philanthropy:

"John rearranged the great Platter's hit, "Only You." He did a masterful job on it and could have saved it for himself. He actually recorded the guide song for the album. But he gave it to Ringo to include on the album *Good Night Vienna*. The song was also released as a single, and shortly rose to number six on the charts. It was a special gift and it really helped Ringo's solo career."

Part of the reason why John always had an affection toward Ringo can be traced back to Ringo's singular reception of Yoko Ono into John's life. Unlike George, Paul, most of the Beatles' inner circle, and practically the entirety of the general population, Ringo did not pass judgment; he simply accepted John's choice of partners. In effect, Ringo offered virtually no objections to the presence of Yoko Ono. And John was keenly aware of this offering. In a long view back at the Yoko situation, it's clear that much of that famous rift—John and Yoko on one side and the rest of the world, it seemed, on the other—was instigated by Paul and George, at least in terms of the Beatles family's shunning of Yoko. Paul was more silent about his sentiments, of course, as he was with most forms of confrontation, but George, always a man who didn't mince his words or shield his facial expressions, was not. John, who would mentor George during the post-Beatles years, was especially upset at George's frequent irreverence toward Yoko, even to her face. John remembered one get-together with anger and disappointment:

"To be insulted, just because you love someone. And George, shit, insulted her right to her face in the Apple office at the beginning; just being 'straightforward,' you know, that game of, 'Well, I'm going to be up front because this is what we've heard, and Dylan, and a few people said she'd got a lousy name in New York, and you gave off bad vibes.' That's what George said to her, and we both sat through it, and I didn't hit him, I don't know why, but I was always hoping that they would come around. I couldn't believe it, you know. And they all sat there with their wives, like a fucking jury, and judged us. Ringo was all right, so was Maureen (Ringo's first wife), but the others really gave it to us. I'll never forgive them . . . although I can't help still loving them either."

It was typical of John to end any of his diatribes about the Beatles with an outpouring of some affection, even when he was disgusted with them. The comment about "loving them" was part of the strong, silent bond that was forged over the years and would never be broken.

George's candor on bringing Yoko into the mix was part of an underlying change that would mark his new attitude in the post-Beatles years. Once subservient to John and Paul, George became more independent in the late sixties. The ties that bound him to John's leadership were slowly disintegrating. There was a clear reason for this: Harrison was maturing. The trip to India and public notice of his songwriting talents had inspired him to become more independent. His relationship with John was complex. John loved George but was startled when George started displaying Lennon-like frankness, especially in public interviews. Despite their differences over Yoko, John and George's friendship was woven through the threads of their common bond—an interest in music that was more eclectic than the other Beatles. That's why George was never hesitant to answer John's call to play his magical guitar on many of John's solo efforts.

❖

John's relationship with Paul always seemed warm and genuine during the 1964-66 tours. If there was any resentment simmering between the two in the Beatles' heyday, it was certainly disguised. But all the time I spent with the boys touring North America, I never witnessed anything between the two of them that even bordered on dislike, mistrust, backbiting, or malevolence. In fact, during the last filmed interview that Lennon and McCartney ever gave together, which I had the honor (unknown at the time) of conducting in 1968, the two of them seemed—despite the rumors that were already swirling—committed to each other as musicians and as human beings.

That may be why the later controversies between the two—which were oh-so-real—surprised me, especially because of their penchant to support each other and compliment each other so publicly, and privately, in the past. I have a vivid memory of visiting the Beatles' office in London's West End in 1968, where Paul introduced me to one of Apple's first clients, Mary Hopkin. He stood beside her like a proud teacher with his star pupil. Paul was so proud of Mary's potential that he played for me a tape of her song, "Those Were the Days"—a song that would later sell millions of copies. He was very quick to add, "Ya'know, Larry, Mary is going to do very well. Both John and I discovered her talent. And John is as equally impressed. He has that ability to spot talent, ya' know."

In addition to that mutual respect, there was another aspect of the John-Paul relationship that is worthy of mention, as author Bruce Spizer elucidates:

"John showed tremendous generosity and respect toward Paul in terms of sharing credits. A great example of that is the recording of 'Give Peace a Chance.' Paul had no creative piece of that song, yet John gave him a fifty percent share. Conversely, that was part of Paul's offerings to John, but in the case of 'Give Peace a Chance', Paul had no role whatsoever in the song's creation."

The obvious generosity and mutual respect could perplex any believer in the theory that Paul and John were always rivals. That widely held theory is simply not true. Bitter rivalry did occur, at times and in very pointed occasions, but it mostly came after the Beatles break up and was motivated by separation, petty jealousy, a pair of protective wives, and the development of the clique-like relationship that John had developed in the post-Beatles years with George and Ringo.

Beatles historian Martin Lewis sees the beginning of the actual estrangement between John and Paul as a result of the vacuum created by the breakup:

"[As Beatles], they were always trying to prove to each other they could do even better. They wrote like people spoke, and they knew they had that magic. . . . And even as 1970 approached, amidst all that rancor was creative juices. The anger that came out in the early seventies was more about personal differences. . . . They were arguing like divorced people. They had a creative love affair [and] now they were having a public divorce."

Veteran broadcaster and media executive Scott Regan says that it's easy to forget how long they were together:

"John once said, 'When you say John, Paul, George, and Ringo, it's just part of me.' So he knew about unity. They played and wrote together from 1956 to 1970. John and Paul were together almost as many years as they were old when they first meet . . . that's fourteen years, almost half of their lives."

The physical separation of the two—and all the competitive energy that it stimulated—was aggravated by and led to a startling war of lyrics and art that began in 1971. The same battle of words would come full circle, as it should, after John's murder, with a touching song by Paul for John.

It all began in May of 1971. Chris Carter, host of the radio program *Breakfast with the Beatles* in Los Angeles—and considered one of the world's finest scholars on Lennon and McCartney music—recalls the tit-for -tat scrap:

"[The cover art on McCartney's album] *Ram*, released in the spring of 1971, was credited to Paul and Linda McCartney. The cover of the album has Paul holding a sheep by its ears, but the back cover displays two beetles fornicating. Apparently enraged by the art work and lyrics, John inserts a postcard in his next LP, *Imagine*. The card shows John holding a pig the same way Paul is holding his sheep."

The illustration duel was kids' stuff compared to the lyrical aggression that began with Paul's song, "Too Many People," on the *Ram* LP. Carter says:

"There is a clear shot across the bow on this one, with references to John's lifestyle and his new more eclectic life. . . . Look at the words":

TOO MANY PEOPLE GOING UNDERGROUND

TOO MANY REACHING FOR A PIECE OF CAKE

TOO MANY PEOPLE PULLED AND PUSHED AROUND

TOO MANY WAITING FOR THAT LUCKY BREAK

THAT WAS YOUR FIRST MISTAKE

YOU TOOK YOUR LUCKY BREAK AND BROKE IT IN TWO

NOW WHAT CAN BE DONE FOR YOU?

YOU BROKE IT IN TWO

TOO MANY PEOPLE SHARING PARTY LINES

TOO MANY PEOPLE EVER SLEEPING LATE

TOO MANY PEOPLE PAYING PARKING FINES

TOO MANY HUNDRED PEOPLE LOSING WEIGHT

THAT WAS YOUR FIRST MISTAKE

YOU TOOK YOUR LUCKY BREAK AND BROKE IT IN TWO

NOW WHAT CAN BE DONE FOR YOU?

YOU BROKE IT IN TWO

John's retort, which came five months later on the *Imagine* album, seemed to take off the kid gloves, according to Carter:

"In the song 'How Do You Sleep?' John attacked the nerve center of Paul McCartney—his creativity and talent. The lyrics are pointed . . . especially the reference to Paul's immortal song 'Yesterday'":

SO SGT. PEPPER TOOK YOU BY SURPRISE

YOU BETTER SEE RIGHT THROUGH THAT MOTHER'S EYES

THOSE FREAKS WAS RIGHT WHEN THEY SAID YOU WAS DEAD

THE ONE MISTAKE YOU MADE WAS IN YOUR HEAD

AH, HOW DO YOU SLEEP?

AH, HOW DO YOU SLEEP AT NIGHT?

YOU LIVE WITH STRAIGHTS WHO TELL YOU YOU WAS KING

JUMP WHEN YOUR MOMMA TELL YOU ANYTHING

THE ONLY THING YOU DONE WAS YESTERDAY

AND SINCE YOU'RE GONE YOU'RE JUST ANOTHER DAY

AH, HOW DO YOU SLEEP?

AH, HOW DO YOU SLEEP AT NIGHT?

It didn't end there. Also on the *Imagine* LP, John took the feud to a deeper level when his song "Crippled Inside" waged war against McCartney's sense of conviction. The lyrics are scathing:

YOU CAN SHINE YOUR SHOES AND WEAR A SUIT

YOU CAN COMB YOUR HAIR AND LOOK QUITE CUTE

YOU CAN HIDE YOUR FACE BEHIND A SMILE

ONE THING YOU CAN'T HIDE

IS WHEN YOU'RE CRIPPLED INSIDE

YOU CAN WEAR A MASK AND PAINT YOUR FACE

YOU CAN CALL YOURSELF THE HUMAN RACE

YOU CAN WEAR A COLLAR AND A TIE

ONE THING YOU CAN'T HIDE

IS WHEN YOU'RE CRIPPLED INSIDE

The post-Beatles word wars might seem vicious in retrospect, but the two began seeking each other out in the mid seventies. And as Chris Carter points out, there was a poignant end to the music of discord:

"Paul was severely affected by John's death and expressed it in so many ways, but perhaps none as special as the song he wrote about John. It was on the 1982 *Tug of War* album, and it was called 'Here Today'":

AND IF I SAY I REALLY KNEW YOU WELL

WHAT WOULD YOUR ANSWER BE

IF YOU WERE HERE TODAY

OOH- OOH- OOH- HERE TO-DAY

WELL KNOWING YOU

YOU'D PROBABLY LAUGH AND SAY THAT WE WERE WORLDS APART

IF YOU WERE HERE TODAY

OOH- OOH- OOH- HERE TO-DAY

BUT AS FOR ME, I STILL REMEMBER HOW IT WAS BEFORE

AND I AM HOLDING BACK THE TEARS NO MORE

Ooh- ooh- ooh- I love you, ooh.

What about the time we met
Well I suppose that you could say that we were
Playing hard to get
Didn't understand a thing
But we could always sing

What about the night we cried
Because there wasn't any reason left to keep it all inside
Never understood a word
But you were always there with a smile

And if I say I really loved you
And was glad you came along

If you were here today|
Ooh- ooh- ooh- for you were in my song
Ooh- ooh- ooh- here to - day

Much of the reason for the original animosity involved decisions of business, but a thaw began in 1974. Lennon-watcher Andre Gardner, the New York and Philadelphia broadcaster, recalls the changes in the mood:

"In the seventies, there was the initial estrangement, but during [John's] separation with Yoko, and even after that, [John and Paul] began to talk quite often on the phone. John mellowed toward Paul during the late seventies. The two wives had little room for each other, but the bond of the early success and the history they made came through in manifestations of warmth and surprise friendship."

Sometimes the manifestation of their friendship was literally a surprise. Photographer and family friend Bob Gruen remembers a knock on the door of the Lennons' Dakota apartment in late fall 1978:

"A couple weeks before Christmas, I was at the Dakota. There were no servants there. It was just John and Yoko and Sean asleep in the other room. We were just watching TV and doing other usual [things]—hanging out, drinking tea—and suddenly there was a knock on the door of the apartment, which is kind of unheard of because the Dakota's a high-security building. John and Yoko, twice before [had bad experiences with random door knocking]—once in London when they were falsely arrested for having pot, the police barged into their house; and when they lived on Bank Street, the police tried to barge in and arrest them. So, when the doorbell just rings, they get real nervous, you know. I was the only one there and John said, 'Check it out. See who's there.' And I open the inner door and I heard people singing Christmas carols. And so I called back to John and Yoko in the bedroom. 'Yo. Don't be nervous. It's just some kids singing Christmas carols.' And I opened the outer door, and it was not kids, but Paul and Linda going, 'We wish you a Merry Christmas,' you know. And I was embarrassed (laughing)! I said, you know, 'You're not singing to me,' you know. I said, 'I think you want the guys in the bedroom. Come on in.' And I brought them in and they sang their way into the bedroom. And John and Yoko were absolutely thrilled to see 'em. And they were hugging each other like the way old friends at the holidays do. And I saw no animosity between Linda and Yoko, which is supposed to be a famous [thing]. But when they actually saw each other, it was like, 'Hey, how are you doing? Let's have some tea. What's going on? How ya' been?'"

May Pang believes that few really understand the complexity of John's feeling toward the other Beatles, especially Paul, and that contrary to speculation and rumors, John had a true respect for Linda McCartney and a brother-like relationship with Paul:

"I think he didn't think [Paul] would marry Linda. He thought he would be [with], you know, I guess somebody more glamorous, maybe. I think that is how he thought of it, but he liked Linda. He didn't dislike her or anything.

No matter what anybody thought . . . he loved all the guys and he was very concerned. Even if he had the bickering with Paul, no matter what was out in the press, it was like he didn't worry, but if anything happened to him, he would have been there.

"Business-wise, yes, they had their differences. But they didn't talk about business when they got together. They talked about who was around, what music they were listening to, what's going on, what they were gonna be doing . . . more as brothers talked, but leaving the business out of it."

There is a pattern to Paul McCartney's behavior and John Lennon's reaction to it that is apparent and revealing through the seventies. At various points, Paul reached out and John blinked. The perfect example of this cat-and-mouse game was the so called "secret jam" at the Burbank recording studios while John was producing Harry Nilsson's album *Pussycats*. It was a case of McCartney extending the olive branch by showing up for surprise visits. Beatles historian Chris Carter remembers:

"It was an amazing event. Jesse Ed Davis, on guitar, was there along with Stevie Wonder. Paul had kept showing up. He was at the California beach house and then he shows up at the studio with Linda for this jam. It was John on guitar, Paul on drums, Stevie Wonder on the keyboard, and Jesse on the guitar. They did 'Lucille,' and 'Stand By Me,' and some others. There were other meetings between the two . . . but this session was notable. Paul seemed to feel more comfortable in May Pang's presence. This was the time [John and May] were in California together. It was the only time in the period after the Beatles that John and Paul played together."

A single jam session, unknown to the public, marks the only collaboration of Lennon and McCartney in the post-Beatles years. But more significant than the music is the proof that, once again, across the barriers of creative and marital rivalries, John and Paul become mutual seekers, reveling at their brotherhood and, once again, basking in every brief glory of personal contact they shared.

During the early nineties, twenty years after the cold war between John and Paul, former press secretary Derek Taylor, in and out of the Beatles lives for it seemed like an eternity, lamented those years of estrangement and apparent disengagement. In a phone conversation with me in 2004, Derek wondered:

"Larry, external forces necessitated some rather extraordinary hostility, but through all the bullshit, all the smoke and fire of public scrutiny, John loved Paul, and in his own way, Paul loved John. John was the more sensitive of the two, so he would be the first to make up. But no matter what happened, too much had gone down. And there was a genuine feeling between them, an affection that even public disharmony could not stop."

Through the early days, through the rise to fame, and even after the breakup, the brotherhood of John and the boys—singed by public discord, spousal controversy, and great misunderstanding—remained intact through the time of John's death. Ringo was always close and appreciative. George was more independent, yet willing enough to play guitar even on some of the *Imagine* LP songs that attacked Paul. Paul McCartney was definitely not in complete emotional harmony with John at all times through the years, but in the end there was a truth that no one could ignore. Differences aside, emotions hung out to dry, and discord always appearing around the bend, both men and their legions of fans could never walk away from their musical marriage made in heaven.

EIGHT:
The Man, the Myth, the Truth

> "With all his frailties, fears, high notes and low notes,
> he was like everyman."
> —*Tony Bramwell, childhood friend, Apple executive, and film producer*

> "John is a powerful force. Sometimes, he's rough, if you know what I
> mean, man. But there's no greater person that I know."
> —*Malcolm Evans, the Beatles' Road Manager*

From his early days to the afterlife of the 1980 tragedy, perhaps no human being in the contemporary culture has been written and talked about more than John Lennon. The analysis of his life and times matches the sort of detailed scrutiny usually reserved for the careers of world leaders. To that end, legends persist, myths remain, and clarity is a rare commodity.

The life of John Lennon was a duality: the private man and the public personality. But in his case, the public persona wasn't far removed from the private person, a rare thing at that level of fame. John may have feared the dangers of entertaining people in public, but he was fearless in allowing the world to witness his strengths and his weaknesses. Perhaps he knew that the vulnerability he exposed endeared him to anyone who experienced similar miscues in their own lives.

Yet the burden of the famous is the sense of hero-worship that exists outside their control. The worshippers, in their zeal to idealize or crucify, forget the fact that their idol is a real human being just like themselves. They over-analyze facts just as quickly as they conveniently omit them. They define and compartmentalize. All the while their fantasy expectations blind them from seeing—or even seeking—the real deal.

Few have allowed us to see the real deal so well as John Lennon. Still, the myths persist and the rumors swirl. Was John Lennon a mean bastard? A foolish prankster? An aggressive sex-fiend? A musical tyrant? A drug abuser? A gay man?

The answer to such questions—like the man—is complex. But the clues are out there, and there are many. When it comes to certain lingering myths surrounding John Lennon's legend, there are clear-cut explanations, and I will give them. But to understand and grasp the man as a whole, there is only subtle revelation like the layers of an onion peeling away, and in that revelation, there is truth.

❖

London tabloids portrayed John as always being in trouble with the law. In fact, outside of routine punishments in school and his overplayed marijuana conviction in London in 1968, he had no remarkable legal difficulties. Although he lived his personal life quite dangerously, John paid his taxes, stopped for red lights (after he finally acquired a driver's license), and enjoyed being an upstanding, if not quiet, resident of the two nations he called home. The bad boy reputation that often followed him was a source of great aggravation and agitation and was simply not deserved. His respect for law enforcement, for instance, is underscored by the generous donations he arranged to provide protective equipment for the New York City Police Department.

Still, there was no question that John Lennon had "edge" written all over him, and it often grated others. As we walked down the steps of the Beatles' plane at the airport in Minneapolis on August 21, 1965, a print reporter came up to John to ask him a question, her face only inches away from his. I didn't hear her remark, but I will never forget the response. John slapped her in the face and moved quickly toward the car. Approaching the limo, I asked him, "What was that all about?" Before I could blink, he answered, "None of your fucking business."

Technically, he was right, but I've always had solidarity with my fellow reporters and was especially curious. Slapping a reporter because you don't like their attitude is not something I would advise or endorse. Later on in the hallway at the Leamington Motor Court in downtown Minneapolis, I chided him again about the slapping episode. He said, "The shit asked me if I was faithful to my wife." I replied jokingly, "Instead of slapping her, why didn't you say 'no' and have a laugh over it?" He didn't answer, but a bit of a smile curled on the edges of his lips, a silent message that he knew he had screwed up. Still, being the year 1965, that particular reporter was light years ahead of her peers in her extremely audacious line of questioning. Lennon's extreme reaction to her (while unfortunately physical) simply proved that he was willing to dish out more than he would take. And it never mattered who was doing the dishing.

The risk of instant anger always lurked just below John's surface. And one thing that usually set it off was prying questions—especially those that had to do with fidelity. In the Beatles' rented mansion in Hollywood on the 1964 tour, John was sitting on a sofa chatting with a young woman during a party following the Hollywood Bowl concert. "Long John" Wade, a popular dee-jay from Hartford, Connecticut, walked into the room, tape recorder in hand, and casually approached the woman. He pointed the microphone toward her face and said, "And who might you be?" Wade was holding the microphone with an animated gesture, trying to be funny. The recorder happened to be turned off, but Wade's joking was off limits. Lennon didn't think it was all that funny, especially since he didn't know the recorder was off. He sprung out of his seat and punched Wade in the forearm. Wade looked like he was in shock as the microphone detached from the recorder and flew across the room.

"I was stunned," Wade said. "But what was interesting was how hard John tried in the days ahead to make up for it. He became so accommodating, so friendly." At one point in the following days, Lennon asked Wade to join him for a drink. "He did everything but come on to me," Wade says. "He was a tough customer, but he was the real thing. I was scared to death when he struck out at me, but considering my little prank, as I look back, I'm not surprised."

This pattern of trying to make amends and be loved—after lashing out— was very clear to those around him. May Pang talks repeatedly about John's drunken fits in Los Angeles, and how sweet and tender he became after realizing just how far he had gone toward the precipice of indecency or even violence. It was a character trait that revealed itself consistently, as if a Jekyll & Hyde existed inside him. Those who only see the negative side of things say that Lennon was an ornery bastard. But, as many insiders attest, very often his lashing out was justified and the remorse intensely sincere. Whether John Lennon was reacting to outside forces or just his own gut, you always got the truth out of him. And sometimes the truth can be an intimidating, powerful force.

Even in the early days as leader of the Quarrymen and Johnny and the Moondogs, Lennon often emitted signals of danger ahead. Pauline Sutcliffe remembers how that element of impending peril made John an unparalleled conductor of live musical electricity:

"I thought he was frightening, overwhelming, interesting. I found him quite magnificently attractive. My brother tried to calm him down, and often did. I knew he could be explicit and rude. I never wanted to be at the end of his acidity, but that also made him so electrifying. I used to marvel at my brother who handled that and still loved him."

Upon my arrival at the Hilton Hotel in San Francisco, the 1964 tour's first stop, I was stunned by my initial encounter with John. I had met and interviewed him and the Beatles back in February of that year, and was looking forward to reconnecting with the boys even while wondering what was in store. I was stunned, to say the least, by John's "greeting." Puffing on a cigarette and looking tired, John publicly chided me about my clothing and general appearance, calling me a "fag ass." I roared back, "It's better than looking like a slob like you!" Minutes later, he ran out into the hallway outside the room, spun me around, and rather heartily apologized. In life, there's something to be said for candor. There is also much to be admired for realizing that you've screwed up and doing something about it. Few of the chroniclers of John Lennon's life have ever given him credit for loving more than hating, for creating more than destroying, and, ultimately, for leaving the world a better place.

Many of John's professional acquaintances became his good friends. He was especially tight with Mick Jagger and Elton John. Beatles historian Denny Somach suggests that friends like Elton were willing to put up with John's emotional roller coaster because they respected him as a loyal friend, and they were captivated by his personality and presence:

"Actually the best description of John Lennon was given to me by Elton John. He said, 'John Lennon was my friend—my best friend in the world. He was the greatest, but he could be an asshole at times.' And that's how he described him. Nice guy, nicest guy, but he had his moments when he could be a problem."

More than anything, Lennon saw humor in people and enjoyed chiding and cajoling the people he met and worked with. Vince Calandra, a young producer for *The Ed Sullivan Show* in 1964, remembers an encounter with John in Miami Beach:

"I just know that he had a real dry sense of humor. I didn't find him abrasive or anything. In fact, when they went to Miami, right in the middle of the press conference, he started ragging on me with Ringo, you know, like

'Here's the boob from *The Ed Sullivan Show* following us around,' [as if to say] get him arrested or something. It was a funny, funny remark. I mean, that was his sense of humor. It was warm and it was fun."

Lennon also had an uncanny ability to inject humor into sticky situations, especially those that he created. In the party following the Hollywood Bowl concert in '64, we were chatting with a woman from Capitol records when he suddenly blurted out, "Tell me, can you give me a blow job?" As I blushed in horror, the woman responded, "Are you kidding! No way!" John replied, "Well perhaps you can get me a referral?" The three of us laughed, if a little uncomfortably. John ended the conversation by saying, "Mind you, only kidding, ya' know." Kidding or not, he knew that thinking out loud could get him into trouble, but he also knew that he could always manage to bring prickly situations to a comfortable close.

Nowhere can the caring side of John Lennon be documented more accurately than in his relationship with Malcolm Evans, the very tall and bespectacled man who became a regular as a road manager, along with Neil Aspinall, on the Beatles' tours. Evans had a magnetic personality and was a favorite with reporters and the women who tagged along. His smile and charm could be deceptive; he would have done anything to protect the Beatles. At one point on the touring aircraft, while traveling from Jacksonville to Boston in 1964, a tired Mal Evans sat next to me in the rear of the aircraft with tears trickling down his face. I asked, "What's the matter?" Mal answered, "John got kind of cross with me . . . just said I should go fuck off. No reason, ya' know. But I love the man. John is a powerful force. Sometimes he's rough, if you know what I mean, man. But there's no greater person that I know." I never learned what the dispute was about, but I do know that a few minutes later, a sullen Lennon walked by and embraced Evans.

In February 1965, while in Nassau, Bahamas, for the filming of the Beatles' feature film *Help!*, Evans asked me to join him for a few drinks in town. There, Evans would introduce me to the facts behind a Lennon myth—perhaps the most controversial one of all— that has persisted to this day.

❖

The greatest myth and mystery in Lennon's legacy is whether he had same-sex encounters—particularly with Beatles manager Brian Epstein. Many fans, authors, and screenwriters—amateur sleuths all—believe they know what really happened. But in my estimation, if it were indeed valid, John Lennon, with his determined desire to be blunt and honest at all costs, would have come out years ago.

If you fast forward the tape on John Lennon's life, this story surfaces to the world at large shortly after his death, but it was leaked early and often by those on the musical scene in Liverpool.

First of all, some background. Malcolm Evans would have stood in front of a freight train to protect John Lennon's life, so it will come as no surprise that the lanky Mal was enraged at the accusations that were flying in 1965. It all began with a vacation.

Several weeks after the birth of his son Julian, Lennon took off with Beatles manager and impresario Brian Epstein on a twelve-day vacation to Spain. The pair left on April 28, 1963, for a simple retreat filled with sun and rest. The holiday, however, quickly brought about whispers and innuendo that continue into this century. The question was, and for many still is: Did John Lennon have a gay affair with Brian Epstein?

The whispers were mostly local until John struck out quite famously at the twenty-first birthday party of Paul McCartney. Bob Wooler, a popular local deejay and Lennon friend, said something to John about the Spanish trip. Lennon, ugly drunk, answered with his fists and pounded Wooler. The episode made the papers, but there was no mention of why John hit him. Instead, Tony Barrow, the Beatles' careful and wise press secretary, managed to spin the story so there was no mention of any potential homosexual tryst.

In the end, John apologized to Wooler and blamed it all on too much drink. Years later, he would say that he made his first big national headlines in Great Britain "when I punched a friend who called me a fag."

So, what really happened in Spain?

While it is common knowledge today that Brian Epstein was a homosexual, it is important to note that homosexuality was illegal in the United Kingdom in the mid-sixties. "The love that dare not speak its name" was scorned by most of the world, in fact, and so Epstein was always extremely discreet about his sexual preference. He disclosed his innermost secret to only a few people, and to only one member of the media that I know of, namely, myself.

On a late night during the 1965 tour, Brian invited me to his cottage room at the posh Beverly Hills Hotel. We talked about the Beatles and had some food. Most of his conversation was about his problems with John. He had a sense of losing control of the band and he was clearly worried. Toward the end of the evening, he brought out some wine and said, in a toast, "Here's to you and me." With that, he put his hand on mine. And rather abruptly, but kindly, I called it a night.

Rather naïve at the time, I failed to connect my social time with Brian Epstein to the story I had heard about Spain from Mal Evans a few months earlier. In recounting the entire story in Nassau, Evans had complained to me that Lennon was still aggravated by the rumors, and so was he:

"He's a man, you know, John is, and it's awful what they were saying about him."

Mal's anger, his detailed storytelling of the episode, and Epstein's hand on mine along with his toast "to you and me," all finally clicked later that night. So I wondered, like many have for decades, was it true? Did John Lennon and Brian Epstein have physical sexual relations with each other?

It was a question that was on many minds within the Beatles' circle, and to a lesser degree within the Liverpool music scene. Later, it would be written about by the Lennon biographer, Albert Goldman, in his book *The Lives of John Lennon,* and it was the focus of the screenplay and feature film, *The Hours and Times.* Goldman recklessly stated in his book that John used sex with Brian Epstein to advance his career as the self-proclaimed leader of the Beatles. It was a tawdry assumption, designed most likely to sell books, yet it doesn't make sense in light of the fact that John was already the band's unquestioned leader. Furthermore, Lennon's key power and tool in terms of leverage was his talent. *The Hours and Times* also leads the viewer to believe that Epstein's famous infatuation with John Lennon may have been requited while in Barcelona. Its portrayal of the four-day interlude is more subtle than Goldman's take, but it does have Lennon and Epstein practically flirting with each other, while leaving the big question itself unanswered.

But Lennon's friends and associates have their own views on the matter, based on better primary evidence than either Goldman or the countless other speculators have had access to.

Beatles' insider Tony Bramwell, there from the beginning in Liverpool with John, dismisses it all angrily, saying, "I don't think it ever happened. I think it is furious, pure bullshit." Bramwell, who worked for Epstein and called him "Eppy," explains it this way:

"Brian was close to all of us. He never came on to any of us. He was a very private gay person. Homosexuality was illegal. The terror of being found out was one of his main horrors. Revelation of it would have destroyed everything. It was, after all, a jailing offense."

Tony Barrow, the Beatles extraordinary spin doctor, has his own take on the Spanish getaway.

"No one really knows. John was daring, ever blunt, so determined to be different. I would never say, "never." But knowing both of them, I would say it never happened. There is no question that Brian was attracted to John in a sexual way; Brian was a sensitive man. His cheeks would go purple when Lennon was tough with him, and John could be gruff. He was stand-offish quite a lot, which was John's way of saying, 'I'm not gay, you can't love me, but you can be my best friend.' But remember, there was pressure. John was the reason that Brian Epstein got involved with the Beatles in the first place. Brian had a strong bond with him, but he also knew that his homosexuality itself could shatter the Beatles. He may have wanted John, but as far as I know, it only happened in his dreams."

The timing of the trip was a source of family anguish. Lennon had decided to go to Spain shortly after the birth of Julian. Instead of staying home with the newborn, he elected to take a vacation.

For some, the question of whether or not John Lennon and Brian Epstein had sexual relations on the trip to Spain begins with the question of *why* they even went on holiday together in the first place. Tony Barrow explains the reason for the trip in terms of timing and other circumstances in John's life:

"In those days, if your girlfriend got pregnant, it was quite simple—you got married. [John] wasn't happy about the baby, although I knew he began months later to really love Julian. But the fact that he had to marry was disturbing to him. His decision to go to Spain, although very selfish, was a 'fuck you' to all the things that were happening to him. It's kind of ironic because months later at a West End pub called the Speakeasy, we were chatting after a recording session. Both of us sensitively talked about our infant children, and how good it felt to be fathers. John loved Julian, but he didn't love the circumstances surrounding his birth."

May Pang, who saw all sides of John Lennon, dismisses the speculation surrounding John and Brian as nothing but revisionist history:

"The likelihood of John having an affair with Brian Epstein is absurd, and actually impossible. Even when Phil Spector once tied up and threatened male sex against him, John was terrified."

One thing is certain: if John were alive today, surely he would relish the debate and do his best to leave us guessing, as he tried to do in a 1973 interview:

"I went on holiday to Spain with Brian—which started all the rumors that he and I were having a love affair, but not quite. It was never consummated. But we did have a pretty intense relationship. And it was my first experience with someone I knew was a homosexual. He admitted it to me. We had this holiday together because Cyn was pregnant and we left her with the baby . . . lots of funny stories, you know. We used to sit in cafes and Brian would look at all the boys and I would ask, "Do you like that one? Do you like this one?" It was just the combination of our closeness and the trip that started the rumors."

Cynics who fan the flames of rumor would say that of course Lennon would deny the gossip. But the ultimate truth is in the single revelation that Brian Epstein himself offered to me the night after our uncomfortable encounter in his cottage room. The Beatles were performing that night at Balboa Park in San Diego. I walked up to Brian as he stood outside the makeshift dressing room. His face turned beet red, but I broke the ice by saying, "Thanks for the time last night. I really enjoyed it." Awkward moments are never a pleasure, but in an effort to show my support, I whispered to him, "Did all that talk about the Spanish trip upset you?" He responded, "Larry, I love John, but nothing (pause) *nothing* happened. It was simply an impossibility." I may have been the first and only reporter ever to pose that question to Brian Epstein.

If I knew at the time what a fable would develop from the trip to Spain, I would have pursued the story more aggressively. But in the journalism of the sixties, such talk or even the suggestion of it, was off-limits. And besides, Epstein's brief characterization of the trip couldn't have been more emphatic, or sincere. Meanwhile, the story of the Spanish trip would not surface in the general public for years. In retrospect, Brian Epstein's answer to my question—which I have never reported until now—provides all the truth anyone needs to know.

❖

The people who knew John Lennon best were those who spent time with him. In some cases, that time was short-lived, but quite revealing. In other cases, individuals practically lived with Lennon in their daily lives and got an even clearer picture. Ultimately, the case that's made through these accounts is the most reliable and accurate portrait of the artist.

As a man, Lennon was as confused as the rest of us, but his songs and lyrics tell us about his uncanny ability to "read" other people. Allan Steckler, a veteran music executive who became the only American on the Apple staff in the early seventies, considers John Lennon to be the most interesting human being he has ever encountered. Steckler was so talented as a record and album innovator that the Beatles relied on him to pick and reject talent, design album presentations, and create all relevant marketing art. With an ear for music and a talent for merchandising it, Steckler worked closely with the Rolling Stones, Engelbert Humperdinck, and Badfinger, an Apple group whose career he personally resurrected. He was a man to be dealt with, and served at times as the main liaison between the Apple creative arm and John Lennon and Yoko Ono. He remembers meeting John and Yoko at their home in Tittenhurst Park, U.K.:

"I was blown away by the famous white piano and the white rooms and the forest that backed up into the house. I was intimidated, but he treated me with such warmth and grace. I felt clearly at home in someone else's home, which is not easy to do. John and I hit it off right away."

In the New York office, John and George would often visit Allan and, looking for input, sing to him. "One day," Steckler recalls, "John and George are singing and Yoko chimes in. John very gently says, 'Now, now, Yoko,' lifts her off her feet, and carries her out of the office. It wasn't cruel, just funny. And she was laughing, too."

Steckler always had deep respect for Yoko, whom he believes kept John focused during the recordings of the album *Some Time in New York City* and throughout his collaboration with the New York street group Elephant's Memory.

"It was a difficult time for John Lennon because of all the stuff he was on, and the fact that he was out of it here and there," Steckler says. "But even with all the bad stuff that was going on, he was intensely personal, very human, and wickedly funny. Not nasty—just wickedly funny. He made me laugh a lot."

Like many of the insiders interviewed for this work, Steckler is aghast at the generally accepted image of John as someone who was cruel or mean.

"This man had a genuine sense of compassion, a real sensitivity to other human beings," Steckler said. Recalling the day he brought his ten-year-old daughter to work with him, he continued, "She was playing with the type-writer when he came up behind her and started talking. He was interested in what she was doing, in her life, in her activities. When he left the room, she was stunned that it was John Lennon. I was always appreciative of how John and Yoko treated me, not just as a professional associate, but as a human being."

Lennon's ability to analyze a situation and perceive the real motives of people was always uncanny to watch. How many of us can make instant judgments on people and almost always be correct? Photographer Bob Gruen was, and still is, amazed:

"He had tremendous perception; really quick perception. He could see people and situations in depth, in all their layers very quickly. He wouldn't just take something at face value. He'd see it and immediately know what was behind it, what was going on, what the person's ulterior motives were. And he had a way of expressing it very bluntly, very quickly, and very hilariously. So he would make a little crack . . . he had a way of twisting it into a little pun or a little joke so that it was funny. It was harmless and people could accept it. And yet he lived on this very real level. He didn't do small talk with people. He was really quick with the one-liners, but they were real zingers sometimes. And so he really related to people on a really ground level. I mean he could see bullshit a mile away. And I think he respected and appreciated realness and people who were grounded and could accept who they were and what was going on, and he was pretty open about that."

The perception that Al Brodax had of John Lennon was multilayered and developed over the course of years. Brodax is a legendary figure in the world of movies and animation; he was producer and creator of the Beatles' cartoon TV series and developer of the Beatles' animated film *Yellow Submarine*, now considered a classic in its genre. His contact with the Beatles and their crowd in the sixties was extensive. The award-winning author and entrepreneur has some sharp reflections on John Lennon, punctuated by an unusual journey to a restaurant in London's SoHo district—a journey that became a real trip.

Initially Brodax, a tough guy from Brooklyn and a distinguished veteran of the Battle of the Bulge—with medals and wounds to prove it—was unimpressed by the Lennon mystique:

"I couldn't believe it. At the very first press conference to announce the Beatles' cartoon series, the three other guys answered questions while an oblivious Lennon hid under the table and wouldn't get up. It seemed like he needed attention. More than anything it was a distraction. He truly was not the easiest of the Beatles to get along with, but the animators were in awe when he would come to the studio in London and suggested changing a line or two in the dialogue. He was a combination of brilliant, impatient, and acerbic, but also mysterious and surprising."

Brodax has written a magnificent book, *Up Periscope Yellow: The Making of the Beatles' Yellow Submarine*, and in it he seethes with pride and sometimes anger at the frustration and limitless energy it took to produce the movie. He saves special ire for the machinations and moods of John Lennon in the book. But in person, Brodax offered me these fond memories of a lunch debate with Lennon:

"It was a spur of the moment invitation. He just looked at me and said, 'Brodax, lunch?' I had no choice. He was John Lennon and I never expected that it would turn into an entire afternoon of debate and mental stimulation, impacted by the pot that John smokes, the scotch that I devoured, and the pot that I turned to after the scotch. Our main target of discovery was Aldous Huxley's novels, two of which he was carrying. Huxley's highly intellectual view of the technological future brought us into one of the most inciting and insightful conversations I've ever had with anyone. I attacked Huxley's novel as essay needing validation, and not a page-turner. John roared back, 'Not unlike your research with Popeye, Barney Google, Krazy Kat and other current classics like the Flintstones!'"

As the lunch continued into a drug and alcohol-enhanced debate, Brodax realized who he was dealing with, as he remembers in his book:

"To know John, and few do, is not to try and understand him, but to trade off his perceived elitism for his extraordinary talent, and his acceptance, his impatience and his affinity for remarks that sting in exchange for his company . . . his brilliance. In any event, time with John is unique and memorable. I theorize that his verbal bombshells have a lot to do with his impatience to ignite discussion, to inspire debate."

The unflinching Brodax appreciated John as a brilliant artist, and today reflects that there was something very special about Lennon that is hard to forget:

"He was worth all that irritation to get to know him. In life, you don't meet many people like that. Once he got off of himself, he was a delight to be with. John Lennon was the kind of person you would want to have lunch with every day."

So how do you reconcile a brilliant argumentative intellectual with the man who considered himself the unabashed champion of the world's working class? Taking the measure of a man is always a complex assignment. But in the process, even with the normal contradictions of life, some consistencies emerge. In the life of John Lennon, one trait endured over the years, that gnawing desire to be champion of ordinary people. Sometimes, in that mission, he turned the ordinary into the extraordinary.

Enter Mario Casciano.

Mario Casciano has never graced anyone's published list of John's so-called celebrity friends, but for a few years of John's life, Mario became a friend and more than an admirer.

His story begins in early November, 1974. Mario, a fourteen-year-old student at Edward R. Murrow High in Brooklyn, was a Beatles fan. More than that, he was positively obsessed with John Lennon. At the time of Mario's daring journey into Lennon's life, John and May Pang were living in a penthouse apartment at 434 East Fifty-second Street on the fashionable and quiet East Side of Manhattan.

Casciano heard a broadcast where John described seeing a UFO. From the few details in that broadcast—landmarks, street signs, and billboards that John mentioned—Mario was able to put together the puzzle and find out where John was living. His first gambit was as a pizza delivery boy, but no one was home. Later, in a flight of fancy, he picked up his father's dry cleaning, took the subway to the city, whisked by the door man, and rang John's bell.

John answered the door. When he saw Mario standing there, he yelled out to May, "It's only an average-looking Beatletard." John looked down at Mario and said, "How did you find me?" Mario told him the UFO story. John looked at the dry cleaning and said, "Let me check out the clothes to see if I can find anything useful." Mario will always remember the next few moments:

"So, there I was, my idol bringing me inside. My heart was beating so fast I couldn't even talk. Then he said to me, 'Okay, now that you've found me, now what?' All I could think of was that I would never see him again. So I asked him for an autograph, then another, and a few more for the family. He didn't say much. May came into the room with her cheerful, smiling face. They both got a kick out of me being there. And then, to my shock, John gave me an envelope with some things in it and asked me to bring it over to WNEW Radio, and then pick up something at his office at Columbia records. I was a messenger, a gopher for the day, and I loved every minute of it. I mean, if my friends asked me what I did after school, what was I going to tell them that I visited John Lennon and went to work for him?"

The afternoon visits became a routine for Mario, John, and May. May adored Mario, John smiled when he was around, and Mario, at the age of fourteen and fifteen, was working in the record business, of sorts. When John and May split up in early 1975, Mario continued special assignments for John. He often secured tickets for the circus for John, Yoko, and Sean. Both Mario and John were Beatles fans, and they traded items in their collections. *Yes, John Lennon, the man who founded the Beatles and helped rocket them to fame, was a Beatles fan!* And Mario's friendship with John endured during John's stay-at-home years.

In their quiet, hidden relationship of the late seventies, John and May talked about Mario as a member of the family. In fact, when Mario escorted May into a court hearing where she testified for John in a record company lawsuit, John looked over at Mario and said, "I guess she got full custody of you."

When John died, Mario Casciano was so distraught he couldn't function. He had looked at the face of greatness and found a normal man.

"I loved John. I was just a kid, a teenage fan, determined to meet him. He treated me with respect. He liked me and I liked everything about him. I still am close with May, and we reminisce about Fifty-second Street, that first day, my weird capers, and all that I learned in the next few years after that. After all, my meeting with John, the inspiration he gave me, my working in the music business—it all added up to what I would do in my life. My experience was invaluable."

❖

John Lennon's relationship with the other Beatles was clearly of immeasurable value to him and them, yet it was often questioned by the media and by many fans. His relationship with Paul has been the subject of particularly venomous speculation. Of course, it is well-documented that John and Paul had serious business differences, mostly influenced by their own talents and desires, not to mention their forceful and enterprising wives, Linda and

Yoko. But beyond those occasional disagreements, the two had a warm relationship most of the time that they knew each other, even in the seventies, when their continued communication was accentuated by social gatherings and special one-on-one meetings.

The bottom line: John Lennon cared deeply about each of the Beatles, and that feeling was surely reciprocated despite incidents and comments that have made headlines over the years.

Yoko Ono, Cynthia Powell, and May Pang all verify that John never worried about Paul. He considered Paul his peer. But he did have concerns about George and especially Ringo, whom he felt was drifting in California during the seventies.

For a few months, Ringo lived in the same house with May and John in L.A. John was determined to get Ringo back on a musical track. Both of the boys were abusing themselves with drugs and alcohol, so it was difficult for John to offer counseling. But he had a paternal instinct about Ringo and George, and it came through, according to May Pang, in several ways:

"John always worried about George and Ringo. He was constantly on the phone to George, and heartsick about what Ringo was doing with his life. In California, he watched over Ringo. In New York, at the Apple offices, John made sure he had good time to talk to George, who was a bit insecure about going it alone."

Former Apple employee Linda Reig remembers the visits by George. "John could be a bastard, but when it came to George Harrison, nothing was ever enough. George was a sweetheart, a real gentleman. He came to the office all the time. When he came, John would stop whatever he was doing to spend time with George. I think he viewed him as a younger brother."

On the tours of 1964 and 1965, all the Beatles received equal time in public. I never witnessed any acrimony, not even a sign of discord between John and Paul. But there were differences in their styles away from the public glare. There was a crucial part of John's personality, rarely seen by most observers, that was a major reason for the Beatles' success. In short, John

Lennon did the hard work to make people on the tour feel better about themselves. Such a skill cannot be underestimated in its importance.

I will never forget the late nights when John, exhausted from the grind, would walk up to the front of the plane and comfort the acts who opened for the Beatles and were so often overlooked by the fans and the press. It was John, after all, who even in the duress of touring and the torture of his own fear about going on stage, would kindly place his arm on Ringo's shoulder as he entered the Montreal Forum, where there were death threats against Ringo's life. Ringo was frightened. John reassured him. When a member of the band had a problem, it was John who fixed it, according to former Beatles press officer Tony Barrow:

"First of all, Paul and John got on well, pre-Beatles, during the Beatles, and after. This myth about bad blood is a myth, pure and simple. But the fact remains that during the height of Beatlemania, John did the heavy lifting. When one of the boys was upset over something, Paul would go to John and complain. John would confront Brian. Brian would fix it or try to. And Paul would sometimes look like the good guy because he didn't want to engage in uncomfortable conversations. Both were born leaders, but John was the risk taker in dealing with heavy issues."

A primary challenge in Tony Barrow's job was keeping the Beatles away from controversy. Assigned to the position in 1962, his experience in getting to know John is a clear example of John's ambivalence about relationships:

"I met the Beatles for the first time in a pub in Manchester Square. It was an important meeting and all of them were extremely social and eager to meet me, but John stayed in the background. In general, he was reluctant to meet people that he didn't have to meet, but in my case it was a necessity. He was the last to come up and say hello. Eventually we hit it off, but his experience with me was typical. John Lennon was very mistrustful of people at first glance. Basically you were his enemy until proved otherwise. You had to prove to him you were okay, and until you did that, you were simply not. As press officer, he was my biggest problem, not necessarily because of what he said, but because I always feared I was doing something wrong. His basic attitude was, 'Prove to me that you're a good friend and you're not going to hurt me and then I'll be your friend.' That's the way he was."

Whether it was on stage, in press conferences, or during everyday interactions, John was always exhibiting a high degree of bravado. As I began to know him, I realized that it was all a surface cover-up of a high level of insecurity, the kind of uncertainty that makes great artists greater, forcing them to work harder and achieve excellence, all the while fighting their own fears. It took me awhile to figure that out. Barrow saw it right away:

"Throughout his life, John showed all that bravado as a form of self-preservation. He was very insecure and enclosed himself in a hard shell. It's funny—he didn't crave fame or fortune. He wasn't as ambitious as Paul. He just loved the music, and when he got to know people, and he was really comfortable, he enjoyed people."

As the Beatles progressed in fame and fortune, Lennon actually resented the modernization of the band. John hated tight time schedules, but he respected Brian Epstein's organizational skills. In 1962 and early 1963, against a rising tide of commercial change, Lennon held the band together, but longed for the days of the Quarrymen. Fashion, says Barrow, was a particularly sensitive issue:

"John hated the formalization, the carefully tailored look, the look that brought the Beatles such popularity. He liked being naughty. So he compromised with Epstein. As a measure of the man, you had to give him credit for trying desperately to stay honest to his roots."

❖

The source of John Lennon's fascination with and attitude toward women is a topic for a team of psychoanalysts. But there is no doubt that he loved women and that he loved to push their buttons. Part of the Lennon mythology are the scurrilous rumors that he forced himself on women, or that he somehow abused them. While his actions and words involving women were not always of exceptional manner, it's impossible to say that he ever approached misogyny, as some may like to believe.

There was the innuendo that surrounded John on the trip to India in 1968, for example, with rumors spread that he had tried to assault young actress Mia Farrow, who was there with her sister Prudence. Paul Saltzman, the young film producer who took numerous photos of the entourage at Rishikesh, sets the record straight:

"John would have never done anything like that. The truth is that Mia Farrow bolted from the ashram after claiming the Maharishi brushed by her in a suggestive manner. She did eventually come back. There was no evidence that John had ever harassed or stalked Mia or her sister Prudence. If anything, he treated them with great respect."

Still, the public rumors lingered. But as Yoko Ono remembers, the public image and the private view can be worlds apart:

"John could not do anything to hurt people, and if he did, it stuck in his mind and he always felt that he had to correct it."

That need to right wrongs was displayed throughout his life. For his first thirty-five years, John's experiences with women were disappointing, to say the least. The lack of a full-time mother, a hurried-up first marriage, and the convenience of casual sex had given John a warped and distorted view of women and their status in society. Yoko remembers him talking about it often in his years with her:

"He was a different person when he was touring. He told me a lot of stories of what was going on. He was totally honest with me. He said, 'If I can't be honest with you, what's the point?' He was telling me all sorts of stories, but he wasn't like that with me."

His attitude toward women changed over the decades, as evidenced by a sensitive story Yoko shared with me:

"One night I fell asleep and then I woke up and it was early morning and light was coming into the room, and he was crying. He read this book all night, which was a book that's called *The First Sex* by Elizabeth Gould Davis, and it's about showing what the woman had to go through in history and how there were many women who did things, but the credit was given to the men or whatever. He was crying. He said, 'Look, I didn't know that women go through all this,' and he can just cry because of that kind of very, very sensitive soft side. I think he had that side and that side kept me going with him."

That very private side was rarely seen by others. Lennon's courage in the face of trouble and his cowering attitude toward death and tragedy was an easy target for observers and biographers who didn't want to find the complete man.

❖

John Lennon saw many things more clearly than most of us, but one thing he never saw was his own legend. Daringly brave and quietly insecure, the John Lennon of the sixties and seventies could never really comprehend his place in history. During the early seventies, the other three Beatles registered number one solo singles before him. Downtrodden from the immigration struggle and battling back from his drinking and drug binges, the master creator was unsure of his future and unaware that his impending triumph of the human spirit would remain a legend for the ages. Yoko Ono told me that John would have been surprised that the world has created such a pedestal for her husband. But she emphasizes that, as he did in life, John Lennon would have wanted the truth of his existence to be told.

Pauline Sutcliffe, however, cautions that real and genuine fans sometimes disdain the truth. "Some fans and admirers make their own truth. They don't realize that even John might be embarrassed if he saw all the stuff that was going on today. I think he'd be pleased on the one hand, but on the other hand, it wouldn't fool him because he was also brutally honest with himself. I just think that someone as gifted as John also was complex. I think the truly gifted people are complex. The hero worship is very one-dimensional. John would have not liked that because he was about much more than that."

No doubt the myths of John Lennon's life will continue. The truth, of course, is always harder to find. In his case, it has stung with disappointment and rung out with joy. To Mark Hudson, the well-known producer for Ringo Starr and a studio companion of John Lennon in the tempestuous Los Angeles days, there is no mystery at all:

"It is very simple and clear cut. John wasn't afraid to say the truth. John Lennon was the truth. He was saying to people, 'I'm not trying to save the world. I'm trying to say what's in my heart.' As far as the inner core of his personality, he was a tough guy who really wasn't tough at all. He was loving and caring."

Detractors and self-appointed moralists have been harshly critical of John's public pronouncements and private indiscretions. Perhaps what they despised the most was the bravery he displayed in standing out alone on the issues, making himself a convenient target. Beatles scholar Martin Lewis sees Lennon as not just a brilliant and magnificent musician and artist, but as a bearer of truthful insights into ideas and causes:

"I think John has left a legacy of what it is possible to do when you achieve a surreal thing that we call fame. Prior to John Lennon, the vast majority of people that achieved prominence tended to revel in that fame, and did things related just to their fame. It was very rare for people who had achieved fame to use that fame as a soapbox for such a broad variety of issues. Few decided to lend their names to good causes. They never fused their fame with their cause. The key to John was his integrity. No one doubted that he believed what he said when he said it. He was a passionate believer of what he believed."

The ultimate question that has a thousand answers remains: Why was John Lennon so special? Beatles historian Mark Lewisohn has perhaps the most solid and forthright answer:

"He was a man who understood the way human beings operated. He had enormous talent aside from his musical talent. He had an attitude and a lack of compromise, along with a sense of humor and artistic drive. He would try anything. Did he know he was great? He acted on impulse. You don't win every time you act on impulse. But he won most of the things he did and he did them with absolute honesty and integrity."

To know him was one thing; to play with him was another.

The real John Lennon was seen by the man widely considered to be among the greatest rock and roll drummers of all time, Alan White, who since 1972 has been a staple of the popular group Yes.

John discovered Alan's talents in a London club when the drummer was just twenty years old. When Alan received a phone call asking him to join John at Heathrow Airport to fly with him to Toronto and play in his band, he hung up the phone, assuming it was a joke. When the second call came and he realized it was the real thing, he started packing. Thirty-six years later, he remembers that fateful journey with the wonderment of a young man:

"So I arrive at the VIP lounge and sit down next to John Lennon, Yoko Ono, Eric Clapton and Klaus Voorman. I was so nervous to be in such grand company. On the airplane, we rehearsed under the tutelage of John, who made me feel so welcome. None of us had ever played together before when we recorded *Live Peace in Toronto*."

A few months later, Alan White became a part of music history, although he didn't know it at the time: "I was invited to the Lennon studios at Tittenhurst to join the others in recording the tracks for *Imagine*. It was fascinating that John gave us the lyrics for every song. He knew he was sending some strong message and he was so considerate. He wanted to make sure none of us objected to the message of peace in 'Imagine' and to some of the other songs, especially 'How Do You Sleep?' with its references to Paul McCartney. Recording those tracks and my later work with him on 'Instant Karma' was a thrill, but mostly an education on what he was all about."

White was amazed at John's desire and willingness to let the players play:

"I had to pinch myself. He said I was his little drummer boy and as long as I was doing my thing, feeling the music, he never interfered. This was an inspirational man who was incredibly great to play with. He could sense when good things were happening. Of course, he offered creative input, but also wanted it from us. I stayed at the house and will always remember how he made me feel a part of the family."

When it came to bringing talents together to make music, there was no equal to John Lennon. In a stunning revelation, White says that the actual recording of the song "Imagine" was one of the first three takes, testament to Lennon's commitment to free-flowing creativity:

"He was just incredible to be play with, and incredible to be with."

Alan White's experience once again reinforces the view that John Lennon was eager for true and genuine camaraderie, without his own ego standing in the way of creative collaboration.

The truth about John Lennon, from this reporter's perspective, is this: for all of his bravado, alleged superiority, covered-up insecurity, raw talent, and complex and sometimes abusive personality, under it all was a man reaching out for friendship and love, most of the time offering it without qualification, and above all, in his every endeavor, leveling with all of us.

The man was unique. The myths are many. The truth is what he left behind.

NINE:
The Music Is the Passion

"John's life was filled with a litany of tragedies. His life paralleled the
lives of millions of others and his music reflected their lives."
— *Scott Regan, media executive and 45-year radio veteran*

"The guy had more rock and roll in him than I had ever witnessed. In
my mind I was saying 'I want to be John Lennon.'"
—*Mark Hudson, musician and producer, on seeing John Lennon perform*

On the 1965 Beatles tour of America, young George Harrison gave me a
treat: a short show-and-tell on how his fingers moved so skillfully and lov-
ingly over his guitar. Smiling and confident, George said to me, "Ya' know
Larry, for people like us, the music is the passion."

For John Lennon, there were many passions. Peace. Equality. Art.
Conversation. Food. Sex. But in the beginning and at the end, there was one
burning obsession in John Lennon's life above all others: music.

Like most great artists, almost all of John Lennon's musical efforts mirrored the trials and triumphs of his life. And because his life was so daring
and eccentric, he trailblazed a creative path that no one could have imagined
before him, but that thousands have traveled after him.

Mark Hudson, a member of the band the Hudson Brothers and the producer for Ringo Starr, Carole King, and many others, first saw John Lennon at a Beatles concert in Portland, Oregon in 1965. The experience would inspire his dream of being in the music business.

"John came out wearing a black leather jacket and chewing gum, his nostrils were flared, he looked like he was feeling good about that time of his life. In a wild gesture, he threw his hat to the crowd. The guy had more rock and roll in him than I had ever witnessed. In my mind, I was saying, 'I want to be John Lennon.'"

Hudson was not alone in that reaction, according to historian Denny Somach:

"One of the things I found out in doing my book and my radio show was that just about every major musician you talk to today, from Billy Joel to Joe Cocker to the Eagles, will tell you that when they saw John Lennon and the Beatles, and this is usually how they phrase it, 'John Lennon and the Beatles on *Ed Sullivan*,' and they decided that night that's what they were gonna be. Because here's a guy that came from a little town in northern England, started a band whose members wrote their own material, played their own instruments and conquered the world. And what he did was, he made it. . . . I mean, without seeing John Lennon and the Beatles, they never would have been in the business. I think that's his single greatest contribution."

Years later in Los Angeles, after he had formed the Hudson Brothers band, Mark Hudson got to meet John at a party and remained, without shame, in awe of him:

"He was a magnetic figure. Just to meet him was a thrill. But most of all, he gave people like me so much inspiration, so much encouragement to write and produce. Genius filled his eyes and his heart was filled with joy as he made the rounds of the party. It was in the early seventies. I fawned all over him and he said, 'Hudson, have a seat will you.' At that point, I gushed and told him what a giant he was and he simply said, 'Calm down Hudson, calm down.' I think he enjoyed the fact that someone wasn't afraid to express their feelings to him."

John's uncanny ability and commitment to express his own feelings through music inspired thousands of people like Mark Hudson to do the same, helping create an unprecedented generation of powerful songwriters. Some were inspired to pull the best out of their own talents and styles; others just copied the Beatles' sound. On the 1965 tour, George, Ringo, and Paul were reluctant to chat about their copycat competitors. John, in his usual candid fashion, was not.

I asked John, "Does it bother you that certain groups will copy you completely?" He replied, "No, because everybody knows. Only the dumbest people don't know that they are copying us. You just sort of laugh. You see imitation of you going around. They are never really making it. They may have a hit but nobody is fooled for long."

At certain times in his life, John himself may have been better off copycatting his vitality and clarity and musical brilliance during the Beatles' prime. For much of the seventies, his life path meandered into confusion, and his music followed.

These periods of depression, substance abuse, and personal conflict resulted in John's most mediocre music, according to Chris Carter, one of the nation's leading scholars on Lennon's music:

"No question, when John was happier and healthier, he created his best work. When his life was confused, his message and method were often confused. The parameters and levels of his talent were measured by his own personal place, his own personal truth. When his mind was clear and he was in get-serious mood, he became the brilliant composer and lyricist that marked the early collaborations with Paul."

Yet at his best, Lennon could harness those same, troubling aspects of himself to create some of the most honest and accomplished music of his career. The classic 1965 Beatles' song "Help!" provides a dazzling example of a blockbuster hit that also served as a portrait of where John was at emotionally and intellectually at the time. And according to John himself, it was not a pretty place:

"When '*Help!* came out in '65, I was actually crying out for help. Most people think it's just a fast rock-and-roll song. I didn't realize it at the time; I just wrote the song because I was commissioned to write it for the movie. But later, I knew I really was crying out for help. It was my fat Elvis period. You see the movie: [I was] very fat, very insecure, and . . . completely lost. And I am singing about when I was so much younger and all the rest, looking back at how easy it was. Now, I may be very positive—yes, yes—but I also go through deep depressions where I would like to jump out the window, you know. . . . Anyway, I was fat and depressed and I was crying out for help."

Scott Regan, the top deejay in Detroit in the sixties, remembers when he first recognized Lennon's genius for reconciling conflicting emotions by turning them into beautiful music, and how essential that ability was to Lennon and the Beatles' greatness. Regan recalls coming to the realization while sharing a ride with me and Beatles' manager Brian Epstein after the band's 1964 concert in Kansas City:

"[Brian] said, 'Is there anything you want to ask me?' I said, 'What is it that makes the Beatles music so great?' He replied, 'They mix the happy and the sad, the good and the bad.'

"All their songs had that spontaneous real feel. Lennon understood the simplicity of rock-and-roll . . . the clarity of it."

❖

The painful breakup of the Beatles in 1970 catapulted John into a new stage of his life, one where he often struggled to find his voice, and where his path sometimes meandered into the deepest, darkest parts of himself. The solo music he created during that period was sometimes brilliant, sometimes muddled and unpleasant, just like his life.

"When a band breaks up, it's a very emotional time," says Chris Carter.

"For some band members, it is like losing a limb. They are looking for direction. John was doing that along with the other Beatles."

John's first solo effort, *Plastic Ono Band*, ranks with the best music he made with the Beatles, and for good reason, says Carter:

"In 1970, he was glowing over his marriage and was generally upbeat and creative. Considering that he was on his own for the first time in ten years, it was a reflection of his personal happiness that *Plastic Ono* was so creative."

The music he produced on that storied album also reflected a struggle to deal with ghosts that had haunted him since long before the formation of the Beatles. Prior to recording *Plastic Ono Band*, Lennon underwent an intense period of "primal therapy," a technique developed in the late sixties by Dr. Arthur Janov. The therapy aims to purge patients of the toxic remnants left over from early-childhood conflicts. Janov encouraged clients, like John and Yoko, to confront the original traumas in their lives for the first time, and in doing so, learn to cope with them and finally move past them. In May of 1970, John reflected on Janov's techniques:

"Janov showed me how to feel my own fear and pain, therefore I can handle it better than I could before, that's all. I'm the same, only there's a channel. It doesn't just remain in me, it goes round and out. I can move a little easier. I still think that Janov's therapy is great, you know, but I don't want to make it into a big Maharishi thing. If people know what I've been through there, and if they want to find out, they can find out, otherwise it turns into that again. I don't think that anything else would work on me. But then of course, I'm not through with it; it's a process that's going on. We primal almost daily. You see, I don't really want to get this big primal thing going on because it is so embarrassing.

"The thing in a nutshell: primal therapy allowed us to feel feelings continually, and those feelings usually make you cry. That's all. Because before, I wasn't feeling things, that's all. I was blocking the feelings, and when the feelings come through, you cry. It's as simple as that, really."

There's no doubt that confronting his earlier traumas helped him produce some of his most amazing music on *Plastic Ono Band*. The album's lyrics remain sensational and revealing. They offer a musical biography of some of the most important and painful moments of his life, and the people responsible for them.

The song "Mother" poignantly addresses the parents who abandoned John when he was still a toddler:

MOTHER, YOU HAD ME, BUT I NEVER HAD YOU

I WANTED YOU, YOU DIDN'T WANT ME

SO I, I JUST GOT TO TELL YOU

GOODBYE, GOODBYE.

FATHER, YOU LEFT ME, BUT I NEVER LEFT YOU

I NEEDED YOU, YOU DIDN'T NEED ME

SO I, I JUST GOT TO TELL YOU

GOODBYE, GOODBYE.

CHILDREN, DON'T DO WHAT I HAVE DONE

I COULDN'T WALK AND I TRIED TO RUN

SO I, I JUST GOT TO TELL YOU

GOODBYE, GOODBYE.

MAMA DON'T GO.

Lennon looks at his early relationship with British society on another song on the album, the stark "Working Class Hero":

AS SOON AS YOU'RE BORN THEY MAKE YOU FEEL SMALL

BY GIVING YOU NO TIME INSTEAD OF IT ALL

TILL THE PAIN IS SO BIG YOU FEEL NOTHING AT ALL

A WORKING CLASS HERO IS SOMETHING TO BE

A WORKING CLASS HERO IS SOMETHING TO BE

THEY HURT YOU AT HOME AND THEY HIT YOU AT SCHOOL

THEY HATE YOU IF YOU'RE CLEVER AND THEY DESPISE A FOOL

'TILL YOU'RE SO FUCKING CRAZY YOU CAN'T FOLLOW THEIR RULES
A WORKING CLASS HERO IS SOMETHING TO BE
A WORKING CLASS HERO IS SOMETHING TO BE.

And he's at his irreverent best in the song "God," where he rejects the very idolatry that made him one of the world's most famous and influential people, also making reference to personal heroes Elvis and Bob Dylan (whose real name is Robert Zimmerman).

I DON'T BELIEVE IN KINGS
I DON'T BELIEVE IN ELVIS
I DON'T BELIEVE IN ZIMMERMAN
I DON'T BELIEVE IN BEATLES
I JUST BELIEVE IN ME
YOKO AND ME
AND THAT'S REALITY.

Even with its raw language and painfully honest confrontations with difficult topics, *Plastic Ono Band* failed to become a hit album. But for the same reason, it remains John Lennon's masterpiece as a solo artist. Andre Gardner, longtime host of the premiere Beatles radio program in Philadelphia, says the album served up a dose of stark reality that was difficult for many fans to swallow:

"*Plastic Ono* is amazing, wonderful rock and roll. Many radio stations didn't play the songs because of the language, so from a sales perspective, it wasn't a huge success. But as real art, it doesn't get much better than Plastic Ono Band. . . . Remember that John Lennon bared his soul in the name of rock and roll. How many artists were willing to do that?"

Mark Hudson agrees:

"I mean, if you look at it, the album is about purging. He deals with every crisis—his mother, his father, the Beatles breakup, references to tensions with McCartney. He refers to God, mantras, his wife—all the things that he encountered—and in the end, he's really saying, 'It's all about Yoko and me . . . I believe in me.' This is as close to a brilliant musical autobiography as you'll ever get."

That soul-searching music on *Plastic Ono Band* was, as Andre Gardner assessed, too hot to handle for many radio stations. John admitted a few years later that his choice of words on some of the album's cuts frustrated efforts to get airplay. But, characteristically, John made no apologies:

"I put 'fucking' in because it fit. I didn't even realize that there were two in the song 'Working Class Hero' until somebody pointed it out. When I actually sang it, I missed a verse, which I had to add in later. You do say 'fucking crazy.' That is how I speak. I was very near to it many times in the past, but, I would deliberately not put it in, which is the real hypocrisy, the real stupidity."

Still, consistent with his character, John was sensitive to the public's reaction to his words. It would take decades for reviewers and average fans to appreciate the creativity in *Plastic Ono Band,* and he hoped to avoid that delay with his next album. So when recording *Imagine,* he decided to get his message across without infuriating people with profanity.

Shortly after the album was released—one day before his thirty-first birthday in October 1971—John said, "*Imagine* was a sincere statement. It was 'Working Class Hero' with chocolate on. I was trying to think of it in terms of people."

Some of the album *Imagine* was recorded in the U.K. at John and Yoko's house in Tittenhurst in Ascot, produced by legendary record producer Phil Spector, and featured George Harrison's superb guitar on five tracks. The album dealt with many of the themes that infused *Plastic Ono Band,* but John took measures to make sure that fans would listen—specifically by leaving out bad language. That approach seemed particularly important with a song like the album's title cut, whose "red" ideas were potentially more offensive to many people than any blast of "blue" language, according to John himself:

"The song says, 'Imagine that there was no more religion, no more country, no more politics,' which is basically 'The Communist Manifesto.' I am not particularly communist, nor do I belong to any movement. 'Imagine' was the same message as 'Working Class Hero,' but sugarcoated.

"Now, I understand what you have to do. Put your political [ideas] across with a little honey. This is what we do above all, Jerry (Rubin), Yoko and the others—it is to try and change the apathy of young people."

The strategy worked. Though it never reached number one on the charts, the cut "Imagine" became one of the most revered songs in the history of contemporary music. An anthem that captured the hopes of a generation, it served as the musical theme song to many political rallies in the seventies.

The song also served as a sign of the increasingly vital role Yoko played in John's life and art. The lyrics were, in fact, inspired by passages in Yoko's book, *Grapefruit.* Beatles historian Denny Somach says that, while Yoko was very involved in writing "Imagine," she never received a publishing credit:

"Yoko had a lot to do with writing that song. When they went to submit it to their publisher, it was listed as a Lennon/Ono song. They rejected it. They said he was just trying get out of giving away fifty percent of the publishing. So they refused to put her name on it."

Indeed, Yoko Ono receives little credit for any of her positive impact on John, and much blame for what many fans perceive as her negative influence on his art and his life. But the music tells a different story. Because when John began to stray from Yoko in the early seventies, his music began to suffer from a lack of direction.

In early 1972, John launched work on the album *Some Time in New York City.* Chris Carter says the album reflected Lennon's increasing anxiety and decreasing sense of self-respect during the period that would culminate in his infamous "Lost Weekend," which began in the summer of 1973.

"It was the low point in John's career. He shocked the music world and the rest of the world for that matter when he sang 'Woman is the Nigger of the

World.' Just the title shook up a lot of people. The songs had a ring of protest to them and came at a time when there was sort of an overall Beatles backlash in the country. There was a bad reaction to the album.

"This whole period of 1972 and 1973 was difficult, especially 1973 when the other former Beatles had hit singles. John capped off 1973 with the album *Mind Games*, which was a light album, a weak album. This period in his life was marked by his 'lost weekend.' May Pang was in the studio for a lot of this and her organization helped. But John and his music were in a bad way during this time. The magic and creativity of *Plastic Ono Band* was missing.

"And then there was *Walls and Bridges*."

Recorded in July and August of 1974, *Walls and Bridges* features the fine songs "#9 Dream" and "Steel and Glass," plus the beautiful and often overlooked "Bless You." Carter saw the record as a reflection of improving conditions in Lennon's life at the time.

"It was some of the best music from John. He was beginning to get serious. . . . He was coming out of his grief and gloom and feeling good again. The music—I would compare it to *Plastic Ono Band*, which was his finest. *Walls and Bridges* was less slick than *Plastic Ono*, and Phil Spector was not involved. But the album was outstanding in its variety and scope."

May Pang calls it the most productive period of his solo career, but *Walls and Bridges* also represented the bridge John built back to Yoko— artistically, emotionally and, in the end, literally, thanks to its song "Whatever Gets You thru the Night," a duet with Elton John that represented Lennon's first post-Beatles number-one single. Denny Somach traces how the song came about, and how it helped reunite John and Yoko:

"He made a deal with Elton. Elton said, 'If you [do] this record, I'll sing on it. It's gonna go to number one, and if it does, you have to agree right now to come out and sing at Madison Square Garden with me.'"

So on November 28, 1974, when Elton was headlining Madison Square Garden in New York City, right before the last song, he brought John

Lennon out and they sang "Whatever Gets You thru the Night," "Lucy in the Sky with Diamonds," and "I Saw Her Standing There." That was also the day that he and Yoko reunited. Their backstage meeting planted the emotional seeds for John to return to Yoko a few months later.

Yoko gave birth to their son Sean in October of the next year, with Elton John serving as the boy's godfather. John Lennon essentially retired from public life with his son's birth, and spent the next five years raising Sean.

During that period, while the other Beatles were still cranking out records, many people began to vilify Yoko Ono as the reason that John had turned from one of the most brilliant artists of his age into a silent hermit and nanny.

But doubts about the artistic and emotional benefits of John's relationship with Yoko vanished with their collaborative album *Double Fantasy*. The record was released on November 17, 1980, just three weeks before an assassin ended John's life.

Walter J. Podrazik, a professor and Beatles scholar from the University of Illinois, sees the album as one of the highlights of Lennon's life:

"There were many tragedies around the assassination. Two sons lost their dad. A wife lost her husband. From the standpoint of popular culture, death transformed the reintroduction of John Lennon. There was a lot more left in him. He showed that in *Double Fantasy*.

"John only did seven songs. He wasn't into quantity but quality. I've always thought his best work on that album was 'I'm Losing You'—it is such a powerful example of his ability to present the range of individual emotion from fear to absolute love.

"The song '(Just Like) Starting Over' was history in the making. He was saying, 'I'm back.' This romantic song is a reaffirmation of his commitment to Yoko, a message that as a person, you are more complete when you are with someone you love. It's a deeply personal song, a special one."

One doubt John never escaped was his own misgivings about his voice. As amazing as it may seem, John Lennon—one of the lead singers of one of the most popular musical groups of all time, and the voice of his generation—never felt that his singing voice was adequate.

This insecurity flared up in the studios in Los Angeles and New York where he recorded *Rock 'n' Roll, Some Time in New York City, Walls and Bridges* and *Mind Games*. He still had great confidence in his songwriting abilities, composing all the songs for *Mind Games* in less than a week. But recording the music, particularly the vocal tracks, turned out to be a painfully different story. May Pang clearly remembers it:

"He was told by Yoko and others that he wasn't in great singing voice in 1973. He was smoking non-stop. He was worried about his voice, always saying, 'Me voice is fucked up,' and he was obsessed with it. Harry Nilsson encouraged him though, and that's why Harry, although a horrible influence in other ways, could be a great help."

Though John's anxiety over his vocal abilities peaked in the early seventies, it had haunted him since his earliest days with the Beatles, when he would go to great lengths to punch up or cover up what he saw as his vocal deficiencies. "Beatle Brunch" host Joe Johnson remains fascinated that John didn't hear his voice as the rest of the world did:

"John hated his voice, and would often use electronic methods to modify, disguise it, or enhance it. He was always asking Beatles' producer George Martin to put something on his voice. It is most evident on songs from *Revolver* like 'Tomorrow Never Knows' where his voice was put through a Leslie speaker. Even years later, on songs from the *Rock and Roll* album, his voice has a delay echo effect on all the tracks. No doubt part of that was by design, an attempt to capture the feel of fifties rock songs like 'Heartbreak Hotel.' But it is sad for fans to think that John felt he had to distort his voice for his own comfort level, when we know he had one of the most beautiful voices ever."

John Lennon's musical life divides into two broad phases. With Paul McCartney and the Beatles, he explored the frontiers of a positive new musical energy and took rock and roll to heights of popularity and artistry no one had thought possible. On his own, he expanded the musical and lyrical vocabulary of autobiography, self-exploration and confession.

Deejay Scott Regan remembers Lennon and the Beatles' impact:

"The sixties evolved out of the Beatles. They affected the sixties and reflected the sixties. After the amazing music of Lennon and McCartney in the early part, they started moving toward a different sound, moving toward Eastern spirituality.

"*Sgt. Pepper* ushered in the Flower Power era. None of it was mainstream, but as the seventies began, Lennon made it mainstream. His two most significant spiritual songs were 'All You Need Is Love' and one of his final ones with the Beatles, 'Across the Universe.'

"Then, on his own, it all started to flow—'Working Class Hero,' 'Imagine.' Within a few years, he transitioned to the confessor and musical orator of human challenges. John's life was filled with a litany of tragedies. His life paralleled the lives of millions of people and his music reflected their lives."

John and his music continue to thrive decades after his death—on the radio, in the work of all the musicians he influenced, in popular attitudes about spirituality and war and justice, and even in academia.

Since the spring of 1981, a few months after John's murder, Professor John Stevens of the Berklee College of Music in Boston has been teaching a course entitled "The Music of John Lennon." For twenty-four years, enrollment for the course has been "standing room only," with a long waiting list each semester. Stevens, a Beatles fan since he was a teenager, is not surprised that Lennon and his music continue to enrapture:

"John let us in on everything. In *Plastic Ono Band*, *Imagine*, and *Walls and Bridges*, he tells us the story of his life. Let's face it, he's one of the few people we wanted to know about.

"In his music, especially on *Plastic Ono Band*, he tells the story of his shattered childhood and his constant war against the establishment. In the song 'Imagine,' he was able to get controversial messages across because the music was so beautiful—the presentation was so soft that people didn't care what he said, even though he said 'Imagine no God, imagine no countries.' So he accomplished the near impossible: with beautiful music, he was able to get these thoughts on the table for discussion and said that maybe we should open our eyes."

Stevens, who confesses to once wearing little round glasses and emulating John's style as a young man, says his students seem to really appreciate that Lennon was able to relate the events of his life to the world through music:

"Well, they are fascinated by the fact that after his stunning success in the Beatles years, that his music was so impressive considering that it just consisted of piano, bass, and drums. And they are obsessed with the quality of his voice, but more than that, in the sixties and the seventies, how his lyrics and tone serve as a reporter of the things that he and the Beatles were going through."

Stevens says that by connecting his music to his own life, Lennon was able to touch all the people who were experiencing the same emotions and difficulties that he was. And that by making that connection, John opened up a spiritual realm in which everyone could recognize their even deeper connections:

"The music is as searing and powerful today as it was then. There is a timelessness about it, a stark, naked truth about where the world still is, a reflection of the hopes and failures of all of us. That's it, isn't it?"

His question declares the unanimity of spirit that John Lennon embodied. And it underscores the truth that, near the end, it was his love of life and the musical message surrounding it that brought him back from the brink of disaster to a personal triumph that would eclipse the vast commercial success of his lifetime.

TEN:
Triumph of the Human Spirit

"I have to be honest—let them know what I am made of. I'm not all
that perfect or anything and they have to know that."
—*Yoko Ono, quoting John on his relationship with his fans*

"He was so enthusiastic about his new music. He looked healthy, very
energized and ready for whatever came along."
—*Paul Drew, veteran broadcast executive and music manager*

There are few people who can tolerate the failures of a successful person.
After all, *we* lament that if we had the riches and fame, happiness would be
just around the corner. In the human condition, happiness is often elusive,
regardless of social or economic position. From a different perspective, "having
it all" can lead directly down the road to deprivation. Material wealth is
hardly the protein of a life well lived. It is overrated and, surely in the case
of John Lennon and his "boys", hardly the reason for real happiness. And so
it is that the curious and the people who report to the curious have a fascination
with the impact of wealth and celebrity.

John Lennon lived the most public and private of lives. During his time
with the Beatles, he worked, slept, ate, relaxed, and carried on his personal

affairs under a spotlight of international superstardom that has rarely shone so brightly on anyone. But during his last five years, John managed to duck out of that spotlight and lead a largely secluded existence, shared, for the most part, by only his wife, his young son, and a few others.

During both the height of his fame and the quiet times with Yoko and Sean, John managed an even more impressive feat: going out of his way to engage regular people on their terms. Unlike so many superstars, John Lennon insisted on presenting himself as just a regular guy to those he encountered. He knew no other way to be.

As someone who experienced Beatlemania both as a fan and as a behind-the-scenes journalist, I was always impressed by the composure shown by John, Paul, George, and Ringo amidst all the giddy—and sometimes dangerous—frenzy swirling around them. And it infuriated me when the Beatles were blasted by journalists who chided their appearance and demeanor and questioned their talent.

John Lennon bore more of the negative treatment than the other three Beatles combined. With his public activism on behalf of peace and civil rights, and his odd, often misunderstood antics, he gave opportunistic reporters and ignorant gossip columnists plenty to write about.

When I first met him, I could tell why he rubbed many people the wrong way, because at first he kind of rubbed me the wrong way. But many of the things that put off others—his blunt and candid tone, his intolerance for bullshit—quickly drew me to him. I could tell he was terribly flawed and always hurting about something. Many great artists experience similar struggles. And many great artists attempt to comfort their agonies with excessive quantities of drugs, alcohol, and sex, as John certainly did.

But what made John Lennon different from all but a few superstars was not just his willingness, but his insistence on sharing his life with others. He shared the moments of doubt, pain, humiliation, and discovery—in all their glory and pathos—with his fans through his songs. And he went out of his way to share simple moments of everyday life with regular people, whom he'd stop to have a drink with, offer a smoke to, or engage in casual conversation with for a few moments or hours.

In one case, the encounter with regular folks stretched across three days. It was the happiest I ever saw him.

It was May 16, 1975, and, after calls by myself and radio station executive Gene Vassall, John had agreed to come down from New York to Philadelphia to take part in a charity marathon run by a Philadelphia radio and TV station where I was working. What other superstar would agree to participate in such a local event outside of his hometown? And what other superstar, besides John Lennon, would travel to the event by train, and by himself?

When the automatic door of the Amtrak Metroliner opened, he emerged in a white coat, grinning from ear to ear.

"Mr. Kane, I prezooom," he laughed.

"Hey John,' I answered. "Welcome to my to town!"

He looked different than the last time I'd seen him. His hair was still shoulder-length, but thinning at the top with a bald spot on his scalp. His eyes seemed less piercing through his glasses. His complexion was pale and he appeared more gaunt than usual.

But despite his appearance, I was overcome with the simple joy of seeing him. John Lennon, riding coach on a public train, had emerged into my world.

As we walked up the stairs, I asked, "How are you?"

"A little better now," he answered. It seemed an odd reply. But if I'd known what John Lennon had put himself through in the first half of the seventies, I would have been surprised to see him still walking, maybe even breathing.

As we strolled through the cavernous train station en route to a waiting limousine, few people recognized him, but those that did ran feverishly up to him for autographs. I was at the peak of my early success as a news anchor at WPVI, the top-rated TV station in Philadelphia in 1975. So more people actually recognized me than him. Instead of being put off, he was thrilled for me. "You are like a fucking rock star!" he exclaimed with joy.

In the limo, we talked. No tape recorders. No cameras rolling. And the usually animated man was subdued. "Thanks for coming," I said. "Needed to get me ass out of the house," John replied. "Been back a few months. Time to get out. Need a rest."

John seemed tired, but his spirits were high. His wife was four-months pregnant with Sean, a life conceived just a month after John returned to New York and ended his eighteen-month "lost weekend."

"You know Larry, I may have been the happiest I've ever been," John explained to me in the limo of his time in L.A. "I loved this woman. I made some beautiful music and I got so fucked up with booze and shit and whatever."

I was puzzled. "Why did you return?"

"I love Yoko, too. Finding where you belong can be most difficult, if you know what I mean, young fellow."

Our conversation was interrupted by our first stop—the Liberty Bell. I wanted to show John the great symbol of the American Revolution, which was then housed in the rear of Philadelphia's Independence Hall.

As I recited my brief history lesson, John's eyes lit up like a child's, as they always did in moments of enlightenment and learning. Then his stare hardened and his lips pursed. "A cruel war," he said of the Revolutionary conflict, then added, "just like the war in Vietnam—oh shit, they'll crucify me ass for that!"

"Don't worry," I said. "Only you, me, and millions of people know how you feel about the war."

We both laughed. He was referring, of course, to the relentless pursuit of the United States Justice Department to deport him based on a previous marijuana conviction in England. It was a thinly disguised campaign by the Nixon administration—which abhorred John's embrace of the anti-war movement—to remove Lennon from the country.

Ironically, John's visit to Philadelphia and his ensuing good works gave me the opportunity to solicit letters of support from members of Congress in the area we covered—Pennsylvania, New Jersey, and Delaware—and from the mayor of Philadelphia, Frank Rizzo. Later that year John would get his green card, but not before an arduous legal battle. But on that Friday afternoon, John was in a good mood and ready to rock and roll in more ways than one.

We climbed back in the limo and resumed the trip toward the radio and television station where the charity marathon was getting underway. No crowds of fans greeted us as the limo pulled into the parking lot. After all, no one, not even the deejays and my fellow TV journalists, really believed that John Lennon was coming to participate in their charity marathon. Over the course of the weekend, thousands of people would crowd into that same parking lot, hoping to catch a glimpse of the former Beatle. Many of them ended up getting a great deal more than that.

The WFIL Radio Helping Hand Marathon was broadcast in cooperation with WPVI, the television station where I served as anchorman, and would benefit the National Multiple Sclerosis Society. The two stations shared a building at 4100 City Line Avenue, where the city of Philadelphia meets the posh suburbs of the Philadelphia Main Line.

John Lennon's 56 hours in the broadcast studios working for the Marathon tell you a lot about the man—his love of people, his willingness to give of himself, his utter belief in equality, and his intense desire to let people know that he was not a god but just a human being like everyone else. In a decade filled with equal measures of success and personal disappointment, he seemed happy to be back in a positive forum, a place where others' needs were at the center of attention.

When he arrived at the studios, John launched into his best deejay impression, even offering his own brand of broadcast weather reporting: "The weather is mostly sunny today, partly cloudy tonight, and occasional pain tomorrow." What John didn't know was that our television news director, Ron Tindiglia, was in his office listening, heard John's unusual weather report, and had a brilliant idea that would come into play later in the weekend.

Still one of the biggest stars in the world, John spent much of the first afternoon at the station paying tribute to everyone who contributed to the marathon. He announced hundreds of names on the air, thanking those who had donated fifty dollars or fifty cents. At one point, a listener offered a large donation if John would say "Gay people are beautiful." John immediately said, "All gay people are beautiful. . . . I've met a few uglies, too."

Outside the crowds began gathering in the parking lot. Station employees had to move their cars out to make room for all the arriving Lennon fans. When he heard about the gathering throng, John went out into the parking lot and auctioned off his own socks, unwashed and fresh off of his feet, making a joke of his celebrity in the name of charity.

Harry Bluebond, then 24, was among the crowds of people who came to see John Lennon that Friday:

"John was signing autographs and taking donations. I was fascinated by his presence, because it was really so different from what I expected. It was not the performer I was watching, not the man I idolized as a teenager and young adult, it was a real person. He was so natural. He was as real as you can get."

Upstairs, in the newsroom, I was getting ready for my six o'clock news broadcast when I received a phone call from Frank Rizzo, the tough and popular mayor of Philadelphia. He'd been informed of the crowds outside the station. "Larry Kane," he exclaimed, "should I send Stakeout?"

The Stakeout Squad was the city's elite unit of sharpshooters, brought in to control dangerous situations. "No," I replied, "but we should have a few extra police officers." Within minutes, I could hear sirens in the distance bringing scores of blue-shirted police officers to secure the day for John Lennon.

John was having a blast. He was willing to do anything to help out. When our TV news director Ron Tindiglia asked me if John would want to fill in that night for our popular weather forecaster, Jim O'Brien, who was off on vacation, I replied, "Are you kidding, he would chomp at the bit."

At 5:45 that night, I walked John Lennon into the studio of Action News at WPVI-TV for his debut as a TV weatherman. Station manager Damon Sinclair walked with us, all the while filming the activity with his handheld movie camera. (Portions of his film are included in the enclosed DVD.)

I looked over at John and said, "Are you ready man?" He answered, "Cool baby, cool."

The weather forecast was a three-minute whirlwind of basically unintelligible, but absolutely adorable, Lennonism. John threw the magnetic numbers and symbols all over the board.

"There's a high there, a very low there, and this is a cold front headed toward a warm front. Or maybe not. Got it?"

Through the rest of the newscast, as I read the gamut of news from tragedy to happiness and all other events of the day, John stayed in the corner of the set, and in that devilish way of his, made faces and tried hard to crack me up, which he did several times rather successfully.

It was John's first and last gig as a weatherman, but it was memorable and it was magic. With hundreds of thousands of astonished viewers looking on, John's weather forecast transformed the Helping Hand Marathon into a weekend blockbuster. People watched and listened in record numbers through the rest of the weekend, many just wanting to find out what John would do next.

Back in the WFIL studios John played deejay, dedicating anything for a buck and introducing the hottest songs of the day. At one point, Lauren Lipton, one of our radio newscasters, walked up to him and said, "Hi, I'm Lauren Lipton." John paused, glared at her curiously and said, "I like your bags."

The room went silent. Was he referring to sections of Lauren Lipton's anatomy? Was this some kind of tasteless joke? Lauren didn't know what to say. Then we realized John was referring to tea bags, as in Lipton tea bags. Everyone broke out laughing. Conversation with John was always an adventure.

John remained on the air throughout the weekend. On Sunday, tired and hoarse, he proclaimed to the huge radio audience, "C'mon folks, send some money for the memory of an old man like me."

Though nearly exhausted, he insisted on greeting the crowds that continued to gather outside. Lynn Sherrick, an 11th grader from Montgomery County, Pennsylvania, was returning from a camping trip on that early Sunday afternoon when she tuned into WFIL and heard that John was at the station:

"I screamed at my mother and my thirteen-year-old sister, and I didn't stop screaming. My tactics worked. When we arrived at the parking lot, there were barriers up all over the place, but I squeezed my way through, got very close to John and shared with him some stories of my family. I asked him to sign some money I had, but he wanted the money for the marathon. It was so great to see him up close. I never realized his hair was reddish. He looked great.

"Of course, I had to go home. But I wasn't through yet. I called a friend and had him drive me back. I saw John again! And again he asked for money for the charities. He was relentless, but he was also so friendly. He said, "Write to me." I did and he sent me signed notes back, including a February 12, 1977, birthday wish. I will never forget him."

Joan Erle, a high school senior from New Jersey, was driven to the chaotic scene by her brother Ed. They climbed a barricade from a hospital adjacent to the station. Both of them rushed up to John:

"I was surprised at how thin he was. He looked kind of drawn. But he was so cheerful. He was asking for a dollar for an autograph and put all the money in the collection basket for the charities. What impressed me the most was how charming and outgoing he was to all the people gathered around. I'll never forget the day."

Despite hours without sleep, pandemonium surrounding the building, and the crush of fans inside and out, John never lost his cool throughout the weekend. In fact, he watched the growing money tally for the marathon with the eye of a man on a mission. His mission was accomplished. By the end, we'd raised more than we ever had before, thanks in large part, to John Lennon.

But all John could do was thank us. When the marathon ended on Sunday night, John, drained yet overjoyed, turned to Gene Vassal, the station's sales manager and said, "Thank you man. This was so good."

As I bid farewell to him, he came close, in that face-to-face way that John Lennon had, and said, rather softly, "This was special. I needed something like this. Needed to think about other people. Had some fun. This was the most people, just normal people, I've ever met. Thanks. Thanks again."

Over the years, it's become fashionable for rock stars to lend their names and a song or two to charity benefits. What distinguishes John Lennon was how deeply he became involved when he took on a charitable cause.

His most famous effort on behalf of a charity began when he saw a story on WABC-TV in New York by a young reporter named Geraldo Rivera. Using a borrowed key, Geraldo had snuck into the Willowbrook State School on Staten Island with a camera crew to document the abuse suffered there by emotionally challenged patients. John and Yoko were so upset by the reports that they contacted Geraldo immediately. Geraldo remains impressed with their compassion and dedication to this day:

"I met John and Yoko in their Bank Street home in 1971. It was a thrill. I was a huge Beatles fan and a bigger John Lennon fan. We became friends.

"When the Willowbrook investigation went on the air in February of 1972, John called right away with offers of help. Both John and Yoko felt like adopted citizens of New York. They wanted to give something back. John was extra sensitive about the needs of others."

John put on a full-length benefit concert that raised a quarter of a million dollars for the Willowbrook patients. Rivera, who served as one of four character witnesses at John's successful immigration hearing, never forgot Lennon's humanity:

"John Lennon was not a celebrity who just loaned his name to a cause.

When he got involved, he got completely involved. His sensitivity for the victims of Willowbrook is something I will never forget."

Neither will Geraldo's executive producer, Marty Berman, who retains vivid memories of a second appearance by John on behalf of the Willowbrook victims at a festival in Central Park:

"He was as genuine as they get. At the time, in the seventies, we worked with many stars, many celebrities. But he was different. He was a real guy, just one of the guys actually. He just mingled with the crowd, no entourage, just John and the people."

From the very beginning of his career—from the sweaty jams at Mona Best's Casbah to the rancid nightclubs in Hamburg and the triumphant forays at the Cavern—John Lennon always tried to stay close to his fans.

Yoko Ono, the person John grew closer to than any other, says John wanted to interact with fans so they could be inspired by them—so that they could see, essentially, he was really no different than them:

"He felt extremely responsible for his fans. That's why, instead of just showing the best side of himself to them, he went the other way. He said, 'No, I have to be honest—let them know what I am made of. I'm not all that perfect or anything and they have to know that.'

"He didn't want people to just adore him. He wanted to make sure that they understood, "Hey, I'm just this kind of guy and I want to make sure that you don't feel that you're smaller than me.'"

As John headed back home from Philadelphia that May to his pregnant wife in New York, he knew he was beginning a new stage in his life, one that would require him to limit his excesses and freedoms. How he handled that radical shift in focus and responsibilities continues to serve as a model for fathers around the world. As he had in so many other aspects of life, John helped pioneer a new definition of fatherhood.

Mario Casciano, the avid fan who became friends with John when he lived with May Pang, remembers John's transformation:

"He was back with Yoko and she was going to have a baby. He was such a warm guy and I think he had always felt guilty about the absent father he had been with Julian. Let's face it, if it weren't for May, he wouldn't have even kept in touch with Julian. Guilt had set in. He was determined not to repeat that experience."

Yoko's pregnancy seemed almost a miracle to the middle-aged couple. At 43, she had a history of miscarriages and had been told repeatedly by doctors that getting pregnant would pose a serious risk to her health. John had been advised that he was likely infertile. Yet they kept trying. At the urging of a Chinese acupuncture specialist in San Francisco, they changed their diet and avoided alcohol and drugs.

The changes worked, and proof of it arrived on October 9, 1975—John's thirty-fifth birthday—with the birth of Sean Lennon.

John then made another drastic adjustment in lifestyle, transforming himself from high-profile artist to dedicated, stay-at-home father. Yoko was glowing in the aftermath of Sean's arrival. It was an especially happy time for her as she watched a new and upbeat husband take on a difficult challenge.

As the months passed, friends kept inquiring about what John was up to. Few believed that he was actually acting as primary caregiver to a baby. But he clearly loved what he was doing. He boasted of changing diapers and baking bread, saying, "Bread and babies, as every housewife knows, is a full-time job. As I watched the bread being eaten, I thought, 'Well, don't I get a gold record or knighted or nothing?'"

He also devoted his energy to his new passion for healthy cooking and eating. Once again, he was ahead of his time, adopting a macrobiotic food plan, and trying to eliminate most of the sugar from his meals.

Photographer Bob Gruen recalls that John was committed to having a healthier body and to avoid overeating by several creative methods of mind control:

"He started reading cookbooks and he started reading books about nutrition and books about food because he said his mind was on food and this way he could have all these fantastic fantasies—like reading cookbooks that described big preparations or fabulous meals. And he could read the whole thing and fantasize the whole thing and not have to actually eat it. That would help get him through another couple of hours without eating."

Raising a child did not, as many revisionist historians suggest, turn John Lennon into a creatively barren couch potato. According to Yoko, John played the guitar, wrote and pursued other creative endeavors on a daily basis.

Beatles' scholar Martin Lewis believes the period represented a time of personal and artistic renewal for John:

"The thing I admire about John Lennon was his uncanny ability to understand his mistakes. In his earlier days he did not treat Cynthia well. He was a poor father to Julian. After the birth of Sean and his settling down, a natural maturity was descending upon John. Those were happy years.

"Despite all the speculation about his house husband role, he started catching up with his life. After an endless cycle of action going back to 1957, he was soul searching. He needed to make personal reparations to Julian which he began to do. He was happy. It was a solid time of self-examination."

One man, Michael Allison, enjoyed more access to John during this period of rejuvenation than anyone outside Yoko and Sean. A wiry, intelligent long-distance cyclist and film documentary producer, Allison was working as an editor on a film project at the famous Brill Building in the heart of New York City's music district. Allison also had a side business, tending to indoor plants and creating indoor environments with trees.

One day, he went to visit a potential new client referred by a friend at the Dakota apartment building on Seventy-second street. When the apartment door opened, Allison saw a thin man of about 5'10" holding an infant in his arms. He said, "Hello I'm John and this is Sean."

Allison knew exactly who he was looking at, but remained as nonchalant as he could:

"It was a like a blind date. I had no idea that I was coming to John

Lennon's house. I was a big Beatles fan and a big John fan, but that day I was oblivious to who it was. I think he really liked that, that I didn't make a big deal about him. Actually from that time, March of 1976 to the spring of 1982, in all the time I worked for John and Yoko, I was totally understated. I think he respected that I treated him as a human being, not some special entity, not a star."

Allison, who was dubbed "Michael Tree" by John, soon became a daily presence at the Dakota. During that time, he learned something unexpected about his famous client:

"He was a very gracious man. The public toughness was a façade. I knew right away that he was a class act with an intense sensitivity toward the feelings of other people.

Michael Allison's recalls how his role in John's life eventually grew from tree master to friend to trusted confidant:

"I guess he felt very comfortable around me. I would make my rounds in the white room, the kitchen, the Egyptian room, and sometimes I would crack open the door of the bedroom where he would be resting and he would just wave me in. I became, in a sense, a part of the household.

"After his son Julian came to visit in the winter of 1977, John seemed down. He indicated to me that he didn't want to do to Sean what he did to Julian, the absences and all that. He was a good father but he was also strict with Sean, especially during the times when they were without a nanny. But he was especially loving to the child.

"Throughout this time of awakening, several things were happening. He was quietly in communication with May Pang, whose calls I sometimes took for him, and as the time progressed, his feelings for Yoko seemed to intensify."

After fifteen years on the public stage, John relished the quieter, domestic life inside the Dakota. But he also managed to continue to engage everyday life and people. He spent many hours wandering around New York's Central Park with Sean.

Some days, the two wandered even further. Father and son often took the two-hour ride from New York City to the Lehigh Valley of Pennsylvania to explore its woods and parks. Several area residents were astonished to cross paths with John Lennon as he and Sean walked peacefully together.

John kept in touch with old friends through the phone. He talked often with Elton John, who was so instrumental in getting him back to New York. He called me on several occasions. Once, he discussed his forays with Sean:

"You know Larry, I come to Pennsylvania for a little road trip now and then, and I should really get me ass down to Philadelphia to see you."

Another call let me know, in no uncertain terms, that John's days of peace, quiet, and parenthood had not blunted his sharp wit and tongue.

I had enjoyed a successful year-and-a-half anchoring the 11 p.m. news broadcast at WABC-TV in New York. Though a job in New York, the number-one media market in America, was considered the top rung of the local TV ladder—and a stepping-off point for a national network job—I wanted to return to Philadelphia to raise our children. Perhaps I had been inspired by how John put his career on hold in the interests of his child.

But he certainly didn't see it that way. He called me in October of 1978 to berate me for my decision, calling me a "fool" and every other name he could conjure from his almost limitless vocabulary of profanity.

When I explained my family considerations directly and emotionally to him, he paused and seized the moment to tell me how happy he was in the current chapter of his life. Our conversation ended on a warm and pleasant note.

As the reader knows, it was not the first time I was engaged in heated debate with John Lennon. But it was a reminder of one of the most dazzling elements of John's repertoire—he was one of the world's most prolific talkers. If he had survived, there is no question in my mind that John Lennon could have been the greatest talk show host of his generation. *The John Lennon Show.* I would have watched every day.

In the spring of 1979, John and Yoko went public with their domestic bliss, offering what they described as a "Love Letter from John and Yoko to People Who Ask Us What, When and Why." The letter appeared in the *New York Times* on Sunday, May 27, 1979. It read, in part:

"In the past ten years we noticed that everything we wished came true in its own time, good or bad, one way or the other. We kept telling each other that one of these days we would have to get organized and wish for only good things. Then our baby arrived. We were overjoyed and at the same time felt very responsible. Now our wishes would also affect him. We felt it was time . . . to do something about our wishing process—the Spring Cleaning of our minds!

"It was a lot of work. We kept finding those old things in the closets of our minds that we hadn't realized were still there, things we wished we hadn't found. We started to love the plants . . . we began to enjoy the drum beat of the city which used to annoy us. . . . We made a lot of mistakes and still do. . . . We still have a long way to go. It seems the more we get into cleaning, the faster the wishing and receiving process gets. . . . Sean is beautiful, the plants are growing, the cats are purring. . . . We live in a beautiful universe. We are thankful every day for the plentifulness of our life.

"We hope that you have the same quiet space in your mind to make your own wishes come true. Thank you for all the love you send us. . . . If you think of us next time, remember our silence is a silence of love and not of indifference."

Paid for by John and Yoko as an advertisement, the letter also appeared in papers in Tokyo and London. Poetic and thoughtful, the letter served not just as an update, but as a notice that, despite his home duties, John was ready to be active again on the public stage.

In March of 1980, John traveled to Capetown, South Africa, both as a tourist and as an activist to stand up to the architects of the country's repressive apartheid policy. John had expressed his displeasure with South Africa's racist policies earlier, much to the chagrin of the government, which banned his music from broadcast in the mid-1960s. His 1980 visit to Cape Town showed that he was ready to be an activist again.

Another trip that same year showed he was ready to take the public stage again as an artist. With a five-man crew, John sailed his 62-foot yacht Isis to Bermuda with Sean. Their days in the Caribbean were filled with sunshine, shopping, and forays to the beaches. With the turquoise waters surrounding him and the beautiful skies above, John envisioned *Double Fantasy*, a collaborative album of new songs with Yoko. He returned to New York refreshed and ready to record new music.

Paul Drew, the Atlanta broadcaster and music executive who had aided the Beatles on their 1964 and '65 tours and later befriended John and Yoko, remembers getting a call from Yoko in 1980:

"She told me that John had been inspired on his Bermuda trip and was calling her and singing songs. Over a period of several phone calls, she sang the songs to me."

Yoko invited Paul to New York, where he got an inside look at the reborn John Lennon:

"We gathered in a private room in a restaurant. They told me of this wonderful album, where one song would be his, another hers. It would turn out to be *Double Fantasy*. What had amazed me the most, though, was how John looked. He had color in his face. He was talking about his music like a young man eager to show the world his work.

"I had never seen him so enthusiastic about music, even in the early Beatle days. On the trips back in the sixties, he could be moody and alone. In that restaurant, he was as pumped as you can get. He was spending his days with Sean, and his nights at the studio, and you could tell that the joy of the music was part of his life."

In the fall of 1980, John's appreciation of life and living seemed to be enhanced by the beautiful autumn glow of New York's Central Park. One afternoon while walking Sean in the park, Yoko and John ran into broadcaster Geraldo Rivera. Geraldo invited them inside his apartment where they talked for awhile. He remembers how healthy John looked and his sunny outlook:

"They had just finished *Double Fantasy*. John was more relaxed than I had ever seen him. He was mellow, loving the time with his wife and baby. He seemed happy. After all, he had settled all that stuff about always being identified with the Beatles. His music was alive again and he looked very much the part of father, husband, and a star without burdens. It was good to see him. It was the last time I did."

With his single title "(Just Like) Starting Over" a national hit, John was further encouraged by the release of the album *Double Fantasy* on November 17, 1980. The album was produced by Jack Douglas, John's engineer on most of the solo albums. Douglas, now the legendary longtime producer for Aerosmith, says the album experience had motivated John to think ahead in several directions. Douglas remembers:

"John and Yoko were planning a tour for the Spring of 1981, so much so that they had made sketches of what they wanted the stage to look like. John showed his sketch to me. It looked like a giant crab on the stage with the arms of the crab extended over the audience."

Douglas assigned the stage design to tour consultants Dick Hansen and Henry Smith. Hansen, now in the Hollywood film industry, recalls the effort:

"Henry and I came up with the concept and Mark Fisher of a company called Brittania Row did the drawings. Fisher had designed *The Wall* stage for Pink Floyd. The design includes these large arms, actually boom arms with cameras on them. And there was something else: five video screens. The idea was to shoot video of every stop on the tour and make that video a part of the actual show, custom-designed for each town. If you played in San Francisco, the video screens would highlight scenes from that city."

Smith delivered the design to the studio in New York just before Thanksgiving of 1980. The two continued their touring career with Roberta Flack, who ironically was a neighbor of John and Yoko at the Dakota.

While John envisioned a tour, he also had dreams of a Beatles reunion, of sorts. Producer Jack Douglas remembers the pride that John displayed in what he considered a major coup:

"He was proud that he talked Paul McCartney into playing on Ringo's next album. John felt that George had slighted him in a recent book, so George was not invited."

In a poignant memory, Douglas recalls John's fascination with the Beatles, documented several times in this volume:

"John was proud of the Beatles. He became a rabid Beatles fan, and as he emerged with this great album *Double Fantasy*, his thoughts often turned to the Beatles, their success, their music."

Double Fantasy was released on November 17, 1980, to critical acclaim and strong sales. But John would have only a few short weeks to enjoy its success and his artistic rebirth.

Michael Allison remembers the last time he saw John Lennon alive. It was the afternoon of December 8, 1980, a few hours before his life ended in a volley of bullets outside the Dakota apartment building where he had found so much joy:

"He looked healthy and happy and looking to the future. He said to me, 'Michael, we are opening the door slowly to see if anyone is still out there.'"

On his way home, Allison brushed past Mark David Chapman, one of the people waiting for John Lennon just outside the front door of the Dakota. A deranged Beatles' fan, Chapman had twisted his egotism and worship of the band—a sentiment that John Lennon always discouraged—into a belief that Lennon should die at his hands.

Chapman shot four .38 caliber, hollow-tipped bullets into John's back. John Lennon, 40, founding member of the Beatles and the voice of his generation, was pronounced dead a short time later at the hospital.

When the wire report was placed in my hands that night I trembled with anguish. I could barely read the words on the air. As I drove home after midnight, tears rolled down my face and I thought of the Beatles and John. He was a subject of my reporting. But we had developed a special bond, forged by mutual respect and the shared experience of surviving Beatlemania at its exhilarating and wild heights. Like many other people who knew him, I vowed to keep the memory of his incredible talent and spirit alive. I hope this book will play a small part in doing that. I am, of course, not alone in that effort.

As photographer Allan Tannenbaum arrived that fateful night to photograph the aftermath of the murder at the Dakota, he was stunned by the faces of the people in the crowd that had gathered at the scene. They stared up into the stars, looking for a light of hope. Candles were lit and faces were drawn with what Tannenbaum calls the "incredulous look of disbelief." Journalists are known to build walls around their emotions so they can do their jobs without the interference of the normal range of pain and anguish. For Tannenbaum, it was the first time he had covered a story involving the death of someone he knew. Five days later, it unleashed a stream of tears. "I was drowning in tears," he remembers. "I couldn't stop crying. I couldn't stop this combination of sadness and anger. All I could think of was that it was a horrible ending to a wonderful life."

It was a horrible ending, but as history would prove, another beginning in the always amazing and perplexing life of John Lennon.

As you turn the rest of the pages of this book, you will find testimony on the impact of John Lennon's life and death. The people will take the stand. The people are judge and jury on his life. Let's face it—if John Lennon was really addicted to anything, it was the joy and wonderment of people. His faith in humanity allowed him to continue and his spirit to prevail.

His heart stopped beating on December 8, 1980, but the beat of his music and the echoes of his search for the truth continue to resonate. And the people will be the judge of that. Some of them are about to speak.

ELEVEN:
The Lennon Generations Speak

"John showed me that what you believe in and value in your life has tremendous meaning. Follow them, trust in them and don't compromise on the things that are important in your life. When you're gone, all that remains is who you were and the impressions you left behind."
—*Bill Hemsley, Beatles fan*

Young and old, from communities far and wide, the generations that follow the life of John Lennon, took part in this special addition to this book.

In the Spring of 2004, our good friend Joe Johnson, whose *Beatle Brunch* program on the Westwood One network airs on over a hundred radio stations, solicited his listeners to join in paying homage to John Lennon for this book project. The e-mails came in every week until March of 2005. There were hundreds and from them, I was able to select a broad array of viewpoints. It was an interactive diary that I kept and its words, sometimes poignant, sometimes sad and wistful, help bring this story to an end. I want to thank all of Joe's listeners who took part.

In the beginning, I thought that this project would give a people's perspective to John's life. It exceeded my expectations with a scope and depth of insight and emotion that few authors could match.

The Lennon generations speak.

THE SOLDIER

In 1977, while serving in the U.S. Coast Guard, I had a weekend off duty. A friend of mine and I went to New York to see the sights. We were walking through Central Park when I saw this guy sitting on a shaded park bench watching the sky. As I got nearer, I could not believe who this individual was. John Lennon was sitting there, by himself, just taking in the day.

Nervously, as I walked by, I said, "How ya' doin?"

I can remember to this day that Lennon replied, "It's getting better, you know."

Trying to maintain my poise and check my excitement I said, "John Lennon, right?"

"Just John, but mostly daddy these days," he replied.

At this time Yoko Ono approached with what I assumed were coffees. I did not want to be one of those fans, so I took a step back as if to walk away.

"Ah, my fix," said John. "Yoko Ono, this is Young Man on The Street. My wife, Yoko."

I said something lame like, "Nice to meet you."

I was so nervous about protecting their privacy that I just said, "I have to go. Thank you for your time."

As the years have passed, I often reflect on that brief encounter with one of my childhood idols. The conversation has become etched in my memory, even though the whole event lasted approximately three minutes.

As I turned to walk away, John responded, "You took my time and I took yours. Wear it well."

I thought it was very Lennon of him to say that. Now I just think it was profound.

Steven D. Emerson
Edwardsville, Illinois

THE TV PERSONALITY

In some ways it is very hard to believe that it was nearly twenty-five years ago that John Lennon was senselessly murdered. Lennon had and continues to have such a large presence in our lives that it sometimes seems as if he is still here, with us. In a way, I feel that he still is, because he helped to shape our world in ways both profound and simple.

It would be easy and, indeed, unfair, to summarize John Lennon's life just by citing the usual statistics: The Beatles are still the biggest selling group of all time; sales of Beatles' related CDs, books, and videos continue to be impressive; Lennon is a member in good standing of the Rock and Roll Hall of Fame, etc. Clearly, Lennon's influence goes far beyond the record charts and museum halls. For many, Lennon provided an example of how one might live his or her life in a way that is honest, and in a way that is ultimately life affirming and positive. John Lennon was no saint, and he certainly wasn't perfect. But he spent the last half of his life searching for a way to overcome his own insecurities and demons, and to make sense of who he was—not John Lennon, the Beatle, but John Lennon, the person. He continually tried to better himself, and the trials and tribulations that he went through can serve as lessons to us all.

The facts of John Lennon's early life are fairly well known. His father abandoned him and his mother when John was a small child. His mother Julia handed him over to his Aunt Mimi to raise when she began a new family with a different man. When he was in his late teens, and shortly after John had re-connected with Julia, she was killed in an accident. Then the buddy who was perhaps his best friend, Stu Sutcliffe, died of a brain hemorrhage.

It is understandable that Lennon would become an insecure, bitter young man. It is also understandable that his ambition to make something of himself, combined with his extraordinary talents when it came to music, writing, and art, would help him to become a success—although the level of his success certainly could not have been predicted, and was, indeed, astounding.

Equally astounding, perhaps, was Lennon's willingness to grow, and to get to the bottom of his fears and insecurities. To be sure, like many, he initially sought refuge in womanizing, drugs, and alcohol. Even his fame as a Beatle could be seen as an escape from the reality of who he felt he really was. (The clues were all there, but we couldn't see them at the time: his lyric "beneath this mask, I am wearing a frown," from 1964's "I'm a Loser," or his cry of "Help" in 1965.) In fact, it would take all of his Beatle years, plus experiments with transcendental meditation and Primal Scream therapy, a painful separation from Yoko in the seventies, retirement from the public music making that had been his life's work, and the birth of his son Sean, for Lennon to finally come to grips with the pain inflicted on him during his childhood and teen years.

Yet somehow, he did it. In December 1980 John Lennon seemed to be a happy man, content with who he was, and optimistic about the future. I remember quite clearly reading John's interview with Playboy magazine that month. I believe I had just finished reading it that day, December 8th. I remember being so happy that John Lennon was back on the scene after a five year self-imposed "retirement," and I remember being so happy that he seemed happy. The interview was such a stark contrast to the biting, angry "Lennon Remembers" interviews from *Rolling Stone* magazine from ten years earlier. Lennon was back, and it was exciting, not because he was "former Beatle" or "counter-culture leader" John Lennon (in fact, could that term apply anymore?), but because he was John Lennon—husband, father, human being—who was going to help us get through the soon-to-begin Reagan eighties.

And then, there was that night.

One of the truly awful things about John's murder was that it occurred just when he had finally found some inner peace, and was a better man for it.

Of course, another awful thing was that it robbed a wife of her husband, and a young child of his father. (It robbed another child of the opportunity to one day sort out his issues with his largely absentee father.)

Obviously, we also lost a great musician.

Many, myself included, had longingly hoped for a Beatles reunion. Those hopes were dashed. But you know what? In the grand scheme of things, a possible Beatles reunion really was about the least significant thing that we lost. After all, their music lives on, and their legacy continues. They'd already given their all to the public.

What does make me sad about the Beatles is this: it would have been nice if the four of them could have gotten together one day, just as Paul, George and Ringo did for the "Anthology" projects, just for themselves—just to renew the friendships, reminisce, and have some laughs over their wonderful time together. Only four people in the world went through what they went through, and it would have been nice if they, as a group, could have gone over the old war stories, just for their own sake. Not for us, but for them. That would have been nice.

My best friend Richard and I always planned to travel to New York one day (we lived in the Washington, D.C. area) to hang out at the Dakota and "meet" John Lennon. The word was, it was pretty easy to do so, and he was pretty accessible and patient with his fans. I always thought it would be cool to meet him, just to say "thanks" for all of the great music and the movies and books and everything. I was pretty sure he probably heard that all the time, but it felt important to me to give him my own personal "thank you." Needless to say, we took it for granted that he would always be here, and I never got to deliver my message. Until now.

Thanks, John, for everything. Thanks for helping to make the world a better place, thanks for sharing your life with us, and thanks for helping me to be a better person.

We all shine on.

Tony Perkins
Good Morning America
January 2005

A Poet Among Us

Dear Mr. Kane,

Although John Lennon died before my first birthday, I have always felt a strong attachment to his spirit. I took this feeling along with a need to understand the man that I could only know through pictures, film and song with me as I traveled to England at the age of 20 in the year 2000.

The following is a poem that I wrote on March 27, 2002 about my experience at Strawberry Fields in Liverpool. Thank you for giving all of us the opportunity to be a part of your book.

Beautiful Boy
With your witty charm bursting
Out of a devilish grin,
You could even capture
The hearts of Blue Meanies.
And only you could ask the Queen
To rattle her jewelry as you twist and shout.
When you started, you wrote
Songs to Snow White
And before you left, you told us to
Imagine.
All we ever wanted was to spend
A day in the life,
That you mystically possessed.
So twenty years after Chapman
Asked you for your autograph,
On a rainy Liverpool day,
I stood peeping over the brick wall
Which held a sign marked Strawberry Fields.
I was stretching to extended latitudes
Wishing to find something left of you.
On the brick cage that contained your serenity,

I was expected to chalk
A memorial to a man I never knew.
I etched only a few words.
And signed it with love to a
Beautiful Boy.

Sincerely,
Meghann Boser Pierz,
Minnesota

The Mother with the Memories

If you're like me you look back on aspects of your life through photographs, scrapbooks and memories. My childhood wasn't typical and it wasn't easy but I have many memories that wrapped me warmly and helped the young child I was through rough times. My bedroom wall was decorated in Beatles memorabilia and I was a Lennon fan at six years of age.

Through my wacky youth Lennon was a constant. Words, music and outcry. When John Lennon died I felt a deep pang. His legendary talent made me joyous, comforted and free.

When my fourteen-year-old son plays Lennon on his MP3 player, I know the world is still better for having had JL in it!

Hillary Robert
Keyport, NJ

What Would John Do??

It wasn't John Lennon's looks that caught my attention. It wasn't the fact that he was a Beatle either. It was his fascinating character. His personality is what got me hooked. In him, I saw this very outspoken, humorous man. I saw depth and an overflow of opinions that were just waiting to be let out. When I look at this man, I do not see a "Saint" or an angel sent by God, as others might. I see him for who he is, flaws and all. And the fact that he did not mask those flaws to anyone, is what inspires me to be myself, whether people like it or not. I always ask myself, "What would John do?" It works!

Thank you dearly, Mr. Kane, for giving us Lennon fans this opportunity to be heard!

Sincerely,
Kimber Austin
Saskatoon, Saskatchewan, Canada!

THE DOCTOR IS IN

I listened to the Beatles from the start—I was fourteen and very impressionable. I was always amazed by John's blunt and humorous responses to people, sarcasm with wit, saying what you see. I'm very candid with people and don't believe in double standards or fake people. I've tried to pass this along to my children who are all Beatles fans as well. I am a psychologist by training and the CEO of a mental health business—so I can point out what's wrong and make it palatable with humor—"living is easy with eyes closed, misunderstanding all you see." Thanks

Dr. Chuck Meseck
Milwaukee

A CHANGE IN THE WIND

Hi Larry . . . I heard about your book on *Beatle Brunch* a few weeks back and knew that I had to e-mail you. What a wonderful tribute; I wish you great success. Following are my thoughts on how my life was changed by John Lennon:

I am 51 years of age, so the Beatles are old friends; family, really. Born and raised in Manhattan, as were my parents, Dad and I were watching Monday night football when Howard Cosell announced John's death. I was 27 years old. I remember looking at my Dad crying and screaming, "If this city can kill John Lennon, it can kill anyone . . . It's time to leave and I hope you'll

261

all come with me . . . but this time next year, with or without you, I'll be living somewhere else!" These are not 'light' words coming from a native New Yorker . . . but John's death was devastating. Its magnitude felt enormous to me. I had no idea where I was going, but I knew within every fiber of my being that within a year, I would be gone. I vividly remember for weeks and weeks, maybe months, thereafter, no matter what time of day or what I was doing, I would feel tears just streaming from my eyes. They were endless. I felt like I grieved for months.

The following April, I moved to Phoenix . . . I should say, we moved to Phoenix. My parents, my sister, our dog and I. We have not looked back since. This past May, my husband (who I met here in Arizona) and I celebrated our 18th anniversary. My parents turned 76 this year and celebrated their 55th anniversary. My sister married 5 years ago. We are, one and all, very active participants in our respective communities. I can state, fairly confidently, that none of these things would have happened had we not left the city. Had John's death not occurred when, and how, it did our lives would be dramatically different.

Since that time, with an interesting frequency . . . when I have challenging things with which I am confronted that require decision or action . . . or . . . if there is something unpleasant occurring in my life . . . seemingly out of nowhere, appears a John Lennon song . . . on the radio . . . in an elevator . . . over the speakers in a department store. I just smile. I used to say it was such an interesting 'coincidence.' I know better now. It's absolutely on purpose. I know, at some level, we really are all connected, and while I would give anything to reverse what happened to John, unquestionably I am not the only person whose life was changed that day . . . I am confident that many 'dominoes' been touched . . . and gently touched each other . . . all because of the gentle breeze of the life of John Lennon. I am simply one of those very grateful dominoes.

Kris Lecakes-Haley
Phoenix, Arizona

HIS MOTHER GAVE HIM THE BAD NEWS

John, for me, held the mystique of The Beatles. His wit, his voice, and his outspokenness attracted me from the start. The Beatles were his band, and their perception from the outside originated from his belief that they were the best band in the world. It was confidence and frailty, coldness and compassion, and honesty and sense of justice that got me about him.

The day he died hit me particularly hard. I remember my Mom coming into my room to wake me up. It was earlier than usual, and she was crying. She grew to love the Beatles (by osmosis), and knowing how much I loved them she knew it was going to be a rough day at school. Upon hearing what happened the previous night in NYC, I immediately felt like a close friend was gone. I know, I know—I didn't REALLY know him. But his music—and persona—touched me. Like I previously mentioned, it was his mystique that I most identified with. Another huge part of my sadness was that I'd never see him perform live. It was just one of the most senseless acts in recent history. I can only imagine his reaction to what happened September 11th, not to mention the recent political climate.

There will never be another John Lennon. An obvious statement, I know. But there are so many performers trying to carry his torch, and only a handful come close to his sincerity of purpose. He was a musician, a leader, a biting wit, a TRUE activist, and he had a huge set of balls on him.

Here's to John Winston Ono O'Boogie Lennon. I miss him, but thank God for his legacy.

Thanks for listening.
Ray Whitaker

MESSAGE FROM MAINE

Dear Larry,

You'd like to know how John Lennon affected my life? This might take a while! I wouldn't be the person I am now without John. To this day, John

Lennon still influences me, both my inner life and my outer life, on a daily basis and I love it that he does. Maybe people can even see it. I wouldn't have it any other way.

My best friend and I saw John Lennon "live in NYC" when that concert happened at Madison Square Garden, and when John asked everyone to sing along, I said to my friend, "Remember this moment: we're singing with John Lennon!" (I figured if we're in the same room with him, no matter how large that room is, and it's the same moment in time, and John asks us to sing with him, and we all sing the same song together at the same time in the same room . . . that counts! So . . . we sang with John Lennon!)

That's just one little anecdote, of course. John still adorns my living room walls to this day. That man became a part of my life when the Beatles hit America back in 1964 (when I was eight, about to turn nine), and it was John Lennon who taught me how to sing, how to read (and write) poetry, how to be a thinker outside the norm, how to dress (and how to dress as boldly as I felt and show it off to a world that wasn't ready for it, just as he did), how to be artistic, how to take chances, how to LIVE. He taught my heart to feel love for the first time . . . and it's a love I'll cherish in my soul forever, from lifetime to life!

When I was in Liverpool back in the mid-1980's, I visited Beatle City, the museum, and John's black suit—the one he wore on *The Ed Sullivan Show*—was standing up on a life-form (*sans* fake head or hands; just the suit, standing there). The ENERGY that came off that black suit was unlike anything I'd ever experienced! It was roped off, of course, and you couldn't touch it . . . but I did try. Never did get the chance to touch the fabric, but really, I didn't have to. The shape of it, the form of it, was John. Like he was standing right there in front of me. So close!!!!! That was the John that changed the world . . . especially mine.

I remember listening to one of the New York FM stations one night (it might have been WPLJ when it was deep-cut rock, before they changed over to a more Top-40 flavor), and there was this DJ who said, "Okay, folks, I might get FIRED for telling you this, but I'm bursting at the seams, and I just have to share this with all of you. I went to a party on Saturday night and JOHN LENNON was there. IT WAS LIKE BEING IN THE SAME ROOM WITH GOD." And everyone who heard that DJ knew that he was telling the truth, no exaggeration.

The charisma, the talent, the energy, the life force that John Lennon exuded couldn't help but influence anyone who had ever known him. John lives in my soul and he will always help to keep me as bold and artistic and alive as I dare to be. From John, I know that if I have limitations in this world, they're only my own fault!

Thanks for letting me share that. Let me know if you got this, if you can. Keeping John alive,

Sincerely,
Audrey Sparkes
Bangor, Maine

Just in Time to Break Her Heart

Seeing the Beatles on *The Ed Sullivan Show* in February of 1964 was the most invigorating and exciting thing I had ever seen and I still love watching that footage because it brings back those incredible memories. The images of them on that stage, shaking their mop-top heads as they sang "She Loves You" was breathtaking. They had such great energy. I was a seven-year-old little girl from L.A. and totally into the pop scene, sitting cross-legged on my living room floor squealing and bopping up and down as the Beatles sang. I loved the Beatles and didn't realize at the time what a phenomenon they actually were.

They were so different from the music my parents listened to, that everyone felt this was a "passing fad." But the Beatles ended up steamrolling everything in their path, to completely revolutionize popular music forever. I remember thinking since we laughed at our parents' music, our kids would probably laugh at our music. But that has never happened. The generations of Beatles fans keep on coming. That tells you how timeless their music is and what a gigantic impact they have made on society. The Beatles personified a culture that was shifting dramatically.

I didn't truly appreciate who John Lennon really was until he died. By that time, I was 24, married and living in Seattle; I loved *Double Fantasy*, his new album, and was elated that John looked so good and that he was working again. I even envisioned him working with the Beatles again.

Then on the morning of December 8, 1980, I woke up with the flu, and had to stay home from work. I spent the day in bed listening to the album and reading John's recent *Playboy* interview. It was a very long article and I kept dozing off and dreaming about him, waking up periodically to find the article still in my hand. I couldn't put it down. I was surprised at what I learned about John from reading that article. He revealed so much about himself. I read about his painful childhood and could relate because my childhood was so similar. I couldn't believe it. Suddenly I began to see a much deeper reality about him that spoke to me, and I understood who he was, not as a Beatle or even the legendary "Man of Peace," but as a man. I was very touched.

I had rediscovered John Lennon on a personal level, and was excited for his future. Something clicked and I felt a deep connection to him that was full of compassion, love, and understanding.

My husband flew through the door around 9 p.m. after I had gone to sleep, and woke me with the tragic and unbelievable news that John Lennon had just been murdered in New York. He was shaking. The shock dropped me to my knees, devastating me beyond description. I sobbed all night long and then for days after, sitting in front of the TV set watching all the footage. The grief was unbearable.

It seemed as though John Lennon had reached me just in time to break my heart. That emotion developed into a passion for discovering him—reading about him, talking to people who knew him, listening to rare tracks, watching his interviews, visiting the places he knew and loved, going to his art exhibitions and tribute events. His spirit is with me everywhere I go.

I soon felt I should be sharing all these experiences with other fans, and I began to write. For the last four years I've been writing for *Daytrippin'*, a popular international Beatles fanzine. This is my way of helping to keep his memory alive, and honoring his quest to connect with the world in an honest way. I still feel his presence. He's still here in some way and I think he wants us to know that. I hope at the end of the day that I've contributed somehow to his legacy, which will go on forever.

Shelley Germeaux
West Coast Correspondent
Daytrippin' Magazine

MEMORIES OF A RADIO MAN

I can remember the first time I heard the Beatles. It was 1977 and I was about four years old. My Dad and I were in his red Volkswagen Rabbit on Ohio River Boulevard in Pittsburgh when "All You Need is Love" came on the radio.

Right about the time, John and Paul sang the "She Loves You" chorus during the fade out, I asked my Dad who this was and he gave me a crash course on the Beatles. As soon as we got home from whatever it was we were doing that day, he pulled out *Abbey Road* and *Let it Be* and my life has never been the same since.

The reason why I love the Beatles is because they made me want to do what they did. Not necessarily be in a band that rocked and changed the world, (although if the chance had presented itself . . .) but rather be part of a group that makes a difference.

In fact, I use the Beatles as an analogy for my career in communications. Starting out way back when I was at a station in State College. Coming back and working at a small newspaper in Sewickley and part-timing at a station in the Steel City after graduating from Penn State was the Cavern and the clubs in Hamburg. And now, five years into my time here at CNN Radio,

267

well thus far, it has been playing on *The Ed Sullivan Show*. OK, I admit doing something like a sportscast or a music feature (sometimes on the Beatles) isn't as cool as releasing the "Paperback Writer"/"Rain" single, but, for me, it has become the next best thing.

It is a given that each Beatle brought his own special magical element to the mix, but Lennon was always my favorite. Maybe it was his voice (raw and unapologetic in "Twist and Shout" dreamy and hypnotic in "In My Life" and literally perfect in "Strawberry Fields Forever") maybe it was his lyrics, maybe it was the cocky way he marched to the beat of his own drummer.

Whatever that certain *je ne sais pas* was that he had, it hasn't faded. Look at him smirk on the cover of *Rubber Soul.* He's still as cool now as he was then. All of the Beatles were great, but I think that Lennon was the one who helped the other Fabs realize how great they were in the early days. He was the older brother the others looked up to, (notice how Paul looks at John during the "We Can Work it Out" video) when they were becoming bigger than, well you know Who.

Using Lennon and the Fabs as an inspiration to push myself further, I can't wait until I do my *Rubber Soul, Revolver* and *Sgt. Pepper.* And finally, one day when I retire, I think you can guess what I will say when I am literally and/or figuratively handed a gold watch. . . .

John Lorinc
CNN Radio Atlanta

Deep Thoughts From Indiana

How John Lennon affected my life. . . .

John Lennon impressed me in the way he was not afraid to speak his mind, even if I didn't always agree with what he said. I truly admired his sincerity; he certainly was not a phony! . . . He had great zeal about his beliefs and world view, and really cared. . . . And even if I didn't agree with some of his views, I respected that he seemed genuinely committed to his beliefs, and was not afraid to express it, even in unique, often unconventional, ways that people didn't quite understand. He didn't seem concerned what people thought of him, and I admired that boldness.

He also greatly affected my life through his marvelous, gorgeous music, and his fabulous, kind of haunting, voice that I still love to hear, and always will. I loved his way of not being afraid to experiment with new sounds in the recording studio, being daring enough to create some of the most original, and greatest music in history. . . . I dearly loved the man, and I miss him so much.

Sally Dee Perry
Indianapolis, Indiana USA

MEMORIES OF A COLD MORNING

On Dec. 9th, 1980 I was 11 years old and my parents woke me up very early. It was a school day but this was earlier than normal, it was still pitch black outside, and they didn't wake my younger brother. By the way they were acting I could tell something was very wrong. They seemed uncomfortable and hesitant but my father, finally, gently said "Last night John Lennon was shot." I struggled awake, I asked if John was okay, I asked if they caught the person who shot him, I was so confused. My parents were at a loss. They took me into their bedroom and sat me down in front of their small black and white TV and I watched the news about John. That morning there was no other news. I was completely numb.

I found out later that both of my older sisters had called from college in the middle of the night to ask my parents "How are you going to tell Tom?" because at the age of 11 I was known to all who knew me as "the kid who loves the Beatles." My birthday party the summer of 1980 had been a Beatles party, complete with guitar shaped cake that said "BEATLES" and Beatle movies on a movie projector borrowed from the library. I remember the presents I got that year: the albums *Abbey Road* and *McCartney 2*, a Beatles poster, a t-shirt with the Yellow Submarine on it, and a songbook of Beatles music with guitar tabs (I had just started taking lessons). I don't wonder that my parents didn't know how to tell me about John, so I watched the news in disbelief.

I read the newspaper in my scratchy sweater while eating my oatmeal. I was still numb. Then my Mother turned on the radio and the first song I heard was "Golden Slumbers." I went into the family room and sat down in front of the radio and listened, and the floodgates opened. I sat there sobbing as Paul sang the song that I still cannot hear without remembering that day . . . "smiles awake you when you rise, sleep pretty darling, do not cry . . ."

I was 11 years old and I would never be a child again.

All the best to you and best of luck with the book,

Thommy Burns
Annandale, Va.

THE TRUTH TELLER

Hi, Larry: I'd like to respond to your invitation and share a story about John Lennon and his effect on my life. You see, John influenced my choice of college major and career.

I was a teenaged Beatlemaniac in 1966 when John made his infamous comment about the Beatles being "more popular that Jesus." Overnight, I saw the Beatles, and John in particular, change from darlings to demonized in the media. With horror I watched footage of the record and book burnings, many carried out by kids my age. It shocked me that this could happen in our country during the Cold War, when we so criticized our "enemies" for doing the same thing.

It was even more saddening and shocking because even I, a fifteen-year-old, could understand that the comment was taken out of context. I watched the news as they broadcast John's explanation over the next few days, and the look on his face as he tried to explain that he wasn't saying the band was "better than Jesus" broke my heart. This gentle and talented man was victimized by the very fame he had been enjoying for so many months. And the media refused to accept his apology and kept on maligning him with glee.

It was at that point that I decided I wanted to change things and become a teller of truth. I wanted to be a journalist, but different from those journalists who twisted the words of John Lennon. I wanted to deal in facts and not sensationalism.

So I continued my studies and concentrated on my writing skills. I became the editor of my high school newspaper. I went on to college and was graduated with a degree in Journalism. I worked my way through college on the city desk of a major metropolitan newspaper. And, though my career in journalism didn't pan out (in those days it was difficult for a woman to make her way in such a male-dominated business), I did use those honed writing skills to become a successful technical writer—where I deal in facts and truth. So many, many years later I am a Six Sigma Master Black Belt, where one of the tools we apply to problem-solving is called a "truth table." I do not believe this is a coincidence.

I tell the truth because others told lies about one of my beloved Beatles. And I guess the truth is that I can thank the late John Lennon for much of what I am today.

Thanks for letting me tell this story. Good luck with the book! I love *Ticket to Ride* and look forward to reading your new effort.

Jill Finan
Rochester, NY

THE HEAD OF THE CLASS

I am 28 years old and John Lennon has been a part of my life since I was an infant. My father is to credit for this. He used to play The Beatles and John

271

Lennon for me and we would dance and talk about love and peace.

Throughout my life I have always been questioned about my passion for John and his quest for peace. I have tried desperately to spread his word to those that don't understand.

I have been a kindergarten teacher for five years. Each year I teach my students about John's message. We learn all about "Mr. John Lennon's" quest for peace by studying his art work and lyrics. At the end of every school year the students are allowed to choose their favorite Beatles song and we put on a performance for their parents. Each year their parents thank me for opening their child's hearts and providing them with a love for the Beatles and John.

John is helping me teach our future leaders about the meaning of peace and love. Maybe we can truly "give peace a chance" as these young minds learn how important it is.

All you need is love,

Valerie Ryan Stanley
Coral Springs Florida

HE PLAYED MY GUITAR

Hi, my name is Michael Lowry. I listen to *Beatle Brunch* regularly and heard you were interested in John stories. Okay, here goes.

I grew up in southwest Oklahoma. In 1963, at fourteen, when I heard the Beatles, I knew a musician's life was for me. I played keyboards already, so I got a little Farfisa combo compact and started a garage band.

Fast forward to to 1972 or '73. Ventura, California is where I landed. I was still seeking my fame and fortune as a musician but life was taking a round about path. Anyway, I recall getting ready to shower one afternoon when a friend came by, burst through the front door and screamed, "You're never going to believe who's at John's at the Beach!" John's at the Beach was a local hot spot for dinner and drinks, mostly tourists ate, but the locals came to drink. Often there was entertainment on the small stage. An old upright piano was out of tune but drinking on barrels and with a sawdust floor, it didn't matter. Anyway, I ask my friend what he was so excited about. John and Yoko are at John's at the Beach, eating. Wow, this is great! Let's go! So we grabbed a couple of guitars and climbed into the back of a friends pickup.

The seaside restaurant was just up the road and it was only around two in the afternoon so the joint was quiet. We pulled around the side and could see them through the window. It was Lennon, all right. Man, were we freakin' out. I think we sang some Beatles songs while sitting in the bed of the old pickup. We debated on how to go about getting in and meeting him. We certainly didn't want to disturb their lunch, besides if we pissed them off, all would be for naught. So we just kind of hung around.

After a while they got up from the dining room and went into the pool table room. We couldn't see it from outside. So I decided, that's where I'll make my move.

I'll never forget what happened next. I entered and walked through the bar to the back. There was a small room with a bar table. A bar table is a very small pool table, not your regular four-by-nine but about three-and-a-half-by-eight. No one was in the bar as I walked through and since no one was stopping me I marched right on back. I glimpsed Yoko sitting very upright in a chair to the left, her back against a wall. There was another fellow standing halfway in the door and the room. I brushed by him and saw John leaning over the table, lining up a shot. Kind of peering down his nose, stretched out across the table. Something silvery glinted in the light hanging from his neck. I took it all in and just stood there, probably agape but nonetheless in the same room as John Lennon. Now, I know courtesy, and house rules forbid talking or moving while someone's taking a shot. So I froze, just starring. After he shot he arose and looked at me, sort of quizzingly. His shot went awry. He wasn't a very good pool player, yet he looked at me, I guess, since I had entered their domain, he was leaving the opening up to me. I had sort of been practicing what to say, now was my moment.

"John Lennon, I've always wanted to meet you and I thought I'd have to go find you, and here, you've come to me."

John replied, "I knew you were here all the time."

The ice was broken and all I can say was it was incredible.

I had recently read the *Rolling Stone* interviews and The Primal Scream, which John referred to often in the *Stone* articles.

I recalled he and Yoko were touring America, looking for Yoko's daughter Kyoko. I believe she had been taken by Yoko's first husband. So, she and John were trying to catch up with them, while doing a bit of Americana. Traveling in a green Oldsmobile station wagon with New York tags.

When I approached John, after the usual accolades about his music and my life changing, I felt comfortable enough to refer to the interview in *Rolling Stone*. We chatted briefly about his moving on past the Beatles and the dangers from within the self. The demons he must have burdened, knowing if he said . . . to jump off a cliff, kids around the world were just crazy enough to do it.

He finally gave me one little piece of advice about living in the past versus the now, he said, "Once you do it, it's done. You never have to go back." Now that may sound like some mumbo jumbo to you, but I know what he meant and how he meant it. It's true, you can't go back, so why dwell on it. Thank you, John.

Now while standing next to him and looking eye to eye, I noticed that little silver coke spoon around his neck. His nose was a little red. I produced a slip of paper and ask for his and Yoko's autographs which I have mounted on the "Imagine" poster. The one in the white room at the white piano.

I'd like to say that Yoko was radiant. She's terribly unphotogenic, but in person up close, damn, she was absolutely glowing. Remember this was quite some time ago. She had an aura about her that was , well you'd have to have been there.

I stood along the wall while John and the other fellow finished their game.

I said, "John we have a couple of guitars and there's a piano up front. Would you play?" His response was simply, "I'm with these other people, if they don't mind?"

So, John Lennon with Yoko Ono sitting beside him sat on the edge of the little stage. He was playing my Martin D-35. He sang some three chord change stuff like "Kansas City" and I think "Bad Boy" and "Blue Suede Shoes." All simple stuff. It was great.

The joint filled up in a matter of minutes as the word spread around the beach that John Lennon was playing. When they reached capacity they wouldn't let any more people in. Pitchers of free beer started going around. What can I say, it was the ultimate. And I was sitting right in front not three feet away from John Lennon. Man if I died, I would have been happy. The dream . . . the thrill of a lifetime. And he was playing my guitar. I felt like it was my own private concert, just for me.

I had started to play the piano but the old thing was so far out of tune I didn't want to ruin the moment. So I missed being able to say I jammed with John. But I'll never forget the moment, when time seemed to stand still. Right in front of me....

John played for about half an hour. When he was done the place roared. When he gave me back my guitar we shook hands.

It doesn't get any better than that.

That's it. It's all true and the feeling is like nothing I can describe. "In my life, there is no one compares to you."

Michael Lowry
Lake Ridge Va

HIS MUSIC—MY VOICE

Hello, my name is Raeanne Garcia, and I am 21 years old. Although John Lennon died nearly 1 year before I was born, his life and music has still affected me in a deep and profound way. His music, thanks to my parents, has been my music. I have listened to it and learned that all this world really needs is love. He was not only a talented man, but a beautiful man, who expressed his feelings and beliefs through his music and lyrics. He was a passionate, artistic, and simple man, whose voice has been the voice for many generations—past, present, and future. Thus, his music has, ultimately, become my voice. I don't think I would be the person I am today without him and his music. John Lennon has taught me to be a dreamer, a creator, and someone who was always be experimenting. Those qualities are what I have taken from him as a human being. I only wish that I could have been born 20 years earlier to experience, in the present, John Lennon and his presence.

Raeanne Garcia
Roseville, CA

THE DEFINITION OF COOL

My name is Matthew Ruta and I am 15 years old and to me John Lennon is the definition of cool. All my friends think I'm crazy idolizing someone from that era. I was lucky enough to have my parents be sort of John Lennon fans. My mother and father bought the *Shaved Fish* album, and every Christmas they always woke me and my siblings playing "Happy Xmas (war is over)" and they were dancing. The song brought them so much joy. I was curious so I "borrowed" the album from them when I was about 11 and I listened to it one day. I found out that this man had the greatest voice ever. While I was listened to the album there was a lyrics list and I found out that this man really meant what he wrote. Through the album I found out that I've heard most of these songs before on the radio or my parents playing them like "Instant Karma," "Cold Turkey," and "Whatever Gets You thru the Night." One song stuck out from the rest, one of the only songs to ever make me cry was "Imagine." "Imagine" was like a private prayer made public.

Later through that week I asked my Mother how popular was this man.

She answered "this man was part of the greatest band ever The Beatles." I listened to the Beatles occasionally but I didn't know what people were in the band. So I got even more interested into them and ironically the same week there was an ad on the television for a Beatles CD called 1. I begged my mom to get it, but she refused. So then I forgot about John Lennon and The Beatles for 3 years and then I was in Poland and they had a lot of Beatles CDs over there and luckily they had 1. It was cheap and I had the money so I bought it and fell in love with it from the first day I got it 'till today. My favorite song on the album would probably have to be "The Ballad of John and Yoko" because it was a song that made me very happy. I've collected many of the Beatles albums on CD. I also found 2 John Lennon records at a garage sale (*Double Fantasy* and *Imagine*). I have John Lennon pictures in my basement I'm obsessed. He also inspired me into some songwriting and to learn how to play guitar. Other fans at school say I look somewhat like him which to me is a great compliment, but being born in 1988 I could never have been a part in his life but he was a big part in my life bigger than probably any other musician or person. I could never have been a part in his life but the closest thing to being a part in his life would to be in a book about his life and listening to his music and loving him.

Please consider this as a valid entry and sorry if that was a little long and sorry about any spelling and grammar mistakes I'm still just a kid.

Sincerely,
Matthew Ruta
Troy, Michigan

THE MORE I LOVE HIM

I started enjoying the music of the Beatles when I was just 11 years old. Naturally, being the almost teenager I was, I immediately fell in love with Paul McCartney. His loving ballads, his killer good looks and his charm wooed me over completely. The other three were all right, but no one was like Paul.

The older I got, the more I started listening to the words of the Beatles' music. There was a message there and I loved it; peace, love and acceptance. Growing up in the "Bible Belt" it was hard to find that feeling of tolerance. Don't let the religious name fool you. The "Bible Belt" is known for their prejudices. But there it was. "All You Need Is Love." How fabulous was that!

And the man behind the majority of that peace and love was John Lennon. I started to appreciate that message more and more. The more I read about Lennon, the more I love him. His values and principles mirror my own in a way. And especially in the days of an unjust war, his words ring so true. He is an inspiration in my life. If it weren't for his words of tolerance, acceptance and peace, I might have gone through life with pre-conceived notions of people I don't even know. To fear someone because of the color of their skin or the way they pray to God or Allah or Buddha . . . whoever. I thank God that John was put on this earth to teach people about the important things in life. And it's so tragic that even despite his pacifist nature, he would be killed in such a horrible way.

I never got the chance to experience John Lennon firsthand. But I am grateful that the music lives on today. When my children sing "All You Need Is Love" it gives me chills. The music and the memory of John Lennon will live on forever.

Thanks for letting me express my feelings, Mr. Kane. It is much appreciated. Thanks for your time.

Sincerely,
Susan Fischer
Mother of two
St. Louis, MO

SHE WAS JUST 17, YOU KNOW WHAT I MEAN

Hey Larry, My name is Katie and I am 17 years old. As you can tell by my age, I wasn't alive when John was alive but what I've learned about him and his music has changed me forever. I got into the Beatles after I did my term paper for US History on them. As I looked up information, it seemed to me that John was the most intriguing member. The first time I saw the Beatles was on my computer on this little video clip of "I Want To Hold Your Hand" from the 1964 *Ed Sullivan Show* and I immediately thought that John was the serious member of the group. The way he sang and his facial expressions made me think that he was very serious. Boy was I wrong! Not only did I find out that John was not the serious one, I learned that he was absolutely crazy (in a good way I mean). I remember the first time I saw the movie A *Hard Days Night*, John was hysterical! I knew I had to find out more about him. So I went to every site that I could find on him and began to learn. That was the turning point in my life.

Over the past couple of months I have developed such a strong respect for John and everything he has done. I know he didn't have the easiest life with not knowing his father as a child and his mother's death just as they were becoming closer. This was all very hard for him to deal with but music was his release. I guess you can say his music has been a release for me also. I know I'm not going through any of that stuff he went through but I have my share of disappointments here and there and I've used Lennon's music to help me get through it! Most of his music I can't relate to because I don't have problems with drugs or a love life like he had but I always seem to find some message that I can say "hey me too, man!" It's not even just his Beatles songs, his solo music is incredible but I'm sure you know that already! John Lennon has changed my outlook on music and life. His songs are nothing that I've heard before and none of today's music can even compare with it. Where in today's music are there classics like "Instant Karma," "Watching the Wheels," "Mother," which are some of my favorites and many others. His lyrics are deep, he put emotion into his music, he didn't just write, he used his heart. I can't think of any other artist who has contributed as much as Lennon has to the world. Maybe some of his actions were uncalled for and didn't fit in to what others believed to be good, but then again Lennon from day 1 was different and didn't exactly fit in. I guess that's what made him so brilliant! His acceptance of being different and doing what he wanted to do, not doing wanted people expected him to do, took him places. To sum it all up, if I could I would thank John for what he has done to American Pop Culture, American Music, and American Life. In many cases, his actions spoke louder than his words, and changed everything. I'm so thankful that I got into the Beatles and them as solo artist because I have been changed for good. John Lennon, You're Brilliant, Thanks for being yourself!

Thank You! Good Luck with your book! I'm sure it will be great!

Katie Marmo
Babylon, New York

A Source of Inspiration

Dear Mr. Kane,

My name is Danielle, and I'm 14 years old. John Lennon has affected my life in many ways. One is that he inspired me to take up songwriting. Also, when I struggle at learning guitar, I think of how good he was at it, and keep going. But the most important way he has impacted my life is simply by being someone to look up to. He had a rough life, and when I think of what he went through, it makes my life look like it's not quite as bad as I feel like it is sometimes. When ever I have a particularly troubling dilemma, I sit on my bed and stare at the poster I have of him on my wall, with the lyrics to "Imagine" on it. In the picture, he is staring ahead, and you can tell he's really deep in thought, possibly about a song, or what he thinks of the world. And somehow, if I just look at that picture long enough, an event from his life, or a line from one of his songs comes to mind, and it's always something that makes me feel a lot better.

He also taught me to voice my opinions. Sometimes I want to say things, mostly about politics and the current situation in the world. Sometimes I don't though, because some people think I don't know what I'm talking about, or because I don't know how to say it. Mr. Lennon voiced his opinions through songs and actions, and never hesitated to do whatever it took to get his point across. When I think about that, I'm not a worried about saying something other people think is totally ridiculous.

That is how John Lennon, the most amazing musician, philosopher, humanitarian, and person the world has ever seen, effects my life every day.

Danielle Betters

MUSINGS FROM MANITOBA

I recently read on Joe Johnson's Beatle Brunch website that you are writing a book about John Lennon and that you are looking for fans to share their stories on how he affected their lives. I would like to share my own with you.

I am sixteen-years-old and I have been a fan of the sixties since my dad got me a tape of the Guess Who. I became aware of John Lennon and The Beatles while watching ads for the 1 CD released in 2000. I was dazzled by the flashy *Sgt. Pepper* costumes and could feel the raw energy and chemistry the four had together during the 1965 Shea Stadium concert. So after seeing that footage, I wanted to see what the fuss was about and stood in the Music World store at the mall, asking my parents if it was a good CD. Because they were children of the seventies, they said that they were not sure and that if I wanted to get the disc, I should get it. It was that day, at the age of twelve, that I traded in the homegrown Guess Who for the four Moptop Scruffs in Liverpool, though I did not know about it until the day I came home from school and squealed with delight at sight of a poster of the four with their instruments hanging on the back of my door. Since then I have spent hours buying and reading books about each member in The Beatles and as a solo artist, listening to "Strawberry Fields Forever" for the umpteenth time to prove once and for all that John says "Cranberry sauce" not, "I buried Paul," sharing the latest Beatles story I discovered with one of local deejays while on the air, running to my room to take notes on what happened on this day in Beatle history and strutting around the block in my new Let it Be t-shirt that my Dad almost did not buy because it took him ten minutes to find a place to park.

One of the hardest questions for Beatles fans to answer has got to be: Who is your favorite Beatle. Each one has/had his own unique personality and dynamics, which it makes it harder and more unfair to put one above the other. But John had a certain magnetism about him that made him unique. Though a crude muleheaded oaf at times, it seemed to cover up the highly sensitive and vulnerable side that he seldom showed. Instead, he channeled his feelings into his creativity that created songs and poetry, which are some of the world's greatest masterpieces. He inspired some of my best poems and when I listen to his songs, it amazes me how he could make a listener feel what he was feeling in a song or make the abstract silly, the silly abstract, the melancholy happy and the happy melancholy. Though I have grown up knowing that John is no longer living, I have always thought his death was a waste of talent, but then again, what death is not?

John has been a major part of my life; he has influenced some of my beliefs, my musical tastes and my writing. Though I don't always agree with him or what he did, I can't condemn him because he always lived by his own rules. Too many talented entertainers have been puppeteered in the past by record executives and mangers so that they don't show any personality that will offend someone.

I hope I have been helpful to you Mr. Kane. Please let me know if I can be of any more help.

Yours Truly,
Heather Robbins
Winnipeg, Manitoba, Canada

THE TEENAGE TRIBUTE CONTINUES . . .

It's amazing to imagine how much influence John had on the world, through everything he did from his music to his peace efforts. John made a profound impression on the hearts and minds of anyone who took time to listen to him with an open mind. I am one of those people though I was born nearly seven years after John's tragic passing. His timeless messages of peace and love still reach out and command the attention of people of all ages. I grew up with the Beatles constantly in the background of my life, always weaving in and out whether it was during long car rides spent singing "Let It Be" with my mom or second grade music class reports about the greatest composers of all time, Lennon and McCartney, of course.

In all of that John has always been an influence in my life through his lyrics. But that's all I knew about him, really, that he wrote amazing songs that made you think, until my school chorus did a tribute to John last year which sparked my interest and I decided to read a few books on his life, not only in the Beatles but during his solo years also.

Immediately I was amazed by what I read. His honesty and his direct approach of saying what he believed may have been harsh at times, but I loved it. I was mesmerized by the things he said about peace and love, and his belief that it shouldn't matter what color your skin is or whether you're a man or a woman, but if you've got something to say people should listen. John's life touched me in a way words could never properly describe, and he'll forever be an important part of my life. John was no saint, but he was an amazing man who shared his music and his heart with the world and he will always be remembered by the people, like me, whose lives were changed by his love.

Mindy Zimmerman,
16 Des Moines, Iowa

UNDERCOVER MAN SPEAKS OUT

I grew up in a town called Stone Mountain, Georgia. It is mentioned in Martin Luther King, Jr.'s "I Have a Dream" speech because it is the birthplace of the Ku Klux Klan. As a teen, I thought the KKK was normal and there to defend us white folks. But I was also a big Beatles fan. Of course, the Fabs owe everything to African-American music. The more I got into the Beatles, the more I got into their social views. I listened to *The Beatle Tapes* album (the David Wigg interviews) religiously. I studied the stories on John and Yoko's *Some Time In New York City lp*. It became increasingly clear to me that if I was going to be a Beatles and John Lennon fan not only did I need to reject the Klan's view, I needed to be like John and actively work against it.

John died when I was 16, a senior in high school. The following year I went to college and became a sociology major, researching how racism works. As I grad student, I spent nearly eight years going undercover with Klan and skinhead groups. Now I am a university professor who leads one of the leading hate crime research centers in America (www.hatecrime.net). The spirit of the Beatles and John & Yoko guide me every day. John said in 1980, "If you want to save Peru, go and save Peru!" He gave me the strength to go from being a fan of a hero, to just doing it myself. Power to the people, right now.

Dr. Randy Blazak
Dept. of Sociology
Portland State University

MAKE A DIFFERENCE!

Well, I'll try to make this as short as possible.

It all started back in 1971 when I first heard the song "Imagine." I truly believed it changed my life for the better, all I wanted was to be positive by being peaceful and loving and not judge anyone for anything or for any reason just to accept them for who they are and at the same time by trying to make this world a better place. We also played the song "Imagine" for our high school graduation back in 1973 which we as a class voted to have that song playing, I know now I was not the only one who imagined great things would come from this song and John Lennon.

I just had a surprise 50th birthday party given to me by my wife and six children, ages 18 to 28. Through out there life I had always talked about how they could make a difference by being a peaceful and a loving person, and which they all are. At the party as the music was playing, I was talking to two of my sons and had my arms around them when the song "Imagine" started to play. Well, before I knew it, me and my six sons were all in a circle with our arms around one another swaying from side to side and singing. We stayed like that through the entire song, but what really stuck me was one son said this is what it's all about, another son started saying how much he loved everyone of us while another continued singing along, we all had tears running down our face, my wife was in the circle for a brief time but stepped back to let me and my sons be together for this moment. Well, we stayed in a circle for a few more moments after the song had ended and then separated, as I turned to look for my wife all of the guests were standing there with tears in their eyes along with my wife who was also crying from watching me and my six sons have one of the greatest moments we ever had.

I know now that not only did me and my wife make a difference and believe in what John Lennon was talking about in that song, but my sons do believe that they can make a difference also because of John Lennon and the song "Imagine."

Ken Bernard
Pawtucket Rhode Island

Barbara and Bill

First of all thank you a zillion times over for your wonderful book, *Ticket to Ride*. It made for very insightful reading on those SPECIAL years . . . I was 14 in 1964 so that should tell you how reading your book affected me . . . awesome Mr. Kane . . . I remember like "yesterday" that turning point "in my life" that Sunday night in February . . . to most people of today its sounds corny . . . but it did change my life . . . my love of music . . . my wanting to be in a band . . . my sense of dress . . . also Larry as I get older it becomes more and more apparent . . . I wept quite a bit when we lost both John and George . . . and I'm not ashamed to tell anyone . . . I am a New Yorker now living in Fla . . . I moved here in 86 . . . that night at the Dakota and the subsequent events in central park are etched in my mind forever . . . it has become a part of me . . . your new book I know will touch me to the heart . . . my thoughts of Lennon are there almost everyday, he was a dreamer for all of mankind to live together . . . but if he were alive today, I feel he would still be an activist, but it's gotten so much worse, I can't think about how he would feel . . . because it saddens me . . . his music made us all think . . . you know they always write about the influence Dylan had on the Beatles and the Beatles on Dylan . . . but I always thought it was mainly Lennon who influenced Dylan . . . of course I'm not as close to it as the experts are . . . it's just my gut feeling . . . I also get upset when people say they were robbed of future Lennon songs, that to me is a selfish reaction to a useless tragedy . . . besides, his songs to this day could have been written 6 months ago . . . it's called timeless music, something we don't see anymore in the music biz . . . I was 21 when I first heard "workin class hero" now at 54 it hits home even more . . . and that line in "Imagine" . . . imagine no possessions really sounds poignant with all of the greed there is in the world today . . . oh Larry I could go on forever, but I don't want to bore you.

. . . hey I know you are a swell guy, I'm friends with a man named Charlie Mills he was the program director at a Philly station WPEN for years . . . he said he knew you when I was buying your *Ticket to Ride* book . . . and he had told me all about you. . . . and I thought I was there in 64-65 . . . you really were . . . looking forward to your new book . . . thanks again for insights of those early years . . . now for recollection of that fateful night in Dec. of 1980 . . . I went to bed not knowing what had happened . . . I was working for the NY telephone back then . . . as a creature of habit which I am . . . I always listened to WNEW-FM for my morning drive . . . Dave Hermann was the morning dj at the time . . . when I got into my car he was playing the Beatles . . . nothing out of the ordinary, then another Beatle tune, then a Lennon tune, I thought it was odd because he never strung together a block of music by the same artists . . . when the last song of the set was over he came back on the air and I immediately realized he sounded depressed, then in talking he referred to Lennon in the past tense . . . I stopped my car and pulled over to the side of the road . . . I knew something was wrong, then he said it . . . John had been murdered . . . I starting crying right away . . . I sat dazed in my car, wondering who on earth would do such an awful thing . . . I sat there for about 45 mins. . . . then slowly drove home . . . my wife said to me why are you back . . . I told her what had happened . . . then we both cried . . . and recollected all the great times we had shared   with each other through his music . . . it was wall to wall coverage on New York TV . . . we were stunned and angry . . . the central park memorial feels like it happened in a dream . . . living in Florida now since '86 makes the whole incident seem like another lifetime to both of us . . . in closing, the Lennon/McCartney songwriting team constitutes the best music of the 20th century and will live on forever . . . and John with all his personal insecurities will live on through his music like a true icon that he is and always will be . . . thank you Larry for giving me this chance to express my deep feelings.

Bill and Barbara Pellegrino
Pinellas Park, FL

BIBLIOGRAPHY

Aronowitz, Al. *Bob Dylan and the Beatles*. Elizabeth, New Jersey: 1st Books Library, 2003.

Best, Roag, Pete Best, and Rory Best. *The Beatles: The True Beginnings*. New York: Thomas Dunne Books, St. Martin's Press, 2003.

Brodax, Al. *Up Periscope Yellow: The Making of the Beatles* Yellow Submarine. New York: Limelight Editions, 2004.

Coleman, Ray. *Lennon: The Definitive Biography*. New York: Perennial, 1992.

Davies, Hunter. *The Beatles*. New York: McGraw-Hill, 1978.

Goldman, Albert. *The Lives of John Lennon*. Chicago: Chicago Review Press, 2001

Goldsmith, Martin. *The Beatles Come to America*. Hoboken: Wiley and Sons, 2004.

Henke, James. *Lennon Legend*. San Francisco: Chronicle Books, 2002.

Henke, James. *Lennon: His Life and Work*. Cleveland: Rock and Roll Hall of Fame and Museum Inc., 2000.

Lennon, John. *In His Own Write*. New York: Simon and Schuster, 2000 (new edition).

Lennon, John. *Imagine*. New York: Hal Leonard Company, 1988.

Lewisohn, Mark. *The Beatles: Recording Sessions*. New York: Harmony Books, 1988.

Lewisohn, Mark. *The Complete Beatles Chronicle*. New York: Harmony Books, 1992.

Norman, Philip. *Shout: The Beatles in Their Generation*. New York: Simon and Schuster, 1981.

D'Dell, Denis, and Bob Neaverseon. *At the Apple's Core: The Beatles from the Inside*. London: Peter Owen, 2003.

Pang, May. *Loving John: The Untold Story*. New York: Warner Books, 1983.

Saltzman, Paul. *The Beatles in Rishikesh*. New York: Viking Studio, 2000.

Somach, Denny, and Ken Sharp. *Meet the Beatles Again*. Havertown: Musicom International Publishing, 1995.

Spizer, Bruce. *The Beatles Are Coming: The Birth of Beatlemania in America*. New Orleans: 498 Productions, L.L.C., 2003.

Stevens, John. *The Songs of John Lennon: The Beatles Years*. Boston: Berklee Press Productions, 2002.

Sutcliffe, Pauline. *The Beatles Shadow: Stuart Sutcliffe and His Lonely Hearts Club*. New York: Pan Books, 2002.

Rolling Stone Magazine. *The Ballad of John and Yoko*. New York: Dolphin Books, Doubleday, 1982.

Solt, Andrew. *Imagine: John Lennon*. New York: Macmillan Publishing Company, 1988.

Taylor, Derek. *As Time Goes By*. London: Davis-Poynter Ltd, 1973.

Wenner, Jann, and Charles Reich. *Lennon Remembers: The Full Rolling Stone Interviews from 1970*. New York: Verso Books, 2000.

Wiener, Jon. *Gimme Some Truth: The John Lennon FBI Files*. Berkeley: University of California Press, 1999.

Wright, David K. *The Beatles and Beyond*. Springfield, New Jersey: Enslow Publishers, 1996.

PHOTO CREDITS:

Front cover: © Allan Tannenbaum/Polaris

Back cover and chapter openers, guitar photo:

DVD photo: AP/Wide World Photos

© 2005 Rickenbacker International Corporation. All rights reserved.

Front flap photo: © Larry Kane

Author photo: Courtesy of Donna Jarrett-Kane

Spine: AP/Wide World Photos

pp. 3, 145, 158–159: © Allan Tannenbaum/Polaris

p. 146: © 2005 Astrid Kirchherr/Star File

pp. 147 (top & bottom), 149 (bottom), 151 (bottom): Getty Images

pp. 148 (top), 151 (top): © Bettmann/CORBIS

p. 148 (bottom): © George Orsino

pp. 149 (top), 152 (top), 153 (bottom): AP/Wide World Photos

p. 150 (top & bottom): © Paul Saltzman/Contact Press Images

p. 152 (bottom): © David Marks, courtesy of the 3rd Ear Music/Hidden Years Music Archive Project, www.3rdearmusic.com

p. 154 (top): © 1983 May Pang

pp. 153 (top), 154 (bottom), 155–157: © 2005 Bob Gruen/Star File

p. 160: Time Life Pictures/Getty Images

INDEX